Against the self-images of the age

ESSAYS ON IDEOLOGY AND PHILOSOPHY

Alasdair MacIntyre

AGAINST THE SELF-IMAGES OF THE AGE

Essays on ideology and philosophy

SCHOCKEN BOOKS · NEW YORK

Published in U.S.A. in 1971
by Schocken Books Inc.
67 Park Avenue, New York, N.Y. 10016

Library of Congress Catalog Card No. 74 130208

Printed in Great Britain

Contents

vi   *Contents*

Introduction

These essays would normally not be expected to appear within the same covers; for the intellectual habits of the age would construe them as belonging to two different and not very closely related genres. I make no apology for this, since one aim of the book is precisely to break with some of these habits. It is true, of course, that those essays which have been published previously appeared in two very different kinds of periodical—professional philosophical journals, such as the *Philosophical Review*, on the one hand, and journals of general intellectual culture, such as *Encounter*, on the other. For the institutions and the organization of our culture runs *pari passu* with its habits of mind, and therefore either one does not publish at all or one accepts being misconstrued in terms of dichotomies to which one may be resolutely opposed.

The particular dichotomy which I am identifying here, for the purpose of opposing it, is that between the detailed, analytical, conceptual inquiries of contemporary philosophy and those inquiries into the truth of *weltanschauungen* which laymen sometimes suppose to be the province of philosophy, but which are so seldom carried on within its bounds. However I should immediately distinguish between a legitimate version of this dichotomy and an illegitimate one. It is extremely important that rigorous attention to analytical detail should not be vitiated by premature attempts to assess the significance of that detail in terms of some larger issue; and it is inevitable that ideological stances should be adopted and ideological criticism should be carried forward—since in neither politics nor religion is the urgency of crises delayed by the exigencies of the calendars of academic inquiry—when crucial detailed work still remains to be done. None the less, on the one hand it is essential to underline that, of the multiplying of distinctions, there may turn out to be no end; and that which distinctions are important can only be assessed in terms of some criteria of larger

significance. On the other hand, every doctrine which is not to be
corroded by intellectual complacency has to expose its vulnerable
commitments in all their piecemeal detail. When J. L. Austin
declared that truth is important but that importance is not, he
perhaps made himself the unwitting ally of those dogmatists
whose doctrines were thereby placed low on the list of priorities
for intellectual examination.

The unity of this book resides therefore in the aspiration to link
philosophical criticism and ideological commitment, and, doubtless, with the project thus generally defined very few will be found
to quarrel. But doubtless also almost everybody—whether those
who believe themselves committed to one of the ideologies discussed in these essays or those who confidently believe themselves
exempt from ideological adherence—will find grounds for
quarreling with the way in which I have tried to carry out this
project. Against those who believe that some particular ideology is
still able to provide the light that our individual and social lives
need, I shall assert that—in the case of psychoanalysis, of
Christianity, and above all of Marxism—either intellectual
failure, or failure to express the forms of thought and action
which constitute our contemporary social life, or both, have led to
their necessary and in the long run not to be regretted decay.
Against those who believe that in our type of society ideology as
such can no longer find living roots or expression, I shall assert
that it is the specific traits of these particular ideologies that we
have inherited which make them no longer viable, and not any
characteristics of ideology as such; and moreover that the belief in
the end of ideology itself masks an ideology which is no less an
ideology for being so often unacknowledged and which is perhaps
less reputable than it might be insofar as it goes unrecognized.

In particular I believe that the nature of contemporary academic
philosophy in the Anglo-Saxon world has contributed in a marked
way to the persistence among us of certain uncriticized ideological
concepts and values. The activity of the philosopher in the Anglo-
Saxon world has been variously defined in the last seventy years in
ways which, although inadequate, point to a truth about the
nature of that activity: "analysis," "linguistic analysis," "conceptual analysis," "inquiries into meaning." Such characterizations
are bound to be inadequate, not only because of their brevity, but
also because the question of the nature of analysis and the question
of the relationship of linguistic expressions to concepts have of
course themselves been central matters for philosophical argument
during this whole period. But it is clear that the procedure of

philosophers has been usually and characteristically to select some set of linguistic expressions or of concepts and to then inquire into their meaning, use, and logical liaisons; the categorization of types of meaning, of use, and of logical relationship being an activity that has proceeded side by side with these more particular inquiries. What has not been sufficiently remarked is the lack of attention consequently paid to the historical and social sources of the expressions or the concepts which are to be the focus of attention; and this has led to distortion in at least two ways. There is, first, the possibility of making judgments about the meaning, use, or logical relationships of some particular type of expression on the basis of an inadequate sample. We may take an impoverished view of the range of types of moral concepts or of moral statements, or we may distort our views of particular concepts by being parsimonious with our examples. When professing to study moral concepts as such or "the" language of morals, we may be merely studying one particular variation on possible moral themes, perhaps that which is dominant on our own social milieu. A second possible source of error is in the loss of insight into changes of meaning and transformations of concepts which can only be studied if we are prepared to give historical depth to philosophical inquiry. These two sources of error may result in our conferring necessity, inevitability, and universality on some conceptual scheme, some way of looking at the world, which is in fact local in both time and place and to which there are alternatives. In doing this, philosophy may thus appear to guarantee one way of looking at the world by seeming to demonstrate its necessity; and this is the key role of inadequate philosophy in underpinning ideology.

I shall therefore move in the argument of the succeeding essays from trying to show that Christianity, psychoanalysis, and especially Marxism fail as ideologies for reasons quite other than those propounded in the end-of-ideology thesis and that the end-of-ideology thesis itself masks an ideology, to arguing that a true perception of the latter fact and an ability to understand the world in more adequate and less impoverished ways depends upon the outcome of inquiry in moral philosophy and the philosophy of the social sciences. This is my task; how inadequately I have carried it out and how urgently it is necessary to improve the argument and to perform the task more adequately nobody is more aware than I am.

I have left those essays, which have already appeared elsewhere, substantially in the form in which they were originally presented

This is not because of laziness, but because to rescue them from their form as reviews or essays written at a particular time or place would require that I should know how to tie these arguments together into a substantive whole. This I do not yet know how to do, but I regard learning how to do it as a prerequisite for further advancing inquiry into these questions.

It remains for me to thank the editors and publishers of the following periodicals or books for permission to reprint: *Encounter* for 2, 3, 5, 7, 8, 10; *New York Review of Books* for 4; *The Yale Law Journal* for 6; *Partisan Review* for 9; *Philosophy* for 12; *The Philosophical Review* for 13; *The Journal of Philosophy* for 14; *The Monist* and The Open Court Publishing Company, La Salle, Illinois for 17; Messrs. Routledge and Kegan Paul and Humanities Press for 18 (from *British Analytical Philosophy*, edited by B. Williams and A. Montefiore); The Aristotelian Society for 19.

Finally there is another kind of gratitude: to Miss Barbara Warner and to Mrs. Betty Griffin who typed and retyped; to the Librarian of the London Library and his colleagues for their patient and scholarly help; and to my colleagues at the University of Essex and at Brandeis University for so much illuminating argument and criticism. I owe a particular debt to the members of the Study Group on the Unity of Knowledge for discussion of several themes in this book, especially of essays 20 and 21, and to the Ford Foundation for making such discussion possible.

ALASDAIR MACINTYRE

Waltham, Massachusetts
January 1971

PART ONE

I

The end of ideology and the end of the end of ideology

The 1950s were a decade of immoderate claims made on behalf of what its defenders took to be moderation. Apocalyptic salutations hailed the arrival of the mixed economy guided by what was alleged—quite falsely—to be Keynesian economic theory; messianic value was attached to the politics of social democracy. As in earlier apocalyptic and messianic moments, it was proclaimed intemperately that nothing but the sober truth was at last being told. The core of this prophesying was the "end-of-ideology" thesis, first advanced by Edward Shils at a Congress of Cultural Freedom meeting in 1954 and later endorsed and developed by Daniel Bell and Seymour Martin Lipset. The central message of this thesis was that in the advanced industrial societies of the West, ideology was at an end because fundamental social conflict was at an end.

In the view maintained by advocates of this thesis, there were no longer any social roots for a politics which proposed a revolutionary transformation of the social order. There might still be Utopian visions of a social order in which the ills of the existing order had been done away—and Daniel Bell at least was anxious to stress the continuing relevance of Utopian vision, provided that it was treated as vision and not as something else; but practical politics must now be a matter of pragmatic compromise with an agreed framework of basic and even not so basic values. This agreed framework depended upon a consensus which had been arrived at by means of the institutions of the welfare state and of the economic and political domestication of the working class. Those rival and competing interests which had been allowed expression within the official political order would therefore no longer breed disruptive conflict; and the presentation of ideological world views which might guide and inform a politics of passionate conflict would henceforth be out of place in the advanced industrial societies.

That the end-of-ideology thesis was a diagnosis which expressed something real and important about those societies in the 1950s is undeniable. The political apathy, for instance, to which its protagonists pointed (and which Lipset, for example, took to be a precondition of the stability of democratic political orders) was not an illusion. Moreover, the proliferation of similar theses among political philosophers and political scientists is itself to some degree evidence of a general frame of mind. Shils in Chicago, Lipset in California, Bell in New York found allies in J. L. Talmon in Jerusalem, who proclaimed that the ideological theorists of the eighteenth and nineteenth centuries—and especially Rousseau and Marx—were the progenitors of the totalitarian politics of the twentieth century (the equation of ideological theorizing with totalitarian politics is a central theme in most of these writers); in Sir Isaiah Berlin at Oxford, who identified a belief in "positive liberty" (to be found in Rousseau and Hegel) as a prime source of totalitarian evils; and in Norman Cohn, who saw in the millenarians of the Middle Ages and the sixteenth century the predecessors of modern Utopians, identifying the source of both movements in the psychological disorders—and probably the paranoia—of the individuals concerned. The end-of-ideology thesis, therefore, was part of a general intellectual landscape. Moreover, it found a counterpart in the avowed beliefs of those engaged in politics. The writings of Anthony Crosland and John Strachey espouse what is plainly the same basic standpoint.

If therefore the sheer weight of this agreement is evidence that the end-of-ideology thesis expressed something implicitly, or explicitly recognized by many perceptive observers of the 1950s, it still remains to ask whether the end-of-ideology thesis diagnosed correctly the nature of that to which it was sensitive. On this point three initial observations are in order. The first is that when such writers spoke of the end of ideology in the advanced societies of the West, what they plainly had primarily in mind was the final demise of the influence of Marxism in these societies. Even if those writers were themselves Marxists, or post-Marxists, none were unwilling to declare their allegiance in Cold War terms, and it is therefore pertinent to ask whether they may not have confused the local demise of Marxist ideology with the local demise of ideology. To ask this question suggests that we ought to inquire whether these authors had freed themselves from the influence of Marxism to quite the extent which they believed they had. For their thesis appears to be that it is because what they take to be profound social changes have occurred that ideology |is no longer possible. In their view of the causal sequence—for which none of these writers seems to argue explicitly—it is possible to perceive the ghosts of the Marxist concepts of basis and superstructure. For otherwise, surely they might have taken more seriously the possibility that it was because ideology was not what it was, that social and political conflict was not what *it* was, rather than vice versa.

I deliberately used in the last sentence the neutral expression "because ideology was not what it was," in order to lead on to the suggestion that, in fact, the end-of-ideology theorists had mis-construed their situation in two related ways. They were right to see that in the 1950s ideology was not what it was; and they were right also to relate this fact to the lessening of social conflict. But not only did they confuse the exhaustion of Marxism with the exhaustion of ideology, they failed to entertain one crucial alternative possibility: namely, that the end-of-ideology thesis, far from marking the end of ideology, was itself a key expression of the ideology of the time and place where it arose. Here again there is a strong reminiscence of classical Marxism. For Marx saw Marxism as having an independence of existing social structures and hence an objectivity which rescued it from the relativity of ideological thought which he diagnosed in his opponents. It was, of course, only in the Communist future, when the social roots of ideological thinking had been finally destroyed, that ideology would finally wither away. But Marxism offers an anticipation of this apocalyptic culmination. This surely is the ancestor of that muted apocalypticism in Bell and Lipset which surrounds the announcement of the end of ideology.

To make good the thesis that the end-of-ideology thesis was itself part of an ideology, and was thus also self-refuting, it is necessary to be clear about what we ought to understand by the expression "ideology." Shils, Bell, and Lipset are all astonishingly brief in their exposition; since I wish to make use of this notion not merely to criticize the end-of-ideology thesis, but for other independent purposes, I shall have to discuss this point at some-what greater length.

I take any ideology to have three key features. The first is that it attempts to delineate certain general characteristics of nature or society or both, characteristics which do not belong only to particular features of the changing world which can be investigated only by empirical inquiry. So for Christianity the God-created and

God-maintained character of the world is just such a characteristic; so for Marxism the laws of dialectical change are such a characteristic. Two closely related queries can always be raised about this feature of an ideology: What is the status of statements about these general characteristics and how do we show such statements to be true or false? And what is the relationship between the truth or falsity of such statements and the truth or falsity of scientific or historical claims about the character of empirically investigable processes and events? How for Christianity are claims about divine providence related to claims about historical events in first-century Palestine? How for Marxism are claims about the dialectic related to claims about the wage levels of the working class under industrial capitalism?

The second central feature of any ideology is an account of the relationship between what is the case and how we ought to act, between the nature of the world and that of morals, politics, and other guides to conduct. That is to say, I am making it a defining property of an ideology that it does not merely tell us how the world is *and* how we ought to act, but is concerned with the bearing of the one upon the other. This involves a concern, explicit or implicit, with the status of statements of moral rules and of statements expressing evaluations.

This latter concern, like the concern with the status of statements about the nature of things, shows that a good deal of what I have characterized as ideology not only overlaps with the proper concerns of philosophy, it *is* philosophy. So that philosophical inquiry is always liable to be a solvent of ideological conviction and commitment by arriving at conclusions incompatible with the positions of a particular ideology. Likewise, the dominance of a particular ideology may limit or inhibit philosophical inquiry. I do not refer only or most importantly to the use of policemen by those who are not only ideologically committed but also politically powerful to threaten or abolish free inquiry. For what I shall treat as the third defining property of an ideology is that it is not merely believed by the members of a given social group, but believed in such a way that it at least partially defines for them their social existence. By this I mean that its concepts are embodied in, and its beliefs presupposed by, some of these actions and transactions, the performance of which is characteristic of the social life of that group. The relatively noncommittal word "group" is used advisedly, for it is itself a matter for ideological debate how ideologies come to exercise such hold as they do upon social life. There is a Christian account of why Christians are Christians and the heathens are not;

and there is a Marxist account of why Marxists are Marxists and the heathens are not. It is for this reason that a good deal of ideology not only overlaps with the proper concerns of sociology, but *is* sociology; and hence, sociological inquiry, like philosophical inquiry, is liable to be a solvent of ideological conviction and also to be limited or inhibited by the dominance of particular ideologies.

This potentiality of conflict between any dominating or even aspiring ideology, and both philosophy and sociology, is not merely a source of tension. Rather, it is one of the signs, although only one of the signs, that an ideology is living and not dead, that it should actually breed conflict both with the philosophy and with the empirical science of its day. Conversely, any situation in which an ideology has no problems of conflict with philosophy or human or natural science is characteristically a sign, not that the ideology in question has triumphantly solved the intellectual problems of the age, but rather that the ideology has become empirically vacuous and has won its freedom from conflict at the cost of becoming empirically and perhaps practically empty.

That this is true of Christianity as it now exists I have argued in two essays in *The Religious Significance of Contemporary Atheism*,[1] and I shall not repeat the argument here, especially as the germ of that argument is to be found in "God and the Theologians."[2] But it is important to stress that it is not just the character of Christianity or just the character of contemporary society, but rather the coincidence of certain features of these two changing characters that has rendered Christianity ideologically vacuous. The attempt to maintain the values and the credibility of Christianity in the intellectual and moral climate of, for example, contemporary Britain has led to a vacuity that was not present when Christians such as Karl Barth or Dietrich Bonhoeffer or Franz Jaegstaetter defined their faith in words and action by contrast with and against Nazi mythology.

An ideology may of course be empirically vacuous, because it is held in such a way that it is unfalsifiable, and yet not be practically vacuous. So it is with psychoanalytic doctrine in a certain social milieu at the present time. In the cultural desert created by the prejudices of the liberal intelligentsia of New York or of the Californian cities, the questioning of the scientific pretensions of psychoanalysis is restricted almost entirely to those concerned with the philosophy of science. The therapeutic needs of such aids

[1] With Paul Ricoeur (New York: Columbia University Press, 1967).
[2] See pp. 12–26.

perhaps make intelligible the extraordinary situations whereby a theory that is certainly no better confirmed—and perhaps not as well confirmed—as witchcraft or astrology should have gained the credence that it has.

Finally, at this point we ought to note that the same doctrine can, during its history, experience vicissitudes as a result of which it alters its ideological character, both in respect to its relevance and vacuity and in respect to the liberating or oppressive character of its social effects. This is peculiarly true of both Christianity and Marxism. But in the advanced industrial societies of the West at least, although it may be dangerous to misunderstand why Christianity and Marxism are for the most part impotent, it is far more dangerous to rest this misunderstanding on the kind of endorsement of the status quo involved in the end-of-ideology thesis.

The ideological character of that thesis is most clearly apparent in Lipset's version of it in *Political Man*. The key notions which carry ideological weight are those of the conflicting interests which have been domesticated within the welfare state and that of the political consensus which provides the framework for that domestication. The key empirical contention is that a large measure of nonparticipation in active political decision-making promotes democratic and peaceful political and social processes, while widespread participation tends to go hand in hand with totalitarianism and authoritarianism. About these notions and this contention the following needs to be said: first, that the crucial question is how an interest is defined and how it is identified. Lipset and Bell, when they speak of the welfare state, clearly have in mind the recognition of trade unions either in their own right or through social-democratic parties as an interest which the political decision-makers must consult. But what about the recipients of welfare? Do they or ought they to constitute an interest with a distinctive political voice? What is quite clear is that the processes of formal democracy can coexist with the recognition of certain institutionalized interests, while the distribution of power and of the goods of which power determines the recipients remains radically unequal and radically unjust. The continuous rediscovery of and indeed the continuous re-creation of poverty in advanced societies ought to make this fact central to any political analysis.

Consensus is a concept correlative to that of interest. The question of which interests are recognized and acknowledged and the question of whose voice is heard in the consensus are the same question. It is not, of course, the case that those whose wants are not recognized and acknowledged as an interest by the established political consensus do not have their needs considered in the course of political decision-making; they may constitute an object of acute concern, especially when they create problems for their decision-makers. If the problems they create are sufficiently intractable, then the attempt will be made to give the problem-makers an institutionalized voice *within* the consensus. So at any given time there will be two types of politics possible: one, the politics of those within; the other, the politics of those excluded. The end-of-ideology thesis is one ideology of those concerned with legitimating only the former.

This exercise is underpinned by the selection of facts and by lack of conceptual awareness. The selection of facts is a matter of the type and the range of variables studied. Lipset never considers the type of nonparticipation in decision-making—which in fact prevails in totalitarian and authoritarian states and organizations as a counterexample to his thesis—with the consequence, that either his thesis must be construed as false or his use of "participation" so loose and undefined as to be useless for his own express purposes. But above all, Lipset never considers how the evaluation and selection of the facts not only results in a political commitment (as Charles Taylor has argued in his paper on 'Neutrality and Political Science'[1] and as Lipset himself acknowledges when he writes that "democracy [he means the parliamentary democracy of the West] is not only or even primarily a means through which different groups can attain their ends or seek the good society; it is the good society itself in operation" *Political Man*, p. 403), but arises from a critical standpoint which is not only methodological but also ideological. The Lipset-Bell vision of the world is informed by a view of rationality which makes liberal, pragmatic man the paradigm of rationality. Hence, the antithesis is framed between the reasonable, empirical approach of the proponents of the end-of-ideology thesis and the partisan passions of *les idéologues* (this deprecating sense of ideology was first used by Napoleon). Now rationality may be and, as I shall argue in a later essay, is one. But what are rational goals for those within the consensus to lay down, explicitly or implicitly, for those outside the consensus are not rational goals for those outside the consensus to lay down for themselves, if only because of the

[1] In *Philosophy, Politics, and Society*, Third Series, edited by P. Laslett and W. G. Runciman (Oxford: Blackwell; New York: Barnes & Noble, 1967).

force of that always to be remembered truism that not only in the end, but even in the relatively short run, nobody can know what an agent wants better than the man himself. Every restriction upon the right of men to speak for themselves in this respect involves either some unjustified claim that others can know better than they what they want, or some claim that their wants are irrelevant, perhaps because what they want is not what is good for them. Hence, the democratic claim of Jefferson or of Robespierre is the necessary political counterpart of any moral regard for human wants.

The ideological antithesis of Jefferson or Robespierre is Burke, and it is no accident that the antithesis between a politics of interests and a politics of ideology is as at home in Burke's writings as it is in those of Bell or Lipset. What Burke failed to see is what Bell and Lipset fail to see: that the costs of consensus are paid by those excluded from it. It is noteworthy that neither Bell in *The End of Ideology*, nor Lipset in *Political Man* or even in his much later article on "Anglo-American Society", in the *International Encyclopaedia of the Social Sciences* sees the place of the blacks in advanced societies as posing a radical question mark. Of them we may say what Michelet said of the Irish when he reproved the English: "Sitting at your ease on the corpse of Ireland ... be good enough to tell us: did your revolution of interests not cost more blood than our revolution of ideas?" (The Irish were for a long time the blacks of the British Isles.) The central polarity of advanced industrial societies is that between minorities who cannot solve their problems and majorities who cannot even face them. One instrument which is of importance in their avoidance-behavior (the behavior which elected Mr. Nixon to the Presidency) is the largely implicit belief that all problems are piecemeal and detailed, to be confronted by an empirical and pragmatic approach and that the transformation of society as a whole is an ideological will o' the wisp. But just this is the belief explicitly articulated and defended by the end-of-ideology thesis. It is thus not merely an ideology, but one that lacks any liberating power.

When I speak of the end of the end of ideology I do not mean of course to dwell merely on the fact that the end-of-ideology thesis is itself ideological. For while the end-of-ideology thesis was sensitive to a widespread mood in the 1950s among not only intellectuals, but also students, it proved to be highly discordant with the mood of intelligentsia of the 1960s when social conflict was at its most intense in the advanced societies in the institutions of higher education. What was notable was, of course, not the birth of new ideologies, but a romanticism which sometimes disclaimed any coherent ideology and sometimes constructed an amalgam of ideological fragments to use for its own purposes. This confrontation of middle-aged pragmatism and youthful romanticism, of a pragmatic insistence on the detailed and the empirical and a passionate attachment to vague and large ideological critiques, is misleadingly characterized as a generational conflict, even if it was in fact accompanied by such conflict. For such a characterization misses the symbiotic character of the phenomenon; the pragmatism of the attitude involved in the end-of-ideology thesis leaves precisely those whom it seeks to educate vulnerable to almost any ideological appeal by its failure to criticize social wholes. Each party to this dispute provides the other with an opponent made in precisely the required image. The children of those who define social reality in technocratic, bureaucratic, and academic terms aspire to a definition of human reality which will escape all institutional constraints. The implicit nihilism of so much student attack on institutions is the natural outcome of the defense of the institutions of the status quo as the only possible ones.

It is partly because of this connection that the end-of-ideology thesis still deserves attention. Those who wish to remake society are under an obligation to learn to frame alternative institutions that will escape the crushing polarities of the present. This is a political task. To perform it in a minimally adequate way it will be a necessary preliminary to understand how we can escape ideological deformation by the social order in which we live. One version of that deformation is to allow the fear of 1984 to revive the politics which glorified 1688.

2

God and the theologians[1]

Bishops provide news items under three kinds of headlines: they comment on our Morals, they forward schemes of Church Reunion, and—much less often—they discuss Christianity in public. The reported comments of the Bishop of Peterborough as well as the Archbishop of Canterbury on the book *Honest to God*[2] make it clear that the charge against the Bishop of Woolwich is largely that his utterances were public and that the first of them was an article in the Sunday *Observer*. To the discussion of speculative theological issues between consenting adults in private the Archbishop obviously would have less objection.

The reactions of his episcopal colleagues however provide only one indication of the importance of what Dr. Robinson said in *Honest to God*. The real interest among large numbers of people usually deeply inarticulate about religion is even more significant. More than one kind of raw nerve was touched by Dr. Robinson's theme. For he drew our attention to the fact that although the death of God has been announced over and over again in our culture, it remains true that God is an unconscionable time a-dying. I do not refer by this to the staying power of ecclesiastical institutions; they probably contribute to the strengthening of atheism as much as they ever did. But the survival of religious modes of feeling and questioning at widely different levels in our culture points clearly to something that Nietzsche and Feuerbach missed.

To put what Dr. Robinson wrote into perspective it is worth recalling that atheism is not all of one kind. Like Christianity it has its rival traditions. There is the speculative atheism which is concerned to deny that over and above the universe there is something else, an invisible intelligent being who exists apart

[1] Reprinted from *Encounter*, September 1963.

[2] Dr. John A Robinson, the Bishop of Woolwich. *Honest to God* (London: SCM Press; Philadelphia: The Westminster Press, 1963).

from the world and rules over it. Such an atheism is concerned to point out fallacies in the arguments for the existence of such a being, to stress the fact that we have no need of this hypothesis; and in general to expose religion as a series of intellectual mistakes. Its patron saints are David Hume and Bertrand Russell. Insofar as it seeks to explain religion it tends to lay stress on the general folly and weakness of human beings; its panacea is usually education, and its grief is that increased education by no means always produces increased skepticism about Christianity.

It is at just this point that a quite different kind of atheism intervenes to inquire why we should ever have expected otherwise. Since argument is not what fathers religious beliefs in the first place, why should learning the difference between good and bad arguments produce skepticism? Religion is misunderstood if it is construed simply as a set of intellectual errors; it is rather the case that in a profoundly misleading form deep insights, hopes, and fears are being expressed. We have to remove the mask of supernaturalist error—to this extent this second tradition presupposes the first. But to do so will be to expose a set of misunderstood truths. Religion needs to be translated into nonreligious terms and not simply rejected. This is the atheism of Feuerbach, of David Friedrich Strauss, and of the young Karl Marx. Its task is not a purely intellectual one; it is rather to transform society so that men will no longer need to resort to religious forms of expression. When the hopes which men have are embodied in secular social forms they will no longer need to appear in disguise as portraits of another and supernatural realm.

What is striking about Dr. Robinson's book is first and foremost that he is an atheist in *both* senses. He devotes a good deal of his space to attacking the notion of a being "out there." He quotes Bonhoeffer as saying that "Man has learned to cope with all questions of importance without recourse to God as a working hypothesis. . . ." But not only this: he is prepared to translate theological statements into nontheological. He says that what we mean when we speak of God is "that which concerns us ultimately"; that to speak of God is to speak of the deepest things we experience. "Belief in God is a matter of 'what you take seriously without any reservation' ", and to assert that God is love is to assert the supremacy of personal relationships. All theological statements can consequently be translated into statements about human concern.

Dr. Robinson explicitly contrasts his view with what he calls "supernaturalism" and with what he calls "religion." Yet, although he is prepared to assert with Feuerbach that "the true atheist is not the man who denies God, the subject; it is the man for whom the attributes of divinity, such as love, wisdom, and justice are nothing," he is unwilling to abandon the word "God" and a great many kindred theological words. Yet I think that we might well be puzzled by this strong desire for a theological vocabulary; for the only reason given for preserving the name "God" is that "our being has depths which naturalism, whether evolutionary, mechanistic, dialectical, or humanistic, cannot or will not recognize." But this is to say that all atheists to date have described "our being" inadequately. And that our accounts of human nature are all inadequate, most atheists would concede. But what, according to the Bishop, is at issue is how to describe our nature and not anything else. So the Bishop is fundamentally at one with Hume and Feuerbach, and at odds with Aquinas, Luther, and Billy Graham.

The second half of *Honest to God* reveals that the Bishop is a very conservative atheist. He wants an atheist Christology, he wishes to retain and to revise the notion of worship, and his moral attitudes are in fact intensely conservative. Sex outside marriage turns out to be just as wrong in the eyes of the Bishop, who says we must ask what the demands of love are, as it ever was for any Bishop who asked what ecclesiastical authority said. Indeed, the combination of radical intellectual doubt with conservative moralism is intensely reminiscent of *Robert Elsmere* and of the agonies of Victorian clergymen. Only Dr. Robinson scarcely appears in agony; he has a cheerful, even brisk style. And he recognizes much less clearly than some of his episcopal critics the implications for traditional Christianity of what he is saying.

But Dr. Robinson is not alone here. The response to his book might suggest that the combination of a religious vocabulary with substantial atheism has a wide appeal. And this is a second reason why *Honest to God* may be important. For the quality of this response may reveal something of the situation of theology in general in our sort of society. Dr. Robinson after all does more than merely quote Karl Barth, Rudolf Bultmann, Dietrich Bonhoeffer, and Paul Tillich; he presents his views as the outcome of a revolution in Protestant theology defined by those names.

So that two questions press on us: is Protestant theology, and not merely Dr. Robinson, essentially atheistic now? And what light does such theology throw upon our social life?

Modern Protestant theology is rooted in catastrophe. The liberal

idealism which easily confused a secular faith in uninterrupted
progress with belief in the actions of a divine providence could
not survive the trenches of World War I. Tillich was an army
chaplain, as Bultmann was to be later on. Bonhoeffer was to be
executed by the Nazis. The problem of evil had to be more than
an academic exercise. Moreover the matter of traditional Protestant preaching with its moralizing and its promise of pietistic
consolations could scarcely survive. Two questions pressed in:
how can we think of God after the Somme, after Auschwitz?
And how can we preach to contemporary man?[1]

The first answer to these questions was Barth's commentary on
Romans, where St. Paul's Greek is conjured into a blend of
Luther, Calvin, Dostoevski, and Kierkegaard. (Not so misleading
either, for each of them had digested large quantities of St. Paul.)
Barth's message is that any attempt to justify belief in God or any
attempt to comprehend God's ways by translating revelation into
terms other than its own is bound to fail. God is infinitely distant
from man and totally other. In revelation he condescends to us:
we can only accept or reject, we cannot argue. Evil cannot be
explained; but we can be redeemed and saved from its power.
At first sight Barth's starting-point in theology is at the opposite
pole from that of Dr. Robinson. And certainly as Barthian
theology has developed systematically, it has remained a keystone
of orthodoxy, by now a major influence among Roman Catholics
as well as among Protestants. But Barthian theology none the less
contains the materials for its own self-transformation. For if the
Word of God cannot be identified with *any* frail human attempt
to comprehend it, the way is open for sympathy with those who
reject human theologies which have attempted to substitute for
the Divine Word (and perhaps Barthian theology among them).
So Barth has always had an interest in Ludwig Feuerbach. If it is
any human work or word which we have to carefully avoid identifying or confusing with the divine, then we are in a very different

[1] It is the recurrence of these two questions together which leads Dr.
Robinson to write sometimes as if he is concerned with whether and what
God is and sometimes as if it is merely a matter of finding conveniently
different images to suit different audiences. So he can say that he does
not wish to disturb those who find it possible still to think of God in
traditional ways. This makes it possible for the Archbishop to present
Dr. Robinson as a mildly erroneous and overenthusiastic champion of some
aspects of orthodoxy at the expense of others. But in fact if Dr. Robinson's
argument is right, the traditional views of God are not merely outmoded;
they are simply false. And in other passages Dr. Robinson recognizes this.

position from that of traditional Protestant pietistic orthodoxy. For none but God can be infallible; and hence no church authority, and not even the scriptures, can be treated as infallible without impiety. This was the basis upon which Barth welcomed radical, scholarly criticism of the New Testament while fundamentalist orthodoxy always rejected it. "We have this treasure in earthen vessels."

At this point, therefore, Protestant theology has had to face up to its own inadequacies. Dr. Robinson is misleading here, for his mosaic of quotations from Bultmann, Tillich, and Bonhoeffer might suggest too great a likeness between these theologians: whereas what is in fact striking is that from quite different standpoints all these theologians converge upon unbelief. Consider them in turn.

Bultmann's theology[1] has three quite separate elements to it. There is first of all his historical skepticism about the New Testament events. Closely connected with this is his belief that the New Testament message is presented in terms of a prescientific cosmology and that consequently the gospel must be "demythologized" before it can be preached to scientific man. And there is, thirdly, his view of what the demythologized message in fact is. The prescientific cosmology is one of a three-tiered universe to which belong notions of a descent into hell, an ascent into heaven, a coming again from the heavens, of angelic and demonic hierarchies, and indeed of miraculous powers. This mythology conceals rather than conveys the message that man is a prey to an inauthentic existence, that Jesus summons him to a decision, by which he can face up to his being as that of one who is going to die and so begin to live authentically. What Jesus really meant turns out to have been an anticipation of Martin Heidegger, and when the gospel is demythologized a theistic existentialism is what remains.

But is this existentialism more than nominally theistic? Bultmann's pupil Kamlah took the final step of pointing out that what Bultmann takes the life of faith to be makes its possibility logically independent of the occurrence of any event in Palestine in the first century and, indeed, of the existence of a supernatural being. Christianity is secularized by stages into an atheistic philosophy. Bultmann's own retention of some elements of traditional Christian

[1] *See* Rudolf Bultmann, *Existence and Faith: Shorter Writings* (New York: Meridian Books; London: Hodder & Stoughton, 1960); *This World and the Beyond* (London: Lutterworth Press; New York: Scribner, 1960); *The History of the Synoptic Tradition* (New York: Harper & Row; Oxford: Blackwell, 1963).

theism appears to have no rational justification within the framework of his own thought.

Tillich's[1] contrast with Bultmann is at first sight sharp. Tillich sees himself as the heir of "the Protestant principle" that no finite being must be confused with the divine. Insofar as secularization has been an insistence that nothing in nature must be identified with God, secularization is a genuine ally of Protestant Christianity. God is not *a* being, who just happens to exist, an additional individual: in denying the existence of God the atheists are in the right. It is true that in his *Systematic Theology* Tillich slips into ascribing to God predicates which we would normally take to imply that God was *a* being. God creates and God reveals himself, for example. But he believes that in doing this he is able to rely on his own doctrine of God. This is two-sided. In the first volume of the *Systematic Theology* there is a good deal of traditional metaphysical play with being and not-being. But the rules of play are all governed by an initial criterion whose implications are far more drastic than Tillich realizes: theological statements are statements about what ultimately concerns us, and we learn the nature of what ultimately concerns us by "an analysis of the concept 'ultimate concern.' . . ." If the object of theological discourse is our own ultimate concern, what of God? It turns out that "God" just is the name for that concern. We get the transition from ontological assertion to ultimate human concern very clearly stated in a sermon:

> The name of this infinite and inexhaustible depth and ground of all being is God. That depth is what the word God means. And if that word has not much meaning for you, translate it and speak of the depths of your life, of the source of your being, of your ultimate concern, of what you take seriously without any reservation. Perhaps in order to do so you must forget everything traditional that you have learnt about God, perhaps even that word itself. For if you know that God means depth, you know much about him. You cannot then call yourself an atheist or unbeliever. For you cannot think or say: Life has no depth! Life is shallow!

Clearly, however, the conversion of the unbeliever is only so

[1] *See* Paul Tillich, *The Courage to Be* (New Haven, Conn.: Yale University Press; London: Collins, 1950); *Theology of Culture* (London and New York: Oxford University Press, 1964); *Dynamics of Faith— World Perspectives* (New York: Harper & Row; London: Allen & Unwin, 1958).

easy for Tillich because belief in God has been evacuated of all its traditional content. It consists now in moral seriousness and nothing more. Even if we were to concede Tillich a verbal triumph over the atheist, the substance of atheism has been conceded. Just as Bultmann's view of the New Testament points toward skepticism, so does Tillich's analysis of the doctrine of God. It seems that Dr. Robinson is not alone as a theological atheist.

But what of Dietrich Bonhoeffer? Those who have written of him have usually dwelt on the posthumously collected *Letters and Papers from Prison*[1] at the expense of his earlier books, and more expressly at the expense of *Sanctorum Communio* and *Akt und Sein*. What Bonhoeffer tried to explain was the specific character of a Christian way of life in a Christian community. In *Akt und Sein* he even tries to solve theological problems by showing the role of the concepts in question in the life of the church. And the life of the Christian community in *Sanctorum Communio* is specified in terms of sociological categories borrowed from Ferdinand Tönnies, the familiar categories of *Gemeinschaft* and *Gesellschaft*. But Bonhoeffer wishes to show not what Christian societies share with other societies, but precisely what distinguishes Christian from other shared ways of life. He rejects the answer which both some religious apologists and secular sociologists would give: that the specific differentia lies in the performance of certain religious practices or in the status accorded to certain special theistic types of explanation. God is not a hypothesis, or if he is treated as one, then it is a hypothesis which has already been discredited. The Christian way of life consists not in any reliance either on ecclesiastical forms or on divine power but in a life of worldly powerlessness, lived totally for others. So we get the final conclusion in his notes in prison that

> The transcendence consists not in tasks beyond our scope and power, but in the nearest Thou at hand. God in human form, not, as in other religions, in animal form—the monstrous, chaotic, remote and terrifying—nor yet in abstract form— the absolute, metaphysical infinite, etc.—nor yet in the Greek divine-human of autonomous man, but man existing for others, and hence the Crucified. . . .

So the distinction between secular atheistic man and Christian man is that the latter acknowledges his powerlessness in his concern for others. But what would it be like to do this in the world of

[1] Dietrich Bonhoeffer, *Letters and Papers from Prison* (New York: Macmillan; London: SCM Press, 1956).

today, of the welfare state and of the underdeveloped countries, facing the patterns of world revolution? One gets from Bonhoeffer's writings no clear picture of what type of action he would actually be recommending now, but one gets the clearest picture of what Bonhoeffer means if one sees it in the context out of which he wrote. For in Nazi Germany, and in the Europe of the 1930s, the Christian role was at best one of suffering witness. The Nazi regress to gods of race made relevant a Christian regress to a witness of the catacombs and of the martyrs. There was available then a simple form in which to relive Christ's passion. Bonhoeffer lived it. And in all situations where nothing else remains for Christians this remains.

But what has this Christianity to say not of powerlessness, but of the handling of power? Nothing; and hence the oddity of trying to reissue Bonhoeffer's message in our world. Consider Bonhoeffer's cry from prison:

> Man's religiosity makes him look in his distress to the power of God in the world; he uses God as a *deus ex machina*. The Bible however directs him to the powerlessness and suffering of God; only a suffering God can help.

Imagine it directed to a church which is providing chaplains for the West German armed forces, as Bonhoeffer's church is, or to a church which chose the right moment to get out of gilt-edged securities and into equities, as Dr. Robinson's did. Only a suffering God can help?

Bonhoeffer's Christianity is then intelligible only in one sort of context. Outside that context it lacks precisely any specific differentia from the way of life of sensitive generous liberals. It does not issue in atheism as the conclusion of an argument (as Bultmann's theology does), and it does not present atheism in theological language (as Tillich's theology does), but it fails in the task for which it was designed and in our sort of society it becomes a form of practical atheism, for it clothes ordinary liberal forms of life with the romantic unreality of a catacombic vocabulary.

We can see the harsh dilemma of a would-be contemporary theology. The theologians begin from orthodoxy, but the orthodoxy which has learnt from Kierkegaard and Barth becomes too easily a closed circle, in which believer speaks only to believer, in which all human content is concealed. Turning aside from this arid in-group theology, the most perceptive theologians wish to translate what they have to say to an atheistic world. But they are

doomed to one of two failures. Either they succeed in their translation: in which case what they find themselves saying has been
transformed into the atheism of their hearers. Or they fail in their
translation: in which case no one hears what they have to say but
themselves.

It is this last alternative which leads to the hothouse atmosphere
of so much theological discussion; it is the former which leads to
Dr. Robinson's conclusions. We can see now that Dr. Robinson's
voice is not just that of an individual, that his book testifies to the
existence of a whole group of theologies which have retained a
theistic vocabulary but acquired an atheistic substance. Yet how
can these continue to coexist? To answer this question we must
look at the social context of this type of theology.

Dr. Robinson writes as if the secularization of the modern
world were an accomplished and a recognized fact. If he were
correct we should expect a corresponding sense of triumph in
secularist writers. In fact we find too often the same uneasiness
that we discover in the theologians.

Dr. Gerhard Sczsczesny's *The Future of Unbelief*[1] caused a
minor sensation when it appeared in Germany. It had its place
in the whole history of the rise of a dissenting intelligentsia in
postwar Germany (a piece of cultural history almost unknown in
England). But Sczsczesny's argument is doubly paradoxical. For
he argues first that we ought to recognize that we are now living
in "a post-Christian era," and the paradox is that if this were
clearly true there would be no need to call upon people to recognize it. Sczsczesny would not have to fight against the cultural
orthodoxy of the CDU/CSU. And when Sczsczesny goes on to
construct his humanist alternative to Christianity the criteria
to which he appeals are ordinary humanist ones. So that unless
people are already convinced secularists they are unlikely to listen
to him. Moreover, he formulates his alternative in terms of fairly
abstract and hence unobjectionable principle. Justice, equality,
and honesty are all commended. Yet anyone who lived through
the German catastrophe must know that the problem is not
whether justice, equality, and honesty are admirable; the problem
is how to embody them in social institutions. And to solve this
problem we have to recognize clearly what our existing social
order is. If we do so we shall see that it is very far from being
completely secularized.

England is perhaps an untypical country. The English have
neither the ecclesiastical political parties of Europe, nor the

[1] Gerhard Sczsczesny, *The Future of Unbelief* (London: Heinemann).

majority churchgoing of the United States. But they experience many of the same pressures, and they therefore find analogous religious phenomena. The number of Easter communicants in the Church of England has risen very slowly but fairly steadily for a decade and a half. Over half the marriages in England take place in Anglican churches. Over half the children eligible for Anglican baptism are so baptized. Between the 10 per cent or so of clear and convinced Christians at one end of the scale and the 10 per cent or so of convinced skeptics at the other, there is the vast mass of the population, mostly superstitious to some degree, using the churches and especially the Church of England to celebrate birth, marriage, and death, and to a lesser degree Christmas. This use or misuse of the churches is rooted in a set of vague, half formulated and inconsistent beliefs.

In 1944–45 *Mass-Observation* carried out a survey in a London borough on the topic of religious belief which was published under the title of *Puzzled People*. In 1960 they quota-sampled the same borough. The inconsistency of both self-styled believers and self-styled unbelievers is perhaps the most striking single fact. In both 1945 and 1960 over 40 per cent of those attending Anglican services said that they did not believe in a life after death, while at least a quarter of those classed as doubters, agnostics, and atheists said that they prayed, and over 20 per cent of them said that Christ was more than a man. Tom Harrisson's account of these people's beliefs in *Britain Revisited* is consistent with the answers that industrial workers gave to Dr. Ferdynand Zweig on religious questions, and in *The British Worker* Dr. Zweig concludes that 80 per cent of workers have some sort of "vague belief." But it would be sadly mistaken to suppose that this state of affairs is confined to working-class adults and children. The survey of contemporary attitudes among the readers of *New Society* (May 1963) showed a majority both for the belief that Christian morality is moribund and for the belief that this is a sad thing. But the majority also believe—what the authoritative exponents of Christianity deny—that divorce should be made easier. So we find among some of the best-educated by our conventional standards a paradoxical wish to hold on to a morality which conflicts with their own morality on matters of central importance. Behind this paradox one senses a belief that Christian theology is false and a wish that it were not, which at other social levels appears as the kind of half-belief which I have described.

The sources of this lack of consistency are several. The folk-beliefs of the English cannot be understood without understanding the whole history of Christianity's rearguard actions, including the highly dubious use of religion in wartime. But we can discover one clue to the immediate causes of the confusion if we notice that 67 per cent of children who are subjected to Anglican baptism decline to 24 per cent who find their way to confirmation; and there is another steep decline to the figures for adult church-going.

It is just not true that children in this country are indoctrinated in Christianity as a result of the 1944 Education Act. What they *are* indoctrinated in is confusion. This confusion is rooted in the fact that on the one hand religious instruction is compulsory, and yet on the other it is clear that schools do not take it seriously in the way that they do basic literacy or subjects such as history or chemistry. Since teachers usually do not even attempt to give any criteria for accepting or rejecting belief, many children naturally remain in a half-light between acceptance and rejection. Secularized? Not at all. The secondary modern school children of whom Dr. Harold Loukes wrote in *Teenage Religion* would suggest, for example, that the question of whether God did or did not make the world could not be answered because nobody else can have been there to see. If they do believe in God, it is often the God "up there" (literally, physically "up") who Dr. Robinson thinks has been incredible for a long time.

Christianity provided pre-industrial England with a common frame of reference, with a sense of over-all meaning and with a pattern which gave form to life. Revolutionary protest from the Levellers to the Chartists could express itself within this pattern just as much as the conservatism of the squirearchy. But industrial society has never been able to accommodate a religious interpretation of its own activities. The founders of atheist humanism hoped for and predicted secularization not merely in the sense of abandonment of religious belief and practice, but in the sense of a transformation of human goals and hopes from other-worldly into this-worldly. The present was to be judged and transcended, not by looking to the justice of heaven but by looking to that of the future. The hope of glory was to be, and in some important measure was, replaced by the hope of Utopia.

But we have neither glory nor Utopia to hope for. The hope that a secular Utopian tradition, whether Liberal or Marxist, sought to provide was never realized. The routines of working-class life, the competitive ladders of the middle classes, absorb us into immediacy. We are dominated by a present to which the idea of a radically different future is alien. What conventional politics promises us is always a brighter version of what we have now. This is why political talk about ends and aims is always doomed to become rhetoric. In this situation the substance of religious belief is no longer with us, but in our ordinary secular vocabulary we have no language to express common needs, hopes, and fears that go beyond the immediacies of technique and social structure.

What we do have is a religious language, which survives even though we do not know what to say in it. Since it is the only language we have for certain purposes it is not surprising that it cannot be finally discarded. But since we have no answers to give to the questions we ask in it, it remains continually in need of reinterpretation, reinterpretation that is always bound to fail. We should therefore expect to find continual attempts to use religious language to mask an atheistic vacuum, and sooner or later someone was bound to try to preserve the religious language and the atheistic content together by suggesting, although not of course explicitly, that the latter simply *is* the meaning of the former. Not that this suggestion could possibly work a cure for any of our ills. The only cure lies in the transformation of our social structures; *within* theological discourse, as Feuerbach and Marx saw, we are bound to remain blind to the human significance of theological discourse. Hence Dr. Robinson's book needs not only to be understood as a symptom of our condition, but to be sympathized with as a desperate attempt that cannot succeed.

If the core of my argument is correct, then we should be able to construct a hypothesis about contemporary moral theology. Either it will remain within the theological closed circle: in which case it will have no access to the public and shared moral criteria of our society. Or it will accept those criteria: in which case it may well have important things to say, but these will not be distinctively Christian. I take it as partial confirmation of my argument, therefore, that when we encounter Cambridge theologians grappling with real moral problems[1] it turns out that their Christianity is residual. This is not to say that they have not learnt from Jesus and from Christian traditions; but rather, that they have learnt in ways that are accessible to the atheist too.

When Professor D. M. MacKinnon writes about extramarital intercourse he judges alternatives in terms of human concepts of integrity and stability. He criticizes some uses of the notion of sacrifice in Christian morality. He argues that Christianity is a

[1] *Objections to Christian Belief*, Four Lectures by D. M. MacKinnon, H. A. Williams, A. R. Vidler and J. S. Bezzant (London: Constable; Philadelphia: Lippincott, 1964).

2

unique source of moral inspiration, because it tries to hold together the truth about what men are and the need for them to be merciful to one another. But he presents these as truths for anyone to grasp, whether Christian or not. And this is true also of the outstanding contribution to the debate from among the Cambridge theologians, which is made by Mr. H. A. Williams in his essay on "Psychological Objections to Christianity."

Williams' attack is directed against the moral forms of contemporary Christianity. He exposes the fake character of a great deal of remorse and searching of conscience by describing its role in providing a welcome barrier to genuine self-knowledge. He brings out excellently the way in which condemnation of overt breaches of the sexual code, whether in ourselves or in others, can be a symptom of a more than ambiguous attitude to sexuality, and how the price of self-knowledge and truthfulness may be a life which conventional Christianity condemns. Williams finds a clue to Christianity in Christ's obvious preference for publicans and sinners over the clergy. Williams could scarcely be more severe in his treatment of his own religion, and if it is necessary to ask whether he goes far enough, it is not because one could go any farther in that direction. It is rather that he never asks what makes traits like conscientiousness and a sense of duty so important to contemporary Christianity. The answer is that these traits belong to the manner in which we act; they do not define the contents of our actions. Injunctions to repent, to be responsible, even to be generous, do not actually tell us what to *do*. And about the content of the moral life Christians in fact have no more to say than anyone else. Christians behave like everyone else but use a different vocabulary in characterizing their behavior, and so conceal their lack of distinctiveness. Thus true self-knowledge for Christians would involve the uncovering of much more than a retreat by individuals into neurotic self-concealment. But even in this Christians only reflect a general predicament.

All those in our society who self-consciously embrace beliefs which appear to confer importance and righteousness upon the holder become involved in the same strategies. The fact that their beliefs make so little difference either to them or to others leads to the same concern with being right-minded rather than effective. Hygienic, liberal, periodical-reading progressives who are against capital punishment and blood sports tend to be quite as nasty as Christians are, in this respect.

And there are many other varieties of the neurotic self-deceiver. When Williams tries to accuse his fellow-Christians of believing not in God, but Nobodaddy, I hope that he makes them wince. But I hope he also makes all those of us wince who have turned conscientious atheism into a substitute Nobodaddy of our own.

The one person in the discussion clearly determined not to wince is the Archbishop of Canterbury. His pamphlet *Image Old and New* misses almost all the points. Dr. Robinson is treated as an unbalanced reformer who has stressed some aspects of the Christian faith at the expense of others. Ascetic retreat from the world and unbreakable rules still have their place. (Why do unbreakable rules always turn out to be about sex and not about war?) But the worst feature of his pamphlet is the paternalistic tone. He calls Bonhoeffer's views "thoughts mature in depth but often incomplete, alas, in their working out" and wonders whether, had he lived, he would not have changed his views. He seeks to spread reassurance.

But reassurance is just what Christians should not be looking for at this point in their history. It is not Dr. Robinson who will be disturbing them, if they are disturbed. The fragility of their religion is due not to the theologians but to its role in our social life. This the theologians only reflect. But it is not surprising that when they reflect it as faithfully as Dr. Robinson has done, all the vices of self-deception which Mr. Williams castigates are brought into play, as they have notably been brought into play in so much of the response to *Honest to God*.

Because all this is so, it is highly important that the theologians should not be left alone with their discussions, to carry them on as *they* please. For the significance of their discussions extends far beyond theology. The public response to *Honest to God* helped to make this clear. But in the next phase when the issues are less immediately newsworthy, the danger is that God will once more be treated as an in-group totem. Once there were organized secularist groups (the Rationalist Press Association, the Ethical Union, and the like) which could have assisted in ensuring that the discussion continued in the public forum. But all these groups essentially became nonconformist churches and share in the general decline of nonconformity. So one gets the pathos of humanist groups in universities which are imitations of the Student Christian Movement. At the moment one cannot dispense with this kind of group, if only because it provides a counter-weight to the Christians. But the danger is that atheism is then treated as if it too is the private creed of yet another minority religious group, whereas atheism is in fact expressed in most of our social life.

The difficulty lies in the combination of atheism in the practice of the life of the vast majority, with the profession of either superstition or theism by that same majority. The creed of the English is that there is no God and that it is wise to pray to him from time to time.

3

Psychoanalysis: the future of an illusion?[1]

The more that is written about psychoanalysis the more puzzled one can become. On the one hand there are the ever new but all too familiar expositions of the system. Dr. J. A. C. Brown's[2] and Dr. Reuben Fine's[3] are among the most recent to hand. Excellent as expositions, the time has come when defensive exposition is not enough. Taken as we are again and again on the same conducted tour of Freud's views, the intellectual boredom is intensified. Yet there is a whole series of books which excite and illuminate, and could not have been written but for Freud. I do not mean by this simply to assert the truism that there are dull authors and that there are exciting authors. The contrasts between psychoanalysts are far more extreme than that. It is rather that what is at first sight the same Freudian methodology appears capable both of crippling the intellect and of liberating it. How so?

Psychoanalysts, like priests, suffer from an initial disadvantage: they have to take care to keep separate the situations in which they must assume the pose of authority from those in which they themselves must accept the authority of rational argument. The pulpit is no place to debate the existence of God and the couch is for free association, not for theoretical objections. And yet— unless the theoretical objections can be answered, the clinical authority of the analyst is faked. It was Karl Kraus who remarked that psychoanalysis is in fact the disease for which it purports to be the cure. One gets a hint that, as so often with Kraus, what looks like an easy witticism will bear closer scrutiny from the curious

[1] Reprinted from *Encounter*, May 1968.
[2] J. A. C. Brown, *Freud and the Post-Freudians* (London and Baltimore: Penguin Books, Pelican ed., 1961).
[3] Reuben Fine, *Freud: A Critical Evaluation of His Theories* (New York: David McKay; London: Allen & Unwin, 1962).

tone which infects the answers that some psychoanalysts make to their critics. There is an important difference between their attitude and that of Freud who wrote:

> Looking back, then, over the patchwork of my life's labors, I can say that I have made many beginnings and thrown out many suggestions. Something will come of them in the future, though I cannot myself tell whether it will be much or little. . . .

This underlying caution was always there to temper Freud's flights of speculative enthusiasm. Unfortunately it appears to be mainly the speculative enthusiasm which his heirs have inherited —at least on the occasions when they respond to criticism.

In order to evaluate this response, we must first understand the critics, and in order to understand them we must set out the features of psychoanalytic theory which invite criticism. We can illuminate the logical structure of psychoanalytic theory by remembering that Freud's contentions were made at three different levels. First of all, Freud drew our attention to hitherto unnoticed types of episodes. He reclassified and redescribed our behavior. He made us aware of what needed to be explained. Secondly, he suggested a correlation between adult episodes and traits and the passions and actions of the world of early childhood. Thirdly, he produced a theory to explain that correlation; or rather he produced a range of theoretical notions, of which the earlier account of the distribution and transformations of libido and the later trinity of id, superego, and ego are the most important. It is often difficult in exposition to keep the distinction between these three levels clear, partly because kindred notions appear at all three and more especially when this is so because the explanatory theory helps to provide a vocabulary for the description of the very facts which the theory is designed to explain. One example of this is the way in which the notion of unconscious motivation is often used *both* descriptively to bring out features of goal-directed behavior in which the agent himself remains unaware of his goals and resists (again without recognizing what he is doing) any correct identification of them—and also as part of the account of the formation of character which is invoked to explain such behavior. Another is the way in which adult behavior may be characterized as Oedipal, an instructive resemblance with child-hood behavior being brought out by a term the use of which already half-commits us to a particular explanation of this resemblance.

This transition from level to level is itself important for at least two reasons. There is perhaps no discipline to compare with psychoanalysis for the way in which the very use of the vocabulary commits the novice—quite unconsciously—to acceptance of a complex theoretical framework. And moreover this is common to all the rival analytic schools, or to all at least which share some sort of Freudian commitment. Melanie Klein differed from Freud about many things, and especially the characterization of early childhood; Freud himself was always prepared to revise his own theoretical apparatus; but what cannot be revised without loss of the theory altogether is the notion of a set of childhood traits, a corresponding set of adult traits, and a theoretical bridge between them. It is upon the concepts out of which this bridge is to be built that attention can therefore be focused.

Central among them is that of *repression*. Freud's own view both of the cause and of the consequences of repression gradually changed. He came in his later period to see repression as a response above all to anxiety, when he had earlier seen anxiety as an effect of repression. And he came to envisage it as only one of the defensive strategems to which the threatened ego might resort. But it retains a central and characteristic place. In a paper of 1908, *Character and Anal Erotism*, Freud wrote that:

> We can at any rate lay down a formula for the way in which character in its final shape is formed out of the constituent instincts: the permanent character traits are either unchanged prolongations of the original instincts, or the sublimations of those instincts, or reaction-formations against them.

To this thought Freud remained faithful; and this required that he remained faithful also to the notion of repression. Dr. Brown has summarized his unchanging view in writing:

> that the unconscious plays a predominant part in mental life, since it takes its energy from the instinctual drives, and its contents are kept out of awareness not because they lack significance but because they may be so significant as to constitute what is felt as a threat to the ego. When this occurs they are actively repressed and can find expression only by devious methods, as in symptoms, certain character traits, and the other phenomena which represent compromise solutions to a conflict between primitive drives seeking an outlet and learned ego and superego behavior patterns which must inhibit them. . . .
> Repression is itself an unconscious process. . . .

The difficulties which critics have alleged against this position are of at least three kinds. There is the too open texture of the concepts; the apparent falsity and the untested character of certain of the factual claims; and the unfalsifiability of parts of the theoretical apparatus. A concept like "repression," for instance, can only be safely used if we are given criteria for its application, such that we can identify at least central cases of repression taking place. For its full use in psychoanalytic theory we should also need criteria to determine when behavior evidences the effect of repression and when memories that have been recalled have been recalled as a result of a cessation of repression rather than from some other possible cause.

But we are supplied with no adequate criteria. We are not told how to recognize the response of repression when it is first made; and when later on the analyst interprets his patient's behavior as manifesting effects of repression, what he will treat as confirmatory of his interpretation is probably a set of further reactions by the patient—dreams, newly recalled memories, changes in attitude to the analyst, and the like. Analysts have discussed with a great deal of care what the criteria of a correct interpretation ought to be.[1] But while they have produced some interesting generalizations about the kind of result that may follow from one sort of interpretation rather than another, what they have not done is to explain how these responses help to confirm the *truth* of the interpretation, as distinct from the effectiveness of it in producing further reactions. To do this successfully we should need the concept of repression and kindred concepts of defense to be defined more sharply in operational terms. More than this we must take care to see that the concepts are not defined in terms of the theory. For if repression is defined or explained in terms of unconscious instinctual drives, as it is in the quotation from Dr. Brown, then the use of the term is already part of our theoretical explanation of what occurs, and we shall still lack an adequate way of characterizing and identifying the occurrences which the theory is designed to explain.

At the level of the empirically observable there are much simpler questions to be put to the analyst. What are the alleged facts which the theory explains? What factual generalizations are entailed by the theory and must be true if the theory is true? Experimental psychologists have expended effort and ingenuity in

[1] See especially Susan Isaacs. "Criteria for Interpretation," *International Journal of Psychoanalysis* (1939); and P. M. Turquet, "The Criteria For A Psychoanalytic Interpretation," *Aristotelian Society Supplementary Volume* (1962).

trying to specify the necessary generalizations and confirm or falsify them. The result of this effort is a sifting out from the Freudian amalgam of particular hypotheses concerning the effects of maternal deprivation at different ages, the preferences of children for one parent rather than the other, the formation of character traits, and so on. When these hypotheses are tested, we find that the Freudian doctrine seems to be a mixture of true and false statements. In so appearing it loses its unity of structure. This loss is further intensified by the separating out in the process of the testable elements in the theory from the untestable.

I am not now referring to the kind of untestability which derives from the too open texture of the key concepts, but to the tendency to specify too many ways in which the theory may be confirmed and not enough ways in which it might be falsified. Consider the already quoted statement from *Character and Anal Erotism*. The instinctual drives may be transformed so that they manifest themselves in one way; or it may be the processes of reaction formation result in their being manifested in a precisely opposite way. The same type of background may result in sadistic, aggressive behavior or in gentle, nonviolent behavior. The hypothesis has become a bet that cannot lose; but by the same token, as Karl Popper has shown, it cannot win. Whatever the behavior, the hypothesis is not falsified, and its unfalsifiability is fatal to its status as a hypothesis.

All this is preliminary to a central argument. The criticisms I have summarized are almost overfamiliar to analysts.[1] But what has been inadequately commented upon is the type of answer which is being made by the analysts and their supporters to the critics. I ought in fairness to the reader to stress that I am going to try to set out the analytic case against the critics at its strongest. That is why I want to attend especially to arguments used by Dr. Brown and Dr. Edward Glover.

Begin with Brown's reply to the charge that experimental evidence does not bear out Freud s hypotheses:

> That two American psychologists should ask college students to recall at random pleasant and unpleasant experiences on the assumption that, if repression were a fact, more of the former than the latter would be recalled is bad enough; that, as Professor

[1] *See* especially H. J. Eysenck, "What is Wrong with Psychoanalysis?" in *Uses and Abuses of Psychology* (London and Baltimore: Penguin Books, Pelican) and B. A. Farrell, "Psychoanalytic Theory?" in *New Society*, June 20 and 27, 1963.

Eysenck assures us, a group of strong and presumably normal individuals were persuaded to starve themselves for an appreciable period in order to prove that Freud's theory of dreams as wish-fulfillments was false because they did not dream of food, strains one's credibility; but that an eminent educational psychologist should solemnly "prove" the Oedipus complex to be a myth by the simple expedient of asking a number of other professional psychologists about the preferences of their own children towards one parent or the other baffles comprehension. Freud at no time said that unpleasant experiences as such were likely to be forgotten; he said that experiences which might conflict with other dominant tendencies of the personality were likely to be repressed, whether as experiences they were pleasant or not; he did not say that for any appreciable period a child showed overt preference for the parent of the opposite sex, because the very word "complex" refers to *unconscious* attitudes which are unconscious precisely because they are forbidden; he did not assert that hunger made one dream of food, although explorers and others subjected involuntarily to hunger have said that it did, and he would certainly have seen through the fallacy of supposing that voluntary and experimental subjection to starvation bears any resemblance in its emotional significance to the involuntary situation in which the basic issue is not primarily lack of food but imminent proximity of death.[1]

Let us concede at once the crudity of the experiments referred to; but even that crudity is a testimony to the difficulty of translating Freudian concepts into terms that will yield testable hypotheses. If the experimentalists have, as Brown accuses, mistranslated the concepts, the only adequate rejoinder would be to produce a correct translation and then await the verdict of experiment. But not only does Brown not do this, he does not even seem to admit the suggestion that there is a need for experiment. Yet until and unless such translations and experiments are provided the best available verdict on psychoanalytic theory would be that of "Not Proven." None the less Brown claims that

> Freud alone amongst the founders of analytic schools understood and made thorough use of the scientific method in his investigations. Freud's approach was as logical and his findings as carefully tested as Pavlov's, but he was able to deal successfully with phenomena inaccessible to Pavlov. . . .

[1] J. A. C. Brown, *op. cit.*, pp. 192–3.

Yet throughout Brown's book what we are offered are confirmatory observations, not crucial tests of Freudian theory.

It is of course not only the opponents of analysis who have recognized the need for more inquiry at this point. Dr. Edward Glover has subjected both the lack of adequate definition of concepts and the absence of prediction and testing from psycho-analytic work to a critique as fierce as that of any experimentalist. But, so he has argued in two recent papers,[1] we should not therefore arrive at negative conclusions about psychoanalysis. For the carefully devised experiments of the ordinary descriptive psycho-logist are themselves suspect, since in the experimental study of variations in the behavior of a particular group compared with a control group, we may ignore the possibility of unconscious factors affecting the behavior of the chosen control, in such a way that the matching and comparison are unreliable.

> From all this follows the somewhat disconcerting conclusion that under present systems of control we have no sound justification for abandoning a causal theory simply because the application of statistical controls appears to show that it is non-specific. When allegedly scientific procedures appear to point conclusively in one direction, the investigator of deep and unconscious factors should not be too perturbed if these conclusions run counter to his own interpretations. Although apparently wrong by the standards of natural science he may yet be right by the standards of depth psychology.

The difficulty with this argument lies in its covert circularity. We cannot trust present experimental techniques because their use neglects the operation of unconscious factors; the only techniques which would be reliable would therefore be those which took account of the operation of such factors. But to admit the existence of the kind of unconscious factors of which Dr. Glover speaks is already to concede substantial truth to the very body of theory which we require to be tested. Dr. Glover's criticism of the experimentalists presupposes that the issue which divides him from them has already been fundamentally settled in his favor. Appearing to concede the need for neutral experiment, he in fact lays down preconditions for the construction of such experiments which ensure that his own positions will

[1] Edward Glover, "Psychoanalysis and 'Controlled' Research in Delinquency," *British Journal of Criminology* (1962), and "Research Techniques in Psychoanalysis and in General Psychology," in *Readings in Psychology*, edited by John Cohen (New York: Hillary House, 1964).

remain basically unscathed. It is this that makes the onus of disproof which he lays upon the experimental critics so unreal.

The inescapable conclusion of this part of the argument is that psychoanalytic theory is in no sense well founded and that it is not science in any recognizable sense. But this is not just because it is inadequately vindicated by experiment. It is much more because, although it clearly is in fact not vindicated, it is presented by its adherents as though its truth were well established. Dr. Brown compares Freud to Newton; Dr. Glover says that "Freud was able to establish some of the most important laws regarding human behavior"; Dr. Fine asserts that general psychology now accepts the core of Freud's work. Brown and Fine give the impression that the rejection of psychoanalysis is eccentric and restricted to an imperceptive minority. But Professor O. H. Mowrer, by any standards a central figure in the development of contemporary psychology, decided in the end for "the basic unsoundness of Freud's major premises." This kind of conclusion the layman all too seldom has brought to his attention.

But it works, so it will be said. Surely, it will be added, it is unforgivable to have treated psychoanalysis primarily as a body of explanations rather than as a method of therapy. Yet the whole argument so far is intended, above all, to raise a question about the therapy. It has often been asserted that the therapy is ineffective; roughly speaking, such evidence as there is points to an insufficiently dissimilar rate of cure for patients who are not treated at all as for those who are treated by analysis. But the evidence is not very good and about it, once again, the important point is not that the claims of psychoanalysis have been overthrown, but that they have never been vindicated. Yet even this is not what is crucial. What matters is that the practice of the therapy presupposes the truth of the theory. The claim that what the patient acquires is genuine self-knowledge of a past still alive in his present can only be made good if the theoretical bridge between childhood and adult life does not break down. The authority of the analyst in his therapeutic role rests on his supposed theoretical equipment and backing as well as his clinical skills. Yet the theory which the therapy embodies is a theory in which neither analyst nor patient have a right to be confident. But without confidence the therapy could not even begin. So how is the confidence to be engendered? Only in unjustifiable ways.

The larger problem is the sociological one. False or unjustified assertions have been propagated in our time with the power of almost omnipotent states to back them up; beliefs now usually discredited but once plausible have often survived into our own age. But I know of no other example of a system of beliefs, unjustified on the basis of the criteria to which it itself appeals, and unbacked by political power or past tradition, which has propagated itself so successfully as Freudian orthodoxy. How did it do it?

Consider the following vocabulary: adjustment, conflict, integrate, relate, relationship. . . . It is the vocabulary of Jules Feiffer's characters. It is also the vocabulary of Feiffer's readers: the vocabulary of a segment of urban, middle-class intelligentsia whose cultural situation deprived them of large-scale theory at the same time as it made large-scale theory an intense necessity for them. The skepticism of an earlier generation had deprived them of religion. The history of their own time deprived them of Marxism and in so doing of their hold upon the public world of political ends. The intellectual may be socially valued for his functional utility; but otherwise, his arena is increasingly that of private life. He needs to make his own experience intelligible: an image of the public world as a mere projection upon a larger screen of the private rages and longings, hopes and fears which circumscribe him. The intolerable character of his condemnation to private life is relieved by an overpersonalization of that life. The ideology of personal relationships invokes a public sanction in the closed system of psychoanalytic theory. And a whole vocabulary of personal relationships enables psychoanalysis to appear, not as one more questionable theory, but as the unquestionable framework which gives life meaning.

Yet if this suggestion—which amounts to saying that psychoanalysis is the folk religion of one section of the intelligentsia—were not only true, but the whole truth, we should scarcely expect the series of encounters between psychoanalysis and the larger world of society, politics and history to be as fruitful as they have been. Two books published since 1958 furnish a record of such encounters. They are Bruno Bettelheim's *The Informed Heart*[1] and Erik H. Erikson's *Young Man Luther: A Study in Psychoanalysis and History*.[2] Both exhibit a certain ambivalence toward the orthodox psychoanalytic tradition. Both return us to Freud himself, but to a different Freud both from the Freud of orthodoxy and from the Freud of each other.

Bettelheim is at once the most striking and the most intelligently radical of Freudian revisionists. He is the most striking because his

[1] New York: Free Press; London: Thames and Hudson, 1961.
[2] New York: W. W. Norton; London: Faber and Faber, 1959.

revisions began in Dachau and Buchenwald. He is intelligently radical in his clear statement of what must be rejected in Freud.

> What struck me first was . . . that those persons who according to psychoanalytic theory as I understood it then, should have stood up best under the rigor of the camp experience, were often very poor examples of human behavior under extreme stress.

So he began to reflect on the nature of environment and on the apparent irrelevance of the explanation of types of behavior in terms of their origin.

> It just would not do under conditions prevailing in the camps to view courageous, life-endangering actions as an outgrowth of the death instinct, aggression turned against the self, testing the indestructibility of the body, megalomaniac denial of danger, histrionic feeding of one's narcissism or whatever other category the action would have to be viewed from in psychoanalysis.

Not only the predictions, but also the values of psychoanalysis were put in question, and a common root was discerned for both errors. This root lay in the attention paid to the pathological, the lack of attention to the normal. Bettelheim stresses how psychoanalytic explanations of genius explain everything but the genius. Work, art, social life: all the normal ends of man evade being treated as the outcrops of infantile patterns.

When Bettelheim discusses his own experience in the camps in detail what is striking is the way in which psychoanalysts' concepts become less and less theoretical, more and more descriptive. The same is true of Erikson's work. Erikson—both in his earlier work *Childhood and Society* and in his study of Luther—uses not the Freudian system, but rather Freud's techniques of observation. He pays attention to the facts which Freud discovered rather than to the theoretical entities alleged to be lurking behind these facts. And he works empirically, generalizing from instance to instance, and making modest predictions based on such generalizations. So he detects a pattern of crises in the development of the child. He makes use of Freud's descriptions to illuminate these crises; but his theory of stages is derived not from the theory so much as from generalizations about the empirical material of a much more modest kind than are some of Freud's own larger statements. The historical material is in his hands not something to which a ready-made psychoanalytic theory is applied. The vindication of

Erikson's statements about Luther lies in *the evidence* about Luther, not in the congruence with established psychoanalytic doctrine. In other words, psychoanalysis need not become the self-enclosed system which it so often is. But how do we avoid this? What is the difference between Brown and Fine on the one hand and Bettelheim and Erikson on the other?

Part of the answer is surely obtained by considering the strain within Freud's own writings between observation and explanation, between the material he amasses and the theoretical forms into which he cast his presentation of that material. The comparison with Newton misled not only his expositors but Freud himself. What Freud showed us were hitherto unnoticed facts, hitherto unrevealed motives, hitherto unrelated facets of our life. And in doing so his achievement broke all preconceived conceptual schemes—including his own. As a discoverer he perhaps resembles a Proust or a Tolstoy rather than a Dalton or a Pasteur. We could have learnt this from reading Freud himself; but the division among his heirs also reveals the fact clearly.

Yet both sets of heirs are legitimate. The sterility and the perversity are as Freudian as the perceptive fertility of a Bettelheim or an Erikson. Freud, too, was a victim of the need to explain, of the need to be Newton. The paradox of the history of psychoanalysis is that it is those analysts most intent on presenting their subject as a theoretical science who have transformed it into a religion, those most concerned with actual religious phenomena, such as Bettelheim (who has written a monograph on initiation rites) and Erikson, who have preserved it as science. The achievement of Bettelheim and Erikson has been to extend our subjection to the phenomena themselves. But in so doing they have not diminished but increased its complexity.

The outcome of Freud's discoveries is to leave us not with a solution but with more problems, among them the problem of how to understand the analysts themselves, and the differences between them.

4

The socialism of R. H. Tawney[1]

The deaths of R. H. Tawney and Hugh Gaitskell occurred so close together that they provide an apt symbol for the end of a period in the history of the British Labour Movement. It was a period in which the Right wing of the Labour Party was hard put to it to provide a rationale for its policies, which would both justify its opposition to Marxism and yet enable it to escape from the platitudes of merely liberal good will. The number of those who might have provided such a rationale were surprisingly few. The Webbs defected to Stalinism from the Fabian Society (consistent elitists who believed throughout their career in socialism imposed from above, they merely changed in their choice of elite); John Strachey only defected *to* the Fabian Society from Stalinism at the end of the 1930s; and G. D. H. Cole was always too much of a Marxist to work within the limitations that the Labour Right imposed upon itself. Tawney therefore stood almost alone.

The present collection of essays,[2] written at various dates between 1914 and 1953, reiterates themes from all Tawney's major work. In *The Acquisitive Society* he criticized capitalism because it encouraged economic power without social responsibility. The right to property had become separated from any obligation to discharge a useful social function. In *Equality* he attacked the view that the natural inequality of man in respect of ability justified inequalities of wealth and status; rather, so he argued, it would be in an egalitarian society that diversity of abilities would flourish most for the common good. In *Religion and the Rise of Capitalism* he studied the origins of acquisitive individualism. The present collection of occasional pieces on social history, on education, and in defense of the programs and performances of British social

[1] Reprinted with permission from *The New York Review of Books.* Copyright © 1964 *The New York Review.*

[2] A review of R. H. Tawney, *The Radical Tradition*, edited by Rita Hinden (London: Allen & Unwin; New York: Pantheon Books, 1964).

democracy, accompanied by a preface by Rita Hinden and by
Gaitskell's address at the 1962 Memorial Service for Tawney,
makes an illuminating book.

The heart of the matter for Tawney is the moral deficiency of
capitalism.

> The revolt of ordinary men against Capitalism has had its
> source neither in its obvious deficiencies as an economic engine,
> nor in the conviction that it represents a stage in social evolu-
> tion now outgrown, but in the straightforward hatred of a
> system which stunts personality and corrupts human relations
> by permitting the use of man by man as an instrument of
> pecuniary gain. . . ."
>
> It is this demon—the idolatry of money and success—with
> whom, not in one sphere alone but in all, including our own
> hearts and minds, Socialists have to grapple.

Sentences like these are scattered throughout Tawney's writings.
One need not be a cynic nor an immoralist to find so much cliche-
ridden high-mindedness suspect. The answer of his admirers
may be to stress, as Gaitskell does in his address, Tawney's
personal goodness—"I think he was the best man I have ever
known." The difficulty is that what both the reminiscences and
Tawney's own writings communicate is a banal earnestness rather
than the manifold virtues ascribed and praised. It is fairly clear
what is missing. The moral denunciation of British capitalism
took its content and its interest not from the morality of socialists
but from the immorality and evil of capitalism. What we miss in
these essays is the social context of the 1920s, of poverty, of un-
employment, of suffering.

Moreover the immediacy of these evils was linked with a hard-
headed, common-sense practicality about their cure. Public
ownership of the coal mines or the railways in Britain was not a
radical solution; that it was the only solution, was implicitly
acknowledged by the lack of Conservative opposition when the
measures were finally put through Parliament in the late 1940s.
But why did it take so long to achieve this solution? A government commission headed by Mr. Justice Sankey and including,
along with Tawney, men of widely different views had recommended the nationalization of the mines in 1919. The reason for
the delay lies in the failure of nerve in Britain's ruling class between the two wars. The politicians of the age—MacDonald,
Snowden, Bonar Law, Baldwin, and Chamberlain—are in perspective tiny and impotent figures. No wonder that in comparison

with them Tawney assumed the appearance of great moral stature. Yet if he appears impressive by contrast, we must also ask whether in many ways he did not share many of the attitudes and indeed illusions of his contemporaries.

Tawney equated capitalism with private capitalism, and private capitalism with the effective sovereignty of the functionless share-holder. He defined socialism on at least two levels, both of which were inadequate. At one level he meant the moral values of fraternity and equality, which are, unhappily, terms too vague and general for political guidance until they are embodied in specific social practices and institutions. At another level he defined socialism by his concept of capitalism: the replacement of private ownership by public ownership or control and the state's acceptance of responsibility for social welfare. Thus he never took stock of the capitalism of the big corporation—the capitalism which may for its own purposes accept trade unionism, the welfare state, and even measures of state intervention and public ownership. He is in fact oblivious not merely of Keynes, but of the kind of capitalist ethos in which neo-Keynsian politics could be made effective.

Yet is it not perhaps absurd to criticize Tawney for being limited by the horizon of his period? Not if what we are criticizing is above all lack of *political* intelligence and imagination. The lack of political imagination is notably present in his estimate (reprinted in *The Radical Tradition*) of the role and achievement of the postwar Labour government. He profoundly underestimates the continuity of that government with the wartime coalition government. He writes of the Labour ministers as if they were by deliberate choice implementing socialist policies, when in fact they were providing the necessary and inevitable solutions to the problem of laying a new basis for British capitalism. He never mentions the frustration and disillusionment that that govern-ment engendered, especially among its working-class supporters. To say this is not to underrate the achievements involved in im-plementing the 1944 Education Act (passing it was the work of the wartime coalition government), or of the handing over of power in India, or of the creation of the National Health Service. It is to say that any intelligent pragmatist, thoroughly but far-sightedly imbued with capitalist values, could not and would not have done otherwise. And it is not only that Tawney underrated the resources of an intelligent conservative defense of capitalism. In his statement of socialist objectives he is curiously blind to how greatly his declared ends and his chosen means were at odds with one another. He cared passionately that workers should extend their control over the work process; and he wanted, probably more than anything else, to democratize the British educational system. Yet the kind of orthodox Labour Party politics in which he put his hope has always been managerial and meritocratic. The Labour Party has shown immense hostility to those rank-and-file trade unionists who have been concerned with issues of workers' control; and it has shown a simple lack of interest in many less radical measures concerned with democracy in industry. In education the Labour Party's support for comprehensive schools and for equality of opportunity did not, when it was in office, prevent it from helping to create through the 1944 Education Act a class system in education which not only favors the middle-class child, but has helped to create new class barriers. Labour is increasingly the political expression not of workers, but of managers and technocrats. It is the party of the other half of our ruling class.

Why did Tawney succeed in concealing from himself as well as from others the extent to which the British Labour Party is merely an alternative Conservative Party? One answer can be found in *The Radical Tradition.* Tawney did not lack that essentially English quality, insularity. It is no accident that there is little in his book about peace or international socialism. In his essay on "Social Democracy in Britain" he asserts that "it is not for a foreigner to discuss" the standing of capitalism in the United States. And he appears to restrict himself not only geographically but theoretically. We have jibes—not arguments—against Marxism, and economic expertise is treated as a topic for a joke. The limits of theoretical inquiry appear to be those which actually exist in the House of Commons, a not very theoretical body.

Tawney thus appears to define politics itself as what might go on in a British Parliament. Since the role of Parliament, and consequently of electoral politics, in the decision-making processes of British life has steadily declined, it is not surprising that already his writings have a curiously antique air. He never even asks whether Parliament may not be among the institutions which need democratizing. And however radical he may be about the economic activities of private capitalism, he is a true member of the Labour Party in being completley complacent about British political institutions.

So a book of essays designed to celebrate "the Democratic Socialist *philosopher* par excellence" is in fact a monument to the impotence of ideals. It is not that Tawney failed to live up to his ideals or to propagate them. He succeeded admirably. Nor is it that his ideals were insufficiently high. It is simply that the Socratic question of whether one would rather have one's shoes mended by a good cobbler or a good man has relevance in politics too. Goodness is not enough.

5

How not to write about Lenin[1]

Discussions of historical method rarely illuminate one crucial point: what kind of *rapport* must the historian have with his subject if he is to write about it successfully? Clearly it is not just a matter of a certain sympathy to be felt by the historian for his subject. A certain lack of sympathy may indeed be necessary. But it must be a lack of sympathy of the right kind. For those who intend to write about Lenin there are at least two prerequisites. The first is a sense of scale. One dare not approach greatness of a certain dimension (and what holds of Lenin would hold equally of Robespierre or of Napoleon) without a sense of one's own limitations. A Lilliputian who sets out to write Gulliver's biography had best take care. Above all he dare not be patronizing. This danger is not entirely avoided by all the contributors to a new set of essays about Lenin.[2]

The second prerequisite is a sense of tragedy which will enable the historian to feel both the greatness and the failure of the October Revolution. Those for whom the whole project of the revolutionary liberation of mankind from exploitation and alienation is an absurd fantasy disqualify themselves from writing about Communism in the same way that those who find the notion of the supernatural redemption of the world from sin an outmoded superstition disqualify themselves from writing ecclesiastical history. How much can be achieved none the less is witnessed to by Gibbon and by Hume, as well as by their successors; and how much is necessarily missed out is witnessed to at the same time. So far as the October Revolution is concerned, a sense of tragedy is as likely to be obliterated as effectively by the spirit of orthodox hagiography as it is by the philistinism so characteristic of much anti-Communism. Indeed orthodox hagiography has had to ignore entirely the truth about Lenin's last days.

[1] Reprinted from *Encounter*, May 1968.
[2] Leonard Schapiro and Peter Reddaway, eds., *Lenin: The Man, the Theorist, the Leader* (New York: Praeger; London: Pall Mall, 1967).

Among Lenin's likes were cats, hunting, tidiness, and Pushkin; among his dislikes bohemianism, religion, and Mayakovsky. He once found himself unable to shoot a fox because "really she was so beautiful." He feared the power of great music to distract his energies and emotions from revolutionary ends. These and other opaque facts about his complex and subtle character are brought out in an excellent essay by Peter Reddaway entitled "Literature, the Arts and the Personality of Lenin." Reddaway also notes the traits singled out by commentators as different as Trotsky, Lunacharsky, and Berdyaev, an overriding simplicity and certainty of revolutionary purpose. "Purity of heart," wrote Kierkegaard, "is to will one thing." It was Lenin's purity of heart that his opponents could not and his critics cannot bear. This trait has been subject of much misunderstanding. It is often treated as a personal characteristic which Lenin simply happened to have, and so it will appear if it is detached from the theoretical judgments which informed it.

Professor Leonard Schapiro, Mr. Reddaway's co-editor, stresses Lenin's "fear that the revolution might be 'missed'. As he saw it, compromises, reforms, concessions by the government, a rise in living standards, could all easily operate to postpone or even render impossible or very difficult" the revolution predicted by Marx. What Schapiro does not discuss is the question of the source of this fear. To this question there may be a surprising answer. Lenin shared the views of those Marxists whom he was shortly to denounce as "economists" apparently up to his receiving in his Siberian exile in 1899 Eduard Bernstein's *Die Voraussetzungen des Sozialismus und die Aufgabe der Sozialdemokratie*. That he then proceeded to refute and denounce Bernstein is well known; in this he was at one with every orthodox Marxist, including his future bitter enemy Kautsky. But in this denunciation he did not continue to believe, as Kautsky believed, that the history of capitalism was moving forward in a law-governed way so that even if the transformation of the labor movement into a revolutionary socialist movement and the subsequent victory of socialism was not quite an automatic process, it was in some sense inevitable. It is difficult to see that Lenin took anywhere but from Bernstein his new belief that in the course of capitalism's development the working class might be domesticated and the trade unions become the instrument of that domestication. Certainly even on this point Lenin did not agree with Bernstein. What Bernstein thought was in fact going to happen, Lenin took to represent only one possibility, but it was the possibility which would be realized unless positive countervailing action were taken. In the very act of attempting to refute revisionism Lenin seems to have learnt from it.

The socialist revolution is then from 1899 onward an urgent matter of will, organization, and an eye for opportunity. Any road is permissible which runs more nearly toward the goal than any other road perceived at the same moment. This single criterion allows for a combination of undeviating purpose and flexibility of both tactics and doctrine. The flexibility of Lenin's doctrine has also another source. Lenin saw threats to the revolution from a number of directions quite as, if not more, clearly than he envisaged the road forward. Consequently he rarely devoted himself to expounding doctrine except in the context of polemic. Since he polemicized from time to time on several fronts and tended to allow his project of the moment to be aimed at defeating one particular enemy once and for all, it is not surprising that the key texts are not merely not entirely consistent with each other, but form, in some way, a collection of fragments. Out of these fragments a monument has been built—and admiration and enmity have both contributed to it—called "Leninism." But "Leninism" has a purely factitious unity. The doctrines of *State and Revolution* (1917), for example, contain elements which are found nowhere else in Lenin. Among these is a strongly stated belief in the possibility of the radical democratization of society immediately after the socialist revolution. This belief is not only at odds with Lenin's general attitude to the working class; it is one that he never seems to have taken seriously when within a year the revolution had occurred and he was proceeding to construct the socialist order. Again if we compare his attitude to the working class under capitalism in *What Is To Be Done?* (1902) with that in *Imperialism: The Highest Stage of Capitalism* (1916) there is at least a crucial difference of emphasis. In the former he sees the natural trend in the development of the working class as being nonrevolutionary; in the latter he sees the nonrevolutionary character of the working class as having to be explained by the use of the superprofits of imperialism to buy off the aristocracy of labor. It is not that these two theses could not under certain conditions be reconciled. It is rather that Lenin tends to confront problems in isolation from each other.

Nor is this surprising. Lenin poses the problem of the transition to socialism. About this Marx said very little, Engels only slightly more, and Engels' remarks on victory through parliamentary elections and the outdatedness of military insurrections were scarcely likely to be appreciated by Lenin. Classical Marxism is a doctrine in which insight into the bourgeois societies of the mid- and late-nineteenth century was bought at the price of all too close a reflection of the categories of that society in its own theories. In consequence when Marxism came to be applied to new situations at the end of the nineteenth century and the beginning of the twentieth century would-be Marxists were left with a good deal of freedom, both theoretical and practical. The phenomena of imperialism, for example, evoked quite different responses from Rosa Luxemburg, from Lenin in 1899, and from Lenin in 1916. In *The Development of Capitalism in Russia* (1899), as Professor Alec Nove points out in his outstanding essay, "Lenin as Economist," Lenin argued against Struve's view that foreign trade can be a means by which capitalism can rid itself of surpluses which it cannot sell on the home market. According to *Imperialism*—and Lenin makes no reference to his own past views—such surpluses *can* at least for a time be exported. But this very inconsistency is a sign of the degree of freedom which Marxist theorists possessed at this period.

This freedom to theorize within a framework which was a good deal less constraining than even the Marxist theorists themselves believed and liked to believe makes the old question of whether Lenin was or was not a genuine and orthodox Marxist one to which rival answers can with equal plausibility be given. Some of these rival answers are discussed by Professor J. C. Rees, who points out acutely how one can frame an impressive case—as Sukhanov and other Mensheviks did—for saying that on Marxist grounds Russia was in 1917 far from ready for a proletarian revolution; but that one could also in 1917 have framed an impressive case for saying that Marxist theory supplied no ready-made recipes for application to Russia and that what was required was a creative remaking of the Marxist categories.

Not all the contributors to this volume are as clear as Professor Rees is about the kind of advantage that we have over Lenin in being able to view his actions as he could not, just because we know what happened next. The shadow of what happened next can far too easily be allowed to obscure what in fact happened. It ought also to be remarked that Mensheviks have been better at writing memoirs since 1917 than they were at making political decisions at the time. For when the worst has been said about Lenin it is clear that there was *no* possibility of Marxist revolution except for that which Lenin seized upon and indeed partly created. We ought not to confuse a proper grasp of the tragic dimensions of the October Revolution with the sentimentality that actually prefers tragic failures of integrity to any substantial achievement and so idolizes Martov and even finds it far easier to come to terms with Trotsky or Rosa Luxemburg than with Lenin, just because in the end they were losers. But of course none the less Lenin lost too. His late protests against bureaucracy, against the low level of Soviet culture and more specifically against Stalin—those protests which the hagiographers cannot take seriously—in no way amount to any kind of renunciation of the revolution, but Lenin did none the less acknowledge some of his responsibility for some of the negative sides of the Soviet Revolution. Yet Stalinism was not in any sense the legitimate successor even of the negative sides of Lenin's work. The claim that Stalin's work continued Lenin's is familiar not only from Stalinist pens, but also in the writings of those critics of Lenin who wish to fasten on him responsibility for a variety of policies which he never envisaged.

To those critics one must concede at least two points. The first is that Lenin of course was always prepared for tactical retreats from socialist principles and was prepared to be almost indefinitely flexible and adaptive; but where Lenin recognized such retreats for what they were, Stalin presented them as advances toward socialism and in the course of doing so redefined socialism away into tyranny. The second is that it is certainly true that underlying such Leninist retreats was a crude utilitarianism: the end of socialism justifies any necessary means. But the key word here is "necessary." The memoirs of Victor Serge, for example, witness to Lenin's personal humanity in 1917–18. There was never in Lenin the sense of pleasure in terror or the sense of gratuitous *personal* hostility so evident in Stalin. It remains true that such utilitarianism corrupts and corrupted, that it formed the moral link between Lenin and Stalin.

Lenin's was a heroic attempt to force a social situation unforeseen by Marx into the categories of Marxist theory, and to do this not merely in theory but in deed. The future as Lenin envisaged it was the same future which Marx had envisaged. The past which Lenin viewed was the past which Marx had depicted. Lenin's task was to remake the present so that it might be a bridge between that past and that future. The intractability of that present, its refusal to be molded in Leninist ways, teaches the moral that Leninism provides us with few, if any, specific political recipes; what Lenin achieved in spite of that intractability carries the moral that this may not be as important as Lenin's detractors have thought.

6

How not to write about Stalin[1]

Miss Stalin[2] both demonstrates and helps to perpetuate one of the
myths of the modern world: the belief that the explanation of
what is puzzling on the public stage lies in the realm of private life.
There is a small grain of truth here. Sometimes a man's relations
with his wife or friends may suggest a new light in which to see
his actions as a revolutionary or a statesman. But in general what
is crucial in the relationship of private to public life is the irrelevance of the one to the other. That Himmler detested cruelty to
animals does nothing to explain the politics of the Final Solution.
Miss Stalin's revelation that her father was exceptionally good at
handling domestic servants is quite as uninteresting, and obviously
so. Less obvious and therefore more dangerous is the suggestion
that two of Stalin's personal relationships may explain at least in
part the development and character of his tyranny.

The first of Miss Stalin's suggestions is that her mother's
suicide may have played a decisive role in Stalin's development.
"What was the effect of my mother's death? Did it simply leave
my father free to do what he would have done in any case? Or was
it that her suicide broke his spirit and made him lose his faith in
all his old friends?" The second suggestion is that the author of the
essential evil in Stalin's career was Beria. Kirov's murder, for
example, so Miss Stalin says, was far more probably the work of
Beria than of Stalin. The two suggestions are linked, for Beria's
ascendancy followed, on Miss Stalin's interpretation, the death of
her mother. It is true that she claims that she is not trying to shift
blame from Stalin to Beria: none the less she writes that "the spell
cast on my father by this terrifying evil genius was extremely
powerful, and it never failed to work."

[1] Reprinted from *The Yale Law Journal*.

[2] Svetlana Alliluyeva, *Twenty Letters to a Friend*. Translated by
Priscilla Johnson McMillan (New York: Harper & Row; London:
Hutchinson, 1967).

Her metaphor is at once revealing and inapposite. Everything we know about Stalin makes the notion of him as somehow spell-bound extremely unconvincing. But Miss Stalin has no other terms in which to think of her father. In particular she seems incapable of thinking in political terms. Hence those of Stalin's political actions which impinged upon her—the imprisonment of Alexander Svanidze or that of Polina Molotov—appear in her narrative as arbitrary and unrelated actions. This appearance of arbitrariness infects even her account of her mother's suicide. She says of her mother's suicide note that she has been told by those who saw it that "it was a terrible letter, full of reproaches and accusations. It wasn't purely personal; it was partly political as well." But either she does not know or she is unwilling to say what the political content of the note was. Her comments are as follows:

> People shot themselves fairly often in those days. Trotskyism had been defeated. Collectivization of the farms had just gotten under way. The Party was torn by opposition and factional strife. One leading Party member after another did away with himself. Mayakovsky had shot himself only a short time before. People couldn't make sense of this, and the memory was still very fresh. I think all this couldn't fail to have had its effect on my mother, impulsive and susceptible as she was. The Allilu-yevas were all sensitive and high-strung . . . (p. 114).

In other words, suicide was breaking out all over and her mother was peculiarly liable to contagion. But there is in fact no reason for believing that Nadezhda Alliluyeva was peculiarly vulnerable to suicide, except that she did in fact kill herself; and suicide was relatively frequent at that period for highly specific reasons, on which her remarks about Party strife throw no light. Party strife had been bitter for many years without bringing comrades to self-destruction.

The hypothesis I would advance about Nadezhda Alliluyeva's suicide is suggested partly by its date, November 1932. It occurred, that is, when the consequences of Stalin's politics of forced collec-tivization and speeded-up industrialization had already become clear, but when the repression and the purges in the Party had yet to begin. Terror in the countryside and increased exploitation of the working class had become central facts of Soviet social life, but the mass killing of Communists would still have seemed novel and horrific even to those who were about to carry it out. Stalinism had laid its economic foundation, to use a different idiom, but it had not yet erected its political superstructure. What was the relationship between these two periods?

The key lies in the nexus between Stalin's economic policies—which were directed toward problems for which, as Trotsky never fully understood, there were no *socialist* solutions—and the political need for purges created by the failure to acknowledge that socialist theory had perforce been left behind when these policies were adopted. In the final analysis Stalin succeeded, not so much because of the ruthlessness of his tactical maneuvers, as because there was no alternative to the substance of the economic policies he pursued during both periods. Certainly there was a gratuitous inhumanity in the implementation of those policies. But the capitulation of so many principled and tough Old Bolsheviks cannot be explained in terms only of weakness, torture, or bribery. It *is* explicable in terms of the incoherence of Stalin's adversaries who could not by applying their socialist and democratic principles frame any more adequate solution. Moreover, many of Stalin's supporters were sufficiently principled to discover in time the gap between their socialist desires and ideals and the form of state which Stalin was actually bringing to birth. Indeed, when the purges came, Stalin's own earlier supporters were decimated as much as were the ranks of the old Trotskyists and Bukharinists.

But though there may have been no alternative of substance to the economic policy which Stalin had pursued since before 1932, what could have been admitted was that what was being built was not socialism. One can imagine that if Lenin had survived to 1930 he would have pursued in a more radical way the approach he followed when he defended the NEP not as socialist, but as necessary. What led to the corruption of socialism was Stalin's insistence that what he was doing was socialist. A whole redefinition of Marxism thereby became necessary. To secure that redefinition a whole generation of Marxists was to be obliterated. Briefly and perhaps cryptically, it is often supposed that Bolshevik history has had to be rewritten in Russia because the purges and the trials made unpersons of so many Old Bolsheviks. The truth is, I suggest, that the purges and the trials were necessary because the history of the Bolsheviks, including the history of their theoretical positions, had to be rewritten so that the true nature of socialism could be forgotten and the Stalinist redefinition could reign unchallenged in a society where not the working class but the bureaucracy ruled.

In 1932 the task of ideological redefinition was only beginning, and the gap between Stalinist deeds and Marxist words was at its most obvious. It was at this point that Syrtsov, Lominadze and Riutin, all of them Stalinists, hoped to depose Stalin; all were imprisoned. In this year Skrypnik, also a Stalinist, committed suicide when Stalin discovered the opposition to him in the Ukranian government, in which Skrypnik was Commissar for Education. Suicide is indeed a much more intelligible reaction among the disillusioned Stalinists than it would have been then among the adherents of Trotsky or those of Bukharin, who must for some years have lost most, if not all, of their illusions. Thus Nadezhda Alliluyeva's suicide falls into its tragic place in the historical sequence. Miss Stalin, who sees only the sequences of personal biography, thus deprives her mother's action of one possible meaning it may have held. Equally she sees Beria as a private author of evil; she does not see that the unfolding of Stalinism created a role for Beria and those like him. The role and not the man determined the scale of the evil.

None the less, to treat the weaknesses of Miss Stalin's memoirs as simply symptoms of a defective point of view, without inquiring about the social roots of that point of view, would merely duplicate her error. Miss Stalin has a religious perspective upon the world, albeit a rather indefinite one, and her devotion to Russia has religious overtones. Indeed, when she wrote her memoir she believed that she would never be capable of leaving Russia. One can understand why the Russia Miss Stalin confronts, the Russia which she claims that her father always loved, was an abstract mystical entity; privilege and wealth have always separated her from social reality. The most characteristic Soviet experience is to stand in a queue for bread; this does not seem to be a thought that Miss Stalin has ever had. It would be too prosaic for her.

There remains one aspect of her book which is of real value. She does reveal in how impossible a position we put the children of major figures. They lead private and not public lives, but their private lives are distorted by the way in which they are exposed to the public gaze. Of Stalin's children one became a drunkard and one has now written memoirs; but one became a hero. Yakov, the son of Stalin's first marriage, who was largely disowned by his father, seems to have been, and not only from this account, a straightforwardly moral and finally heroic figure who defied the Germans in his prison camp and was murdered by them. Miss Stalin when speaking on the power of Truth and Goodness to survive falls victim to her own rhetoric; on her half-brother's simple nobility of character she sounds more truthful than at any other point in her unattractive book.

7

Trotsky in exile[1]

Trotsky learning to fish in the Sea of Marmora from an illiterate Greek boy; Trotsky on a ski trip in the Norwegian Arctic; Trotsky feeding the rabbits among the cacti at Coyoacan: images such as these all contribute to the violent sense of dislocation which is produced by turning from the first two volumes of Isaac Deutscher's biography to the third.[2] But this dislocation is not of course merely a matter of place. Trotsky's physical remoteness from events in the years 1929-40 is only matched by his apparent political isolation. The creator of the Red Army is reduced to the leader of a scattered following of a few hundred militants; the inspirer of the Soviets is a stateless exile. Exile, of course, is not necessarily impotence. But the question must be faced. Is Trotsky in exile, like Marx in the British Museum, a commentator who is also an actor, or is he, like Napoleon on St. Helena, an outcast from the world of action?

What kind of answer one gives to this question will determine the whole perspective in which one sees Trotsky's last decade. To understand Deutscher's answer fully we shall have to look back to his *Stalin*. Deutscher's own statement in the preface to the 1961 edition of *Stalin* of the unity of his work on Stalin and Trotsky justifies us in so doing.

"In attempting to find an historical parallel to Stalin," wrote Trotsky in 1940, "we have to reject not only Cromwell, Robespierre, Napoleon, and Lenin, but even Mussolini and Hitler." "What appears to be established," wrote Deutscher in his *Stalin* (1949), "is that Stalin belongs to the breed of the great revolutionary despots, to which Cromwell, Robespierre, and Napoleon belonged."

The gap between Deutscher's judgment and Trotsky's is a first

[1] Reprinted from *Encounter*, December 1963.

[2] Isaac Deutscher, *The Prophet Outcast* (London and New York: Oxford University Press, 1963).

52

clue to Deutscher's standpoint. For Deutscher believes that there is a "broad scheme of revolutionary development" which is "common to all great revolutionaries so far." The first stage is one in which "popular energy, impatience, anger and hope" burst out, and "the party that gives the fullest expression to the popular mood outdoes its rivals, gains the confidence of the masses and rises to power." There follows a second heroic stage of civil war in which revolutionary party and people are so well attuned that the leaders "are willing and even eager to submit their policies to open debate and to accept the popular verdict." This stage is short. Weariness and ruthlessness combine to open a gap between party and people. The party cannot abdicate without sacrificing the basis the revolution has created for social advance and prosperity; but it can no longer listen to—it must indeed in time suppress—the voice of the people. At this point the revolutionary party is split between those who see government by the people as the heart of the revolution and therefore cry that the revolution is betrayed and those who justify the new antidemocratic use of power as the only way to serve the ultimate interests of the people by preserving the gains of the revolution. This story is one that Deutscher supposes can be told of any "party of the revolution, whether it be called Independent, Jacobin or Bolshevik," whether it is English, French or Russian. It is within the framework of this story that Stalin and Trotsky are made to appear as playing out necessary roles. Trotsky, the caretaker of revolutionary purity, is necessarily doomed to political isolation in the period of the antidemocratic conservation of revolutionary gains. The significance of the quotation from Machiavelli which stands at the head of Deutscher's first volume is now clear: the prophet must be armed precisely so that he can, when the people no longer believe in the revolution, "make them believe by force."

This is the setting for the message that is spelled out in the concluding volume. Trotsky's ideas and methods, so Deutscher argues, belonged to classical Marxism; but the 1930s were an epoch hostile both to revolution and to Marxism. After the Second World War revolution resumed its course—but not as Marxism had predicted. It was revolution from above, brought to Eastern Europe by a foreign army, to China by a peasant *jacquerie*, which none the less inaugurated a socialist revolution. The Soviet bureaucracy—so Deutscher continues—is gradually reforming itself and at some point in this process will be forced to acknowledge Trotsky's greatness. Classical Marxism will then have come into its own. Trotsky is thus honored by Deutscher on two counts:

as the great dissenter whose protest was both necessary and necessarily ineffective; and as the future patron saint of post-Khrush-
chevite Russia. That this is the frame within which the portrait
of Trotsky in his last years is painted entails that Deutscher has
written both a biography and a political tract. The weakness of his
book arises from the conflict between these two tasks.

The strength of the book lies in the meticulous scholarship:
names, dates, places, at this level of fact Deutscher, as always, is a
model of industry. Moreover his style is as magisterial as ever.
He writes with the restrained passion of the deeply committed
writer, whose deepest commitment of all is to objectivity. And yet,
although objectivity can rescue one from many errors, it cannot
either obliterate or conceal the effects of the basic incoherence of
Deutscher's perspective. To exhibit this incoherence it is enough
to look at how Trotsky himself developed his own positions in the
years of exile.

Trotsky between 1928 and 1940 held at least four positions on
the nature of the Russian state. In 1928 he held that political
power, though effectively controlled by the bureaucrats, was still
in some sense in the hands of the workers, because it was still
possible for them to use constitutional means to "regain full
power, renovate the bureaucracy and put it under its control by
the road of reform of the party and the Soviets" (letter to Borodai).
He could write that "the socialist character of industry is determined and secured in a decisive measure by the role of the party,
the voluntary internal cohesion of the proletarian vanguard, and
conscious discipline of the administrators, trade union func-
tionaries, members of the shop nuclei, etc." (letter to the Sixth
Comintern Congress). What matters is the access to political
institutions still available to workers.

By 1933 Trotsky believed that this access was no longer available,
but that Russia was still a workers' state. The cruel repression
exercised by the bureaucracy is not incompatible with their
maintaining the core of revolutionary gains so long as the means of
production remain nationalized; but they have been able by reason
of the backwardness of Russia to produce a tyranny which en-
dangers the revolution. Trotsky by now believed that inside and
outside Russia the Left Opposition had to constitute new political
parties, genuinely revolutionary in the rest of the world, genuinely
reformist in Russia. Reformist, because the bureaucracy was not
as yet a new ruling class in the classical Marxist sense, and the
prospect of a political strategy in which the bureacrats could be
expropriated without force in the long run was not as yet unrealistic.

By the time *The Revolution Betrayed* was written in 1935 the perspective had changed yet again. Certainly Russia is still a workers' state, even though so gravely degenerated. But the bureaucracy can only be overthrown by a political revolution. The portrait of deadening, tyrannical oppression which is painted in *The Revolution Betrayed* could not be bettered. Why then did Trotsky continue to insist that bureaucracy was only a caste, not a class, and why did he make the preservation of nationalized property the criterion of socialism? The answer is that up to this point he always envisaged the bureaucracy's final goal as being the restoration of private capitalism. He supposed that socialism and private capitalism exhausted the political alternatives—wrongly. For in the period immediately before his death Trotsky did come around to envisage, even if only as a theoretical possibility, a new kind of exploitation—the collective class rule of the bureaucracy. This he did not believe to have yet occurred. But his analysis of Soviet totalitarianism became even more radical.

> *L'état c'est moi* is almost a liberal formula by comparison with the actualities of Stalin's totalitarian regime. Louis XIV identified himself with both the state and the Church—but only during the epoch of temporal power. The totalitarian state goes far beyond Caesaro-Papism. ... Stalin can justly say, unlike *le Roi Soleil*, "*la société c'est moi.*"

Although Trotsky continued to defend the view that in some sense the Soviet Union was a workers' state, he had committed himself to predictions about the results of the Second World War, the outcome of which would for him settle the matter. If his view were correct, the Soviet bureaucracy after a victorious war would be overthrown as a result of proletarian revolution in the advanced countries of the West. If the view of those Trotskyists who held that a kind of bureaucratic state capitalism existed in Russia were correct, they would be vindicated by the failure to occur of such a revolution and such an overthrow. It was with this question still before him that Trotsky died.

To read Trotsky's successive evaluations of the Russian state against the background of what was done to his followers, his family, and himself is to understand that theory too can have a dramatic role. For it was not merely Trotsky's person but his theoretical powers that Stalin wished to condemn to death. Stalinism required the pulverization of every independent political voice in Russia and in the international Communist movement; hence not only the Moscow trials, but the extended passion of the

3

Trotskyists in the Siberian camps, where those who had never surrendered, but who had continued to organize strikes, protests, and political propaganda among their fellow prisoners, were in 1938 marched out in groups and shot. Leon Sedov, Trotsky's elder son, died mysteriously in Paris with the GPU not far from his bedside; Sergei, who had reacted against both his father and his father's politics, and who worked quietly as a private citizen in Moscow, died at the hands of the GPU; Zina, one of his daughters —the other was already dead—had committed suicide under intense nervous strain in Berlin some years before. Rudolf Klement, the Secretary of the Fourth International, was in 1938 murdered, mutilated, and dropped in the Seine. If Trotsky was not utterly crushed, it was only because he was upheld by his wife Natalya and by the conviction that no one but he could carry through his task and that the importance of his work was only to be measured by the venom he aroused in Stalin.

Among the many characters with walk-on parts in this drama some are familiar. Those who in 1962 protested at the Home Secretary's inhumanity to that "persecuted progressive," Dr. Soblen, will meet him again in Deutscher's pages as the GPU agent Roman Well. Mr. Kingsley Martin turns up at Coyoacan, but the meeting is not altogether pleasant, because Mr. Martin wishes to defend the honor of his friend Mr. D. N. Pritt over his defense of the Moscow trials. M. Léon Blum appears suppressing protests against the trials and purges. Theodore Dreiser, Romain Rolland, and Louis Fischer play familiar roles as Stalinist apologists. If anyone says that at that time any of them could not have known better, that the threat of fascism and the effectiveness of Stalin's propaganda exculpate these men, the answer is that many who were far from Trotsky's Marxism did know better. The aged John Dewey, chairman of the committee that vindicated Trotsky against Stalin's accusations, comes out of the whole affair with immense honor. So does Charles Beard, the veteran American historian. And they were not alone.

But the dimensions of Trotsky's tragedy and the way in which reactions to it became a touchstone of honor and dishonor only make the re-evaluation of his views the more crucial. An essential piece of evidence is Trotsky's single most brilliant piece of political comment, the pamphleteering on Germany from 1930 to 1933. The diagnosis of Nazism as "the extremism of the center" which Professor S. M. Lipset advanced in *Political Man* is already made by Trotsky. His castigations of the Comintern over its attitude to the social democrats, to the government of Brüning, and to Hitler himself all bore fruit in verified predictions. At the center of his analysis the stress is on the importance of the presence or absence of a politically awakened working class. (Trotsky's advice about the mobilization of the workers was never taken by the Comintern; but a parody of his point was taken, perhaps unwittingly, by Debré and de Gaulle when the *paras* threatened. Was there by the remotest of chances and historical ironies a link in Malraux?) This remains at the core of all Trotsky's analyses. For the Trotsky of the 1930s, as for Marx, socialism can be made only by the workers and not for them.

It is in part because of this that Trotsky, had he lived, would have had to treat his predictions about the aftermath of the Second World War as falsified. He could not but have concluded from his own premises that Russia was in no sense a workers' state, but rather a grave of socialism. The liberalization of Khrushchev would have appeared to him as parallel to the liberalization which has developed in other capitalisms once primitive accumulation has been accomplished. He could never have accepted Deutscher's analysis, which has only one thing in common with his own: the use of nationalized property as a criterion for socialism. Trotsky never believed in the possibility of the bureaucracy's self-reformation. In *The Revolution Betrayed* Trotsky wrote of the bureaucracy that

> To the extent that, for the benefit of an upper stratum, it carries to more and more extreme expression bourgeois norms of distribution, it is preparing a capitalist restoration. This contrast between forms of property and norms of distribution cannot grow indefinitely. Either the bourgeois norms must in one form or another spread to the means of production, or the norms of distribution must be brought into correspondence with the socialist property system.

According to Deutscher it is this latter course that Stalin's successors have adopted. In what way the norms of distribution differ from bourgeois norms he never explains (in Deutscher's view Britain also has surely abandoned bourgeois norms of distribution). But what is most interesting is that both Alfred Rosmer, Trotsky's most able and trusted companion, and Natalya Trotsky herself drew the opposite conclusion. It was for this reason that Natalya Trotsky explained her break with the stunted and ingrown politics of the self-styled Trotskyists by writing: "If this trend continues, he (Trotsky) said, the revolution will be at an end and the restoration of capitalism will be achieved. That, unfortunately, is what has happened even if in new and unexpected forms" (letter to the Political Committee of the Socialist Workers' Party, 1951). Almost her last political act was a letter in *Azione Communista* in November 1961 denouncing the idea that Mao Tse-tung was in any sense Trotsky's heir, and asserting that Russia and China were as far from socialism as Franco's Spain.

One has, therefore, to choose. Either one can see Leon Trotsky in Natalya's perspective or in Deutscher's, but not in both. There seems little doubt which Trotsky would have chosen. The distressing thing to him about Deutscher's biography would have been that it makes him so acceptable to those against whom he struggled for his entire life. What is more, Deutscher's adroitness will make his conclusions equally palatable on both sides of the Iron Curtain. The news that socialism is Khrushchevite liberalization plus nationalized property will not come amiss in Moscow. Both Trotsky and classical Marxism, it turns out, have to be amended to fit in with Russian reality. Trotsky's Marxist predictions were wrong, but Marxism is somehow vindicated none the less and so is Trotsky. I do not understand how. In the West too the news that the Khrushchevite regime is the necessary outcome of the Russian revolution will be welcome. For this can be thrown back at all believers in the possibility of socialism in the West. It is admirably suited for apologists of the status quo. Trotsky, the inevitable protester against the inevitable course of socialist history, can be safely received by both sides as a dead martyr, with a sigh of relief that they have not the living revolutionary to deal with.

What is most curious about Deutscher's anxiety to approve of the present developments in Russia *and* of Trotsky *and* of the letter of classical Marxism, is that Trotsky's own attitude to Marxism was far less hagiographical. Throughout his life Trotsky was prepared to reformulate Marxism. The theory of permanent revolution bears striking witness to this. In the 1930s we see him trying to use the Marxist theory of classical capitalism to understand entirely new situations. In this situation it may have been that Marxism proved a totally inadequate scheme (the orthodox sociological response) or it may have been that it provided a necessary starting-point for a new, more complex, but still Marxist, schematism. The attempts to characterize the Russian bureaucracy pose just this question; the attempt to characterize postwar Western capitalism would have posed it even more harshly. But whatever answers Trotsky might have given, he could never have been an accomplice to Deutscher's worship of the accomplished fact. Deutscher himself sees clearly in his discussion of Trotsky's *History of the Russian Revolution* that Trotsky was no believer in Deutscherian necessity.

The Shakespearean richness of character which is among the chief glories of the *History* brings out the important difference between those actors who are essentially representatives of a social group or class, and who are therefore replaceable, and those actors who are more than this, who cannot be so replaced. Miliukov, the Russian liberal, is essentially a mirror for the Russian bourgeoisie—"grey, self-interested, cowardly." Lenin, by contrast, was both an expression of his party and more than this. Had he been absent, the revolution's chances, so Trotsky argued, would have been very different. Deutscher devotes several pages to trying to refute Trotsky's conclusion on this point and we can see why this is necessary for his whole argument. If from time to time history presents us with real alternatives where my actions can make all the difference, then I am not just part of an inevitable historical progress. Deutscher invokes Plekhanov's determinism on his side and the reminiscence of Plekhanov is suggestive. Deutscher's life of Trotsky, with all its scholarship, its brilliance of style, its perversity about socialism, its service of the established fact, and its determinism, is just the biography that we can imagine a Plekhanov of the 1960s writing. But Trotsky himself evades all the categories of a Plekhanovite Marxism; his image refuses to be accommodated.

The truth of this is reflected in the way that his name continues to haunt all established powers. So-called Trotskyism has been among the most trivial of movements. It transformed into abstract dogma what Trotsky thought in concrete terms at one moment in his life and canonized this. It is inexplicable in purely political dimensions, but the history of the more eccentric religious sects provides revealing parallels. The genuine Trotskyism of Rosmer and Natalya must have at most a few hundred adherents in the entire world. Yet Trotsky's is the name which is continually invoked, at one level by employers who fear rank-and-file industrial agitation, and at another by those super-employers, the Russian and Chinese states, in their polemics against each other. If they were to read Deutscher and to accept his conclusions, they would wonder what the specter could have been which haunted them. But I doubt if it is possible to lay Trotsky's ghost so easily.

8

Marxist mask and romantic face: Lukács on Thomas Mann[1]

The dictatorship of the proletariat, the politico-economic means of salvation demanded by our age, does not mean domination for its own sake and in perpetuity; but rather in the sense of a temporary abrogation, in the Sign of the Cross, of the contradiction between spirit and force; in the sense of overcoming the world by mastering it; in a transcendental, transitional sense, in the sense of the Kingdom. The proletariat has taken up the task of Gregory the Great, his religious zeal burns within it, and, as little as he, may it withhold its hand from the shedding of blood. Its task is to strike terror into the world for the healing of the world, that man may finally achieve salvation and deliverance, and win back at length to freedom from law and from distinction of class, to his original status as child of God.

NAPHTA in *The Magic Mountain*

In *The Magic Mountain* the spokesman of the reactionary Fascist, anti-democratic *Weltanschauung*, the Jesuit Naphta. . . .

LUKÁCS in *Essays on Thomas Mann*[2]

"Lukács, who is anyhow well-disposed towards me (and who plainly has not recognized himself in Naphta) . . ." wrote Thomas Mann in a letter in 1949.[3] That Georg Lukács' essays upon Thomas Mann form part of the elaborate defenses with which

[1] Reprinted from *Encounter*, April 1965.

[2] Georg Lukács, *Essays on Thomas Mann*. Translated by Stanley Mitchell (New York: Grosset and Dunlap; London: Merlin Press, 1964).

[3] For the facts about the Mann-Lukács relationship, see the essay "Zauberberg-Figuren" in *Tessiner Schreibtisch* by Karl Kerenyi (Stuttgart, 1963). For a suggestive, but speculative interpretation see Victor Zitta, *Georg Lukács' Marxism, Alienation, Dialectics, Revolution* (New York: Humanities Press).

Lukács buttresses his inability to recognize himself as he was in his brilliant and many-sided youth lends to these essays a poignancy and a fascination which they certainly do not provide in their role as literary criticism. The pompous, ponderous style in which they are written all too easily conveys the impression of one Grand Old Man saluting another, the Gamaliel of Central European Communism (as a [London] *Times* leader writer once called Lukács) applauding the Nobel Prize winner. Nor is the translation to blame for this impression; the translator has rendered Lukács' professorial prose excellently. And the consequence might well be that the brief, uncomplicated, facile judgments on Lukács, which it has become fashionable to pass in the West, will not be shaken at all by these essays. Yet they are in fact further evidence of the enigmatic and complex quality of Lukács' achievement.

It is common knowledge that Lukács has publicly disavowed his youth. In Hungary in 1948 he was accused by György Somlyó of staging an auto-da-fé with his own early writings. Lukács replied vehemently that those works "which I have transcended with my own development and which were moving in an improper direction" should not receive attention either from himself or from others. He raged when Merleau-Ponty in 1955 discussed his *History and Class-Consciousness* of 1923 and spoke of "treachery" and of the "falsification of a book forgotten for good reasons." This un-Marxist attempt to separate his present from his past, the self from its deeds, has so strong an emotional charge behind it that one cannot but ask, "Why?" Unless one can answer this question posed in a very general way one is unlikely to answer satisfactorily the particular question of why Lukács, consciously or unconsciously, has refused to recognize his own features in those of Naphta. There is, of course, a strong presumption that the refusal is at least semiconscious, even though Mann himself exhibited strong anxiety that Lucács should not recognize himself in Naphta and was completely certain that he had not done so. The reason for doubting whether Mann's assurance was justified is simply that, in his references to Naphta, Lukács seems to rely upon his readers not actually having the text of *The Magic Mountain* available. How otherwise could he so confidently and without explanation characterize as fascist a character who propounds belief in Communism, the abolition of classes, the dictatorship of the proletariat, and a version of the labor theory of value? Of course, Naphta (as Thomas Mann himself insisted) differs from the young Lukács in a large number of ways. Naphta is a Jesuit; Lukács is not. But the young Lukács was deeply involved with Christianity and often writes of God with immense seriousness. The influence of Dostoevski is strong in the years before 1914; so more surprisingly is that of Plotinus and of the German mystics Eckhart and Tauler.

The commonest explanation of Lukács' rupture with his youth assimilates it to the recantations of intellectuals in the Stalinist period in Russia. There would be some room for doubt about the explanatory value of this parallel just because it is still unclear how far we understand the psychology of these recantations. But in any case Lukács' behavior since 1924 bears all the marks of being not so much a response to pressures from without as a continuous self-inspired attempt to destroy what survives in him of his youth. He has, of course, not been able to avoid a continuous return to the subject matter of his early writings. But he voluntarily and long before he went to live in the Soviet Union abjured their standpoint, as a result of the condemnation of *History and Class-Consciousnes*. Ernst Bloch predicted in his original review of it that the Russians would dislike it: "Some of them will say that Marx had not placed Hegel on his feet so that Lukács can put Marx back on his head." None of the Russians was in fact as witty as this. Zinoviev nagged shrilly at the Fifth Congress of the Comintern in 1924 that "we must not let this extreme left tendency grow up into a theoretical revisionism" and picked out Lukács' work in philosophy and sociology for special mention. Lukács was at once confronted with a dilemma whose roots were already obvious in the text of *History and Class-Consciousness*. For there he explains Marxism as the class-consciousness of the proletariat whose articulate representative is the Communist Party. Thus it is entailed by Lukács' own argument that if the Comintern holds that Marxism is not what Lukács says it is, then Lukács must be wrong. Or, rather, either Lukács is wrong or the Comintern is not the true Communist Party. But if it is not, then Marxism is only a theory, only an idea; it lacks any material incarnation. To have grasped this horn of the dilemma would have thrown Lukács back to his starting-point in an unbearable way. And his tragedy resides in his never having been able to return to it. But what was his starting-point and why would return to it have been unbearable?

In answering this question we can also try to answer another. It is a commonplace that in *History and Class-Consciousness* Lukács produced a Hegelian interpretation of Marx that set Marx's own writings in a systematic framework quite different from and incompatible with that in which Engels had set them in *Anti-*

Dühring. When in 1931–32 Marx's so-called *Economic-Philosophical Manuscripts* of 1844 became known, it was clear that Marx himself had defined his own thought near its outset in precisely the terms of that same Hegelian framework which Lukács had once more spelled out. This confirmation of Lukács' interpretation—Lukács could not possibly have known of the contents of the manuscripts in 1923—was a brilliant literary reconstruction for which his disowning of *History and Class-Consciousness* has never allowed him to claim the credit. What, in fact, enabled Lukács to do this was the degree to which he had in his own experience recapitulated Marx's intellectual development. In order to understand this, both Marx and Lukács have to be placed—if in the briefest, most inadequate way—in relation to their own culture.

The seminal period of German culture is essentially philosophical in a way that English culture never is. It is therefore much easier to interpret it in terms of a unity of ideas and imagination, to narrate its history as a series of attempts to frame answers to pervasive questions that were at once Kantian and Faustian. The literary critic of this culture cannot evade, any more than the philosopher can, the relationships and the antagonisms between value and fact, law and inclination, reason and the passions, society and the individual. But the literary critic has to deal with these not just as conceptual oppositions, but rather with embodied, imaginative resolutions of these antagonisms in the Greece of Hölderlin's poems or in Goethe's later writings. One way of recounting Lukács' career would be to set out the history of his continuous reinterpretation of the central features of German culture between 1780 and 1850. If one did this, one would discover a recurrent instability in which the would-be settled views of any one period in his life are undermined by his insights at other periods.

At his worst in his self-willed Stalinist period before the war he writes in terms of the crude dichotomy between idealism and materialism fathered by Engels and by Lenin's *Materialism and Empirico-Criticism*. But these concepts, as Lenin himself understood later, are chameleons of the mind, taking color only from the examples which they are ostensibly used to explain. So in the *Destruction of Reason* Lukács turned instead to the conflict between reason and unreason and tried to use this as an analytical tool. In so doing he continued his campaign against the interpretation of German Romanticism as essentially irrationalist, an interpretation which he stigmatized as anticipating Nazi interpretations of German cultural history. (This did not save him from being himself stigmatized as a revisionist for abandoning the cant about materialism and idealism.) The most important justification that Lukács has ever given for this view has, however, implications which he himself has never understood (or at least admitted). Discussing the Romantic opposition of reason to the passions in *Goethe and His Age*, Lukács argued that this opposition depends upon a falsely partial view of both reason and passions, an opposition which had been created by the rationalists of the eighteenth century. It follows that it is not reason itself, but a distorted view of reason against which the Romantic rebels. Yet if this is so, doubt is then thrown on Lukács' own categories. For in a culture where concepts of reason and the passions are thrown up by the very nature of its social life and its definitive ideas, the man who claims to be able to detect the distortion must warrant his claims by showing how it is possible for him to escape the distorting influences which imprison everyone else.

Neither the young Marx in the 1840s nor the young Lukács in 1918 was able to take Hegel's way out, that of claiming that in him the Absolute has finally broken through the relativities of history so that the thoughts expressed in the *Logic* are the thoughts of God himself, thinking them through Hegel's pen. But both have to try and find a vantage point outside their own society and culture. In order to explain Lukács' attempt to do this one cannot avoid attempting to explain Marx's; and this is not quite the boring rehearsal of stock platitudes about The Young Marx that it might seem to be, since The Young Marx is a plaster figure in whose lineaments it is fairly difficult to pick out the face of the young Marx.

The myth of the plaster figure runs: once upon a time there was a young humanistic Marx who inherited from Hegel and from the Left Hegelians the notion of alienation. This Marx was not yet preoccupied with socio-economics. But as he became so preoccupied, he discarded the notion of alienation. Indeed his break with the Left Hegelians and his discarding of the notion of alienation are sometimes seen as two aspects of the same process. The *locus classicus* for this myth is Lewis Feuer's "What Is Alienation? The Career of a Concept,"[1] and in order to destroy the myth one has only to set two of Feuer's key theses beside what Marx actually says.

So Feuer writes: "In these early writings, Marx and Engels, as Freudian forerunners, regarded love, not work, as the source of man's sense of reality," and he quotes from *The Holy Family* (published in 1845 but written in the autumn of 1844). But

[1] In *New Politics*, Spring 1962.

already in the *Economic-Philosophical Ms.* (written in April to
August 1844) Marx had clearly argued the central relationship
between work and the sense of reality. And indeed the quotation
from *The Holy Family* does not bear an entirely clear sense when
placed in its context.

Secondly, Feuer claims that "the word 'alienation' was absent
from Marx's mature analysis." But in the *Grundrisse in* 1857–58
(unpublished until 1939–41) Marx is still writing:

> The ancient conception in which man always appears (in
> however narrowly rational, religious, or political a definition)
> as the aim of production, seems very much more exalted than
> the modern world, in which production is the aim of man and
> wealth the aim of production. In fact, however, when the narrow
> bourgeois form has been peeled away what is wealth, if not the
> universality of needs, capacities, enjoyments, productive
> powers, etc., of individuals produced in universal exchange?
> What, if not the full development of human control over the
> forces of nature—those of his own nature as well as those
> of so-called "nature." ... In bourgeois political economy—
> and in the epoch to which it corresponds—this complete
> elaboration of what lies within man appears as total alienation.[2]

This survival of the concept of alienation into Marx's mature
writings is important for my immediate purposes; for had the
concept not, as Feuer claimed, survived in them—although the
word is admittedly not used in *Capital*—how could Lukács have
correctly deduced the core of Marx's thought from the later
writings which he knew? The survival of the concept is important
for other reasons. The concepts of work and freedom in the mature
Marx are in fact unintelligible unless related to the notion of
alienation, and to precisely that notion of alienation set out by
Lukács.

Alienation has at least four defining features. First of all men are
divided within themselves and from each other, by not being able
in their work to pursue ends that are their own, by having external
ends imposed upon them. Secondly, means and ends are inverted.
Where men should eat and drink in order to act, they have to work
in order to eat and drink. Thirdly, men reify their social relationships into alien powers which dominate them. In virtue of this
reification they become involved in conceptual puzzles and

[1] Karl Marx, *Pre-Capitalist Economic Formations* (London: Lawrence
& Wishart, 1964), pp. 84–5.

confusions. And finally, men find life irremediably split up into rival and competing spheres, each with its own set of norms, and each sphere claiming its own narrow and therefore deforming sovereignty. But all this makes it clear that alienation is essentially a contrast concept. We can understand what it is to be alienated only if we can also understand what it is or would be *not* to be alienated. Whence did Marx, whence did Lukács derive the notion of a form of human life in which man would create his own ends, in which conceptual confusion and contradiction would be resolved into a clarity about means and ends, so creating a human nature in which the ideal and the actual would at last coincide? The surprising answer may be that the unalienated men of the Marxist feature are the artists of the German Romantic ideal.

"Thus man also creates according to the laws of beauty." So Marx. Marx's description of the senses of reintegrated man finding their own proper aesthetic objects, his attempt to establish a connection between freedom and aesthetic activity, and his belief that in free, aesthetic activity the contradictions of unfree existence are resolved, is a reissue of a theme in Schiller's break with Kant in the "Kallias" letters.[1] Even more, Schiller's concept of *Selbstbestimmung* is an important anticipation of Marx's "self-activity." The Hegelian concept of self-activity is not its only ancestor. It is hardly surprising that Lukács, coming across Schiller's declaration that it is man who plays (and play includes the whole realm of aesthetic activity) who is most truly man, should use this saying to interpret Marx in a sense relevant to his own problems. These were complex.

Both the energy and the "intellectual poetry" (his own phrase) of the young Lukács arise out of the tension between the conceptual and theoretical resources available to him to interpret reality and the impact of the reality itself. In the view of the young Lukács, the poet faced with the inadequacy of the first to the second creates his own reality. But the critic cannot rest content except with a grasp of both poetry and social reality which can only come from a philosophy in which reality is disclosed. Lukács reads the history of past literature and criticism in terms of the attempted resolution of the tension between the realm of intelligibility and that of brute reality. Belief in God plays a key role here, especially in the definition of the tragic vision in which the hero who is confronted by the demands of a transcendence which he cannot discover

[1] Karl Marx, *Early Writings*. Translated and edited by T. B. Bottomore (London: Watts; New York: McGraw Hill, 1963), p. 160–62.

anywhere in the empirical world must live out his tasks in conflict with a reality that never discloses the divinity he seeks.[1] The tragic vision in which meaning can only be conferred on the world from outside it, and yet the world is silent as to its own meaning, recurs in a conceptualized form in classical German philosophy. The tragic hero is transformed in turn into the epistemological subject of Kantianism whose categories can never reveal the *Ding-an-sich*, the Fichtean Ego, and the Hegelian Self. But each of these philosophies finds itself still external to the reality it seeks to comprehend, reduced to spawning metaphysical fictions on a grand scale. It was the insight of Hegel, rendered into realistic social terms by Marx (and Marx's "materialism" consists in really no more than this rendering) that the escape from the contradictions and mystifications thrown up by this philosophy did not lie simply in intellectually dissipating them by greater clarity in conceptual analysis.

In the Hegelian-Marxist view such conceptual contradictions and mystifications express the incoherences of a whole form of life. To overcome them one does not have merely to philosophize more clearly, but to learn to act in a new way: revolutionary *praxis*, as characterized by Marx in the *Theses on Feuerbach*. Here Lukács sees the resolution of his new problems. The *praxis* in which contradiction disappears is that of the proletarian, not just that of the actual workingman but that of the essential proletarian for whom the Hungarian Soviets of 1919 provided a spokesman. So the contradictions of tragedy are overcome; transcendence re-enters the world; the immediate ends of man become meaningful. The Kingdom of God will have been taken by storm. To read *History and Class-Consciousness* as a solution to the problems of *The Soul and the Forms* is to read it as the work of Lukács-Naphta.

Thus Lukács staked his existence on the possibility of integrating art with social life in a *praxis* in which life should itself have the coherence and meaning of art. He analyses bourgeois social reality with the tools derived from Georg Simmel and Max Weber; he understands art and literature in terms of the Romantic ideal. And he invokes Marxism to link the two analyses so that the aesthetic may be at home in the world. But in so doing he creates insoluble problems for his own future activities as a critic, problems that are nowhere more apparent than in his writings on Thomas Mann.

[1] For the best account of this phase of Lukács' thought, see Lucien Goldmann, *The Hidden God* (London: Routledge & Kegan Paul; New York: Humanities Press, 1964).

Lukács' immense sympathy for Mann derives from the fact that the externality of art to bourgeois society is itself a central imaginative theme for Mann; Lukács' difficulty in writing about Mann is that Mann was always ambivalent in his attitudes both to art and to bourgeois society. This Lukács concealed from himself by simply not seeing in Mann's work every tendency which might underline the *necessary* gap between art and social life to the possible nonexistence of which Lukács' whole critical career is pledged. Thus Lukács cannot acknowledge himself in Naphta because the manifestly desperate character of Naphta's enterprise corresponds to the latently desperate character of Lukács' own enterprise. What is desperate and neurotic, of course, is not Lukács' Communism or his wish to resolve the contradictions of theory with the conceptual scheme of a new form of social life; it is his impatience with history, with the slow pace of social development. This he himself was to recognize, but his recognition of this impatience was turned into an acceptance of the subintellectual world of Stalinist materialism and thereby into a disowning of both the origin and the meaning of his own enterprise.

Lukács' arbitrary excision from Mann's work of all that does not fit into the role which he imposes on Mann—that of the bourgeois realist who disowns the decadence of modernism— is most obvious when Lukács simply writes off the opinions Mann professed in his essays. So Mann's expressed admiration for Freud is dismissed and *The Holy Sinner* read as a refutation of Freud. Equally Mann's expressed attitude to Nietzsche has to be discounted. For Lukács wants to see Adrian Leverkühn in *Dr. Faustus* as a contemporary Nietzsche. But of course there *is* a strong element of Lukács' antimodernism in Mann; neither Mann nor Lukács really understands Schiller's notion of art as play, which underlies so much modern art. Both are therefore least at home with music. And Lukács' attack on Schönberg (like his distaste for Joyce) is rooted not in social perceptiveness, but in a clinging to the values of the bourgeois nineteenth century. This clinging is truer of Lukács than it is of Mann. There is in Leverkühn more of Mann than Lukács could allow and Mann's attitude to the narrator, the old-fashioned classical humanist Serenus Zeitblom, contains far more irony than Lukács can detect. This is because there is in Lukács more of Zeitblom than he realizes. In an age when the formality of art and its autonomy have been among its chief safeguards from degeneration (this is what the Nazi attacks on Schönberg and Joyce signify) the attitudes of the older Lukács smack more than a little of the "power-protected inwardness" which he condemns in Bismarckian Germany.

Yet in the latest of these essays, on *The Confessions of Felix Krull, Confidence Man*, that Lukács is a genius still appears. The comparison of the Joseph saga with Felix Krull is full of insight into Mann's handling of character. But it is by now genius that has paid a high price for survival. Lukács most resembles one of Stendhal's characters. Like them, he has lived in a post-revolutionary age in which the price of survival is to pay more than lip service to the values of petty, bourgeoisified despotisms. And the romantic aspiration to embody art in life itself could not have continued to inspire as it has done, if Lukács had not rein-carnated it so often in the Protean doctrines with which he disguises the unchanging inheritance from *The Soul and the Forms* and *History and Class-Consciousness*.

Like Julien Sorel or Fabrice, Lukács has involved himself in countless strategems; like Sorel he has faced the death penalty, like Fabrice he has avoided it. But the declining quality of his writing suggests that time has done its work, that the face behind the mask has taken on the aspect of the mask. Naphta's suicide was one way of paying the debts of romanticism to reality; the long, tortuous, intertwining of enlightenment and deception that Lukács has practiced is another.

9

Marxism of the will[1]

Of the books below[2] the two most important are Gerassi's collection of Che Guevara's writings and Rojo's brilliant biography. Guevara's own reminiscences of the Cuban revolutionary war are interesting, but the reader needs to be well informed already to make much use of them. Debray's theorizing is perhaps only interesting for the contrast between the Debray version of Che and Che as he was, and the Sartre is worth noticing in this context because it helps us to judge how much of Debray is Paris academicism. Finally I notice the American version of Che's diaries merely to note that it differs in important ways from the Cuban version. The publishers on their dust jacket say their edition "was authenticated not by Cubans or Bolivians but by Americans"; here's news for you, Stein and Day—I still do not trust it. James accuses Che of "personal pique"; his publishers join with him in entertaining the suggestion that Castro was jealous of Che, deliberately denied the help he could have given, and so betrayed him. This obscene suggestion does not come well from Americans, who ought at least to realize that the death of Guevara may well cost them as much as his life did.

The death of Che had—and it is difficult to use the word after it has been so cheaply misused—tragic quality. To use a dramatic metaphor is not to suggest anything histrionic about Che's actions

---

[1] Reprinted from *Partisan Review*, 1969.

[2] A review of John Gerassi, ed., *Venceremos! The Speeches and Writings of Che Guevara* (New York: Macmillan; London: Weidenfeld & Nicolson, 1969; Che Guevara, *Reminiscences of the Cuban Revolutionary War* (New York: Grove Press; London: Allen & Unwin, 1968); Daniel James, ed., *The Complete Bolivian Diaries of Che Guevara* (New York: Stein & Day; London: Allen & Unwin, 1969); Ricardo Rojo, *My Friend Che* (New York: Dial Press, 1969); Regis Debray, *Revolution in the Revolution?* (New York and London: Monthly Review Press, 1967); Jean-Paul Sartre, *The Communists and Peace* (New York: Braziller, 1968).

or passions; it is to indicate that those actions and passions are an appropriate subject for poetry as well as for history, because, as Aristotle said, poetry is "more universal" than history. Che was not just an individual, but a representative figure, who lived out a tragic action. A tragic action is one in which a hero encounters a catastrophe as a result of a flaw in his character. By character I do not mean a mere assemblage of psychological traits, I mean rather the incarnation of a role. (What poetry was for Aristotle, sociology is for us.) What was Che's flaw?

To ask this question, I have suggested, is to ask about a role and not about an assemblage of personal traits. That personal traits can explain little in political or social action is made clear once again in reading reminiscences of Che by those who knew him well. He was an asthmatic who developed a will strong enough to take him onto the athletic field and through medical school. He was an ascetic who did not undervalue sex or alcohol. He was an altruist, but without any signs of that self-contempt which so often underpins altruism. I shall suggest later that these traits were not entirely unimportant in relation to some key positions that Che took up; but there are no splendid psychological generalizations to be constructed which will demonstrate that asthmatic, ascetic altruism is the seedbed of revolution. As so often, what is impressive is not the connection, but the relative lack of connection between individual personality and social role. The need to reminisce about Che has in any case obviously little to do with any task of explanation; it is much more as though his friends still have to reassure themselves that it all really did happen, that this living out of one of our political dreams was not in fact only a dream.

The search for such reassurance is perhaps connected with the extent to which the Cuban Revolution was an accidental happening. By this I mean much more than that it did not follow out the patterns of previous revolutions. Regis Debray is able to emphasize that and yet to insist that the Cuban Revolution embodied an experience from which more generally applicable laws and maxims can be extracted. In this he follows Che faithfully and yet there is an important difference in tone between what Huberman and Sweezy call Debray's "comprehensive and authoritative presentation of the revolutionary thought of Fidel Castro and Che Guevara" and what we actually encounter in Che's writings. This difference arises from the stale, academic atmosphere of Debray's arguments. For however authentically Debray may reproduce what is new and Cuban, he does so in a setting and a style which is old and French. So that while in Guevara's own narratives the Marxism-Leninism somehow coexists with a sense of the Cuban Revolution as a chain of improvisations and coincidences, in Debray's writing revolutionary action becomes nothing but matter for theoretical formulas counterposed to other theoretical formulas. Accident has disappeared and with it truth.

We find in Debray a constant reiteration of Sartrian themes. There are the same strange attempts to unite historical necessity and absolute freedom, to dissent from Stalinism and yet to count Stalin among the revolutionary ancestors, and to portray Trotskyism as the villain of the piece; indeed Debray explicitly refers back to Sartre's fifteen-year-old anti-Trotskyist polemic in *The Communists and Peace*. One can well understand why Trotsky's ghost haunts Sartre and Debray. For both Sartre and Debray have a peculiar conception—far more elitist than that of Leninism —of an inert mass of be it workers, be it peasants, who need a leadership of particular gifts to rouse them to revolutionary activity. Sartre in 1952 and 1954 was equally contemptuous of those sociologists who declared that the French working classes were not revolutionary and those Trotskyists who declared that they were revolutionary—but that their revolutionary tendencies were suppressed or inhibited by their reaction to the Stalinist leadership of the Communist Party of France. In Sartre's view the working masses are not, but will become, a revolutionary class precisely because the Communist Party presents them with goals which transcend their immediate needs; so for Debray the guerrilla army is to present the peasants with goals which transcend their immediate needs. It is a doctrine which enables Sartre and Debray to set on one side in the most arbitrary way the question of what workers or peasants do in fact want now. It also enables Sartre to disregard the theoretical positions of Stalinist bureaucrats; his understanding of the falsity of Stalinism seems in his writings of the early 1950s only marginal to his evaluation of Stalinism's political function. So Debray too exalts questions of organization over questions of political goals and programs and sneers at the Trotskyists for their emphasis upon fundamental theory.

In his intellectual style then Debray is unlike Che; but Che himself could not avoid facing dilemmas which in other contexts were responsible for creating Trotskyism, and he could not avoid making choices which were incompatible with Trotskyism. This is because Trotsky himself had had to face at successive points in his career all the dilemmas of those who wish to make a Marxist revolution in an underdeveloped country and because too the failure of Trotskyism to provide a recipe for successful revolutionary practice in the face of those dilemmas is an inescapable fact. *What is the part of the peasantry in the making of a Socialist revolution?* Marx could see no part for them, Mao invented one *ex nihilo* and called it Marxist, and every position intermediate between Marx's and Mao's has been taken up by some Marxist theorist at some time. Trotskyism at the very least represents the thesis of the ineliminable necessity of the participation of an industrial working class in revolution-making. *Can there be socialism in one country?* One paradox of post-Stalin Stalinism is that it may be those who are most repelled by the surviving Stalinist features of the Soviet Union who therefore try to build a socialist revolution in isolation from the Soviet camp or at least in the minimum of contact with it. But in so doing they revive the very thesis of "socialism in one country" on which Stalinism was founded and in this way reject Trotskyism. *What is the place of the revolutionary party?* The orthodox Communist Parties in Latin America are obviously not revolutionary parties; their weakness and their reformism are notorious. But in the struggle waged by peasant guerrillas there is little room for a party at all. Hence Trotskyism once more appears as the ghost of orthodox Bolshevism, repudiating militantly the only militant strategies apparently open in Latin America.

Guevara's position is thus easily defined by contrast with that of Trotskyism, and in this at least Debray is perceptive. But if Guevara offered us a revolution made by peasants, a revolution which creates socialism in one country, and a revolution with a revolutionary army rather than a revolutionary party, he aspired to do so as a Marxist-Leninist, and here is the crux. For if Bolshevism can only appear in the modern world in ghostly form, Trotskyism is indeed its authentic ghost. How then can an anti-Trotskyist position be grafted on to Marxism-Leninism? To answer this question will return us to my initial inquiry as to the tragic flaw in the role acted out by Che. For what Che uses to close the gap between what the Marxist-Leninist must hold on an objective analysis to be a situation in which the socialist revolution cannot yet be made and the revolutionary aspirations of the selfsame Marxist-Leninist who confronts himself with this, as it must seem, defeatist analysis, is an appeal to pure will. Lenin too was confronted with this gap and at every stage wrestled to link the present and the future by means of a consciousness nurtured by the organizational forms of the party. In Guevara, although questions of organization are treated with intellectual respect, it is the voluntarist component of Leninism which is appealed to as never before.

Consider for example the question of planning. Guevara conducted a polemic against the French Communist expert on *planification*, Charles Bettelheim, in which he argued that because of the level that consciousness (in the Marxist sense) had reached in the world at large, the social and political consciousness of Marxists in a country where the objective conditions for a socialist revolution had not yet been reached could none the less enable them to transcend those limitations and to do what seemed objectively impossible. From this premise Che argued further in more general terms for a relative independence of cultural superstructure from economic basis. This led him to quarrel with Bettelheim and other Marxists on economic policy. Material incentives, such as may be provided by a wages structure may be appropriate as the mainspring of a market economy, but are inappropriate to socialism. Centralized planning demands the centralization of major economic decision-making, but it does not require centralized management.

What is to take the place of material incentives and of the dictates of centralized management? A new motivation springing from the new nature of socialist man. Moral incentives must be the mainspring; material incentives must be subordinate. The word "moral" recurs throughout Che's writings. He was the minister who awarded the title "Hero of Labor" to workers who excelled. In his speeches to workers he constantly urged sacrifice and hard work. His personal asceticism put his right to make such calls beyond question. But their theoretical justification is quite another matter.

Behind the Leninist voluntarism we see in Che the revival of an older answer to the Marxist dilemma about morality. Marx himself never raises explicitly the question of the motives of those who seek to achieve socialism. At the turn of the century when Bernstein raised the question of the moral foundations of socialism and turned back to Kant's invocation of duty in order to answer it. Kautsky replied to him with a crude invocation of utilitarianism which relied on an underlying appeal to material self-interest; and Rosa Luxemburg in her polemics against Bernstein avoided coming to grips with this question at all. Bernstein's Kantian answer was in fact more influential than we sometimes realize; and to be Kantian was not necessarily to be a right-wing social democrat. After 1914 Kautsky the orthodox Marxist was far to the

right of Karl Liebknecht, the Kantian and Spartacist. Guevara
was Karl Liebknecht's spiritual heir; like Liebknecht he in the end
bore witness to the fact that moral heroism is not enough. In the
improbable environment of Cuba, Kantian moral theory was
reborn as revolutionary.

Che's moral heroism, his attempt to transcend the material
environment, was the tragic flaw which finally destroyed him in
Bolivia. When he left Cuba he wrote to his children: "Above all,
always be able to feel deeply any injustice committed against
anyone in any part of the world. It's a revolutionary's most
beautiful quality"; and to his parents: "Essentially, nothing has
changed, except that I am much more conscientious, my Marxism
has struck deep roots and is purified." Again the Kantian note is
struck. Conscientiousness took him to his death, because it led
him to ignore political and military facts, and especially Barrientos'
ability to mobilize peasant support.

When I stress Che's moralism, I do not want to underestimate
his intellectual qualities. Americans in particular should read the
speech rejecting the Alliance for Progress made at the Punta del
Este Conference of the OAS in 1961; about that particular
Kennedy cloud-cuckoo project Guevara has proved alarmingly
right. But when Guevara is not being critical of imperialism, he is
all too apt to substitute invocations of honor or of the spirit of
sacrifice for intellectual analysis. Guevara's student admirers are
indeed moved precisely by this and so is John Gerassi who has
done scholarship a service by his collection of Guevara's speeches
and writings. Yet what they admire is just that abstract moralism
which Marx himself ought to have taught us to suspect. Che's
last letter to his parents begins with an allusion to Cervantes:
"Once more I feel Rocinante's ribs under my heels; I'm taking to
the road again with my shield on my arm." Perhaps as he wrote
this he should have remembered that other reminiscence of
Cervantes in a footnote in *Capital* which ends by Marx remarking
that "Don Quixote long ago paid the penalty for wrongly imagining that knight errantry was compatible with all economic forms
of society."

10

Pascal and Marx:
On Lucien Goldmann's Hidden God[1]

The irregular verb which many Anglo-Saxon philosophers conjugate on their way to international conferences runs, "I am sober; you are intoxicated; he is a French philosopher." A tradition of rhetoric and a belief that for Frenchmen clarity is not an achievement but a birthright have admittedly often worked havoc with analytical sobriety across the Channel. But the unfamiliar atmosphere of French philosophy has other more admirable causes. It is in particular more conscious of its background in intellectual and social history, and not just in the history of philosophy. It is therefore often at its best when it is self-consciously historical in its approach. And this, too, is often the best way for us to approach it. History may provide an initial common ground where philosophy itself would fail us. Metaphysical excitement may appear the more justified at the close, if the starting-point was dull and factual. What facts more dull than names and dates?

Every one of Macaulay's Utopian schoolboys knows the name of René Descartes; not even they know that of Antoine Le Maître. But it was in successive years (in 1636 and in 1637) that Descartes published the account of that winter morning nearly twenty years before when he stayed in by the stove and so founded modern philosophy, and that Le Maître withdrew from the world to live in solitary penance at Port-Royal. Both Descartes and Le Maître are significant because of what the future was to make out of them, and the more significant because they came to symbolize two incompatible alternatives for the modern world. It turned out that Descartes had woven into a single rational system some of the dominant themes of the next age, in its life as well as in its thought: the isolated individual as self-sufficient in knowledge and action; the ideal of mechanical explanation; the

[1] Reprinted from *Encounter*, October 1964.

reduction of God to the status of a guarantee that the gaps in rational argument can be filled, and the actions of individuals harmonized; the dualisms of reason and the passions, and of mind and matter. Cartesianism is the new consciousness expressed as a doctrine. From the world to which Descartes gave expression Le Maître withdrew, abandoning his already successful career as a lawyer. His spiritual director was the Abbé de Saint-Cyran, friend of Cornelius Jansen, the Bishop of Ypres, and director of the nuns of Port-Royal, then in Paris. On May 2, 1638, Saint-Cyran was arrested on Richelieu's orders, accused of depriving the state of its ablest subjects, and never left prison.

From the very first, therefore, the devotional and doctrinal movement of Jansenism was recognized by the powers that be as their enemy. Withdrawal from the modern world was a challenge to it. In its withdrawal Jansenism asserts its own counter-thesis: "It is from our separation and absence from the world that is born the presence and feeling for God" (Saint-Cyran). Or again:

> We must have a low opinion not only of the truths which we discover through our own minds, but also of those which God gives us by his divine light. For this light is not the perfect gift of which the Scriptures speak . . . (Barcos).

Most radically of all Jansenism declared that there are divine commandments which the just man who lacks the requisite Grace —and the just man may well lack the requisite Grace—cannot by his own efforts obey. So we get the paradox of the just man who is yet condemned by God, who is yet a sinner. Or at least these positions seemed to the critics of Jansenism to follow from its central thesis—the Jansenists themselves oscillated between denying that this was a correct characterization of Jansen's theology and asserting that it was a correct characterization not only of Jansen's views, but also of St. Augustine's, and therefore orthodox. What matters is the Jansenist assertion of an unbridgable gap between the concepts by means of which the world understands justice and those in which God reveals his will.

God or the World? As always the choice was between a highly specific God and a highly specific world: an Augustinian God and a Cartesian world. How was one to choose? Within the Jansenist movement there were different answers. One, that of Martin de Barcos, was a total refusal of the world. Another, that of Antoine Arnauld, involved the drawing of an almost Thomistic line between the realm in which natural reason is competent and the realm in which only faith in supernatural revelation can guide. Characteristically Barcos wrote to advise other adherents of Jansenism on matters of faith; Arnauld equally characteristically was the author both of *De La Fréquente Communion* (paradoxically named, since the standards of spiritual achievement demanded prior to communion are so high that infrequent communion would have to be the rule) and of the *Logique de Port-Royal*. Arnauld tries to give unto Descartes the things that are Descartes', and unto God the things that are God's. Unfortunately, as Barcos correctly saw, one cannot serve both God and Descartes, at least in any easy synthesizing way. This becomes plainest when one considers the role of God in Cartesianism: the God whom Descartes *uses* to guarantee the existence of the external world and to give the first push to the mechanisms of the physical universe is precisely that God of the philosophers whom the Jansenists contrast with the God of Abraham and Augustine.

The question of compromise with the world arose, too, at the political level. Barcos, the consistent extremist, severed his connection with Port-Royal finally when the compromise embodied in the *Peace of Clement IX* in 1669 was accepted. That Barcos was in some sense right is shown by the fact that neither the Roman church nor the French state was able to compromise with Jansenism from their own point of view and pressed forward to its total destruction. What was it that they could not accept? The Jansenists, especially Barcos, recognized a duty of obedience to their God-given superiors. They asked only to be left alone. But in providing a withdrawal from the world of church, state, and Cartesianism they affronted it. To understand in what the affront consisted we must consider further *who* the Jansenists were. Yet before asking that question it is even more important to note that the possibilities of Jansenism are not exhausted by the alternatives of Barcos and Arnauld.

Suppose that, unlike Arnauld, one recognized the impossibility of a compromise between God and the contemporary world; yet, unlike Barcos, one could not deny the achievement of Descartes and wished to go beyond it by criticizing it. Suppose that none the less one could not but live in the sight of the God of Abraham and Augustine. One would then have to affirm two apparently incompatible truths:

> If ever there is a time when one should make profession of opposites, it is when one is accused of omitting one of them . . .
> (*fragment* 865).[1]

[1] I have numbered the fragments as in the Brunschvicg edition.

It is for failing to do this that Pascal reproves the Jansenists.

Pascal aspires both to reject and to accept the world. He could thus in one and the same period of his life write of the vanity of scientific pursuits and set himself successfully to solve the problem of the cycloid. When Gilberte Pascal wrote her brother's biography, she explained his application to mathematics at that period as an attempt to take his mind off his toothache. Léon Brunschvicg explained Pascal's denigration of science by referring to his failure to convince the Jesuit Noel and Descartes of the significance of his experiments with the vacuum. Both explanations obscure the complexity of Pascal's position:

> One does not show one's greatness by being at one extreme, but by touching both at the same time, and by filling all the space between.

This is not the position of Pascal in the *Lettres Provinciales* in which the Jesuit opponents of Jansenism are met on their own ground. But, on this interpretation, from March 1657 onward Pascal elaborated a new and paradoxical attitude of which the *Pensées* are the expression.

This interpretation of Pascal is the work of Lucien Goldmann,[1] the Marxist editor of Barcos' correspondence, himself an original philosopher of great powers. In Goldmann's view Pascal's final position is an extreme rendering of a coherence implicit in the rest of Jansenism, but only expressed in other writers in one-sided and incomplete forms. He lays great stress on the change in Pascal in 1657; the earlier crisis of 1654 when Pascal had the religious conversion, whose record was the *Mémorial*, had led Pascal into a life which only found its intellectual expression after 1657. Until then he stood with Arnauld in dividing the provinces of faith and reason.

But after 1657 he affirms both a philosophical view of the world which transcends Cartesianism and a view of God which makes all worldly activity worthless. Sometimes these attitudes are combined in the same fragment:

> Descartes—We must say, approximately, "This occurs by figure and motion," for that is true. But it is ridiculous to say which figures and motions; and try to reconstruct the machine. For it is unnecessary, uncertain, and difficult. And even if it were possible, I do not consider the whole of philosophy to be worth an hour of trouble (*fragment* 79).

[1] *The Hidden God*, trs. P. Thody (1964). Lucien Goldmann's untimely death in 1970 robbed us of the finest and most intelligent Marxist of the age.

Sometimes we get an acute criticism of Cartesianism of purely philosophical interest:

> If man were to begin by studying himself, he would see how incapable he is of going beyond himself. How could it be possible for a part to know the whole? But he may perhaps aspire to a knowledge of at least those parts which are on the same scale as himself. But the different parts of the world are all so closely linked and related together that I hold it to be impossible to know one without knowing the other and without knowing the whole (*fragment* 72).

At other times we find the whole of human knowledge brought under condemnation:

> Everything here on earth is partly true and partly false. But essential truth is not like this, for it is wholly pure and wholly true. The mixture that we find here on earth both dishonours and destroys this truth . . . (*fragment* 385).

Is Pascal simply inconsistent? Should his solution have been in a tough-minded way to grasp one of the horns of his dilemma and abandon the other? This would have been the Cartesian solution as it would also have been the Augustinian. But Pascal inhabits two conceptual universes the claims of which he can neither reconcile nor abandon. Torn as he is between two realms, he can see each from the point of view of the other and his own predicament from both. Thus from within Christianity he sees his dilemma as itself prefigured by Christian theology. For does not Christian theology assert that we inhabit two realms, that man belongs both with the angels and the beasts, that if human nature ignores its limitations and seeks to be angelic it becomes bestial, that a hidden God has revealed himself incarnate and so on? The paradoxes of Christianity show it to be divine.

Yet from within the world he can see Christianity in the perspective of his own critique of Cartesianism. His skepticism about clear and distinct ideas ("Too much clarity darkens") and about any allegedly indubitable first principles, even those of skepticism, extends to any alleged arguments for Christianity, even his own. The theory of chances, which he had elaborated to assist his friend Méré at the gambling tables, encounters its limit at the point at which there are no more probabilities, but the stakes are infinite. Yet at this very point a wager cannot be avoided. It is only through a wager that God exists that meaning is conferred on an otherwise meaningless world. Yet it is from the standpoint of that world that we have to learn that belief in God has to accept the status of a wager.

Let Pascal abandon the world and he becomes the ancestor of Kierkegaard, of a self-contained fideism. Let him abandon Christianity and he becomes the ancestor of Hume, avoiding skepticism only by calling nature and custom to his aid. His greatness is in abandoning neither. Why? To understand Goldmann's answer to this question we must turn to his use of Marx and Lukács.

The danger is that we read what Goldmann has to say through our own preconceptions; and where Marxism is concerned no one is without preconceptions. Goldmann's thesis is that Pascal expressed in one particular form a coherent world vision which Lukács was to characterize. That world vision, the vision of tragedy, is rooted in the social history of Jansenism, expressing the attitudes implicit in the predicament of the *noblesse de robe*. Our preconceptions and prejudices might lead us to treat Goldmann's views as just one more explanation of the history of thought in terms of an economic and social basis. But if we did we should miss the concreteness of Goldmann's concerns. He is very far from forcing the interpretation of Jansenism and Pascal into an already existing theoretical structure. Rather it is at least partly through his studies of Jansenism and Pascal that he gives meaning to his theoretical terms. So one cannot fully understand the early theoretical chapters of his book until one has read the later historical and literary studies. Pascal and Jansenism are made to illuminate Marxism quite as much as Marxism is made to illuminate Pascal and Jansenism. Pascal himself would have understood this: "The last thing one discovers when writing a book is what ought to have come first."

The tragic vision, which Lukács described,[1] is the vision of a world where God is no longer present, and yet even in his absence life has to be lived out by the tragic hero with the eye of God upon him. Because God is absent, the hero cannot succeed in the world. Because God, though absent, still regards him, he cannot abandon his task. He is the just man under condemnation, whom the critics of Jansenism saw at the heart of Jansenist doctrine. So long as he responds by refusing the world, he is Barcos. So long as he tries to live in the world and yet also to refuse it, he is Pascal himself.

[1] In *Die Seele und die Formen* (Berlin: Essays Fleischel, 1911). The Lukács whom Goldmann follows is the since self-condemned Lukács of this book and of *Geschichte und Klassenbewusstsein*. Lukács has now (1971) altered his attitude to his work of this period yet once more.

The Lukács of 1911 saw the tragic vision as one form of aesthetic insight; Goldmann sees it as capable of embodiment only when it expresses a form of social life which can recognize its own crisis in this vision.

The *noblesse de robe* (as contrasted with the *noblesse de cour*) was composed of those lawyers and administrators whom the French monarchy used in achieving hegemony over the rest of the nobility, strengthening itself by this alliance with the Third Estate and the townsmen. During the seventeenth century the monarchy breaks this alliance and becomes an independent power, balancing class against class and governing through its own *corps de commissaires*. The *noblesse de robe* thus find themselves on the defensive; their allegiance to the crown and to the established order is the condition of their flourishing and yet now the crown has less and less use for them. They can less and less live out the only role they know, and yet they must recognize the legitimate authority of the power that is abolishing that role. The congruence of this social experience with the tragic vision is clear. (One is reminded of Milton who does not just have to justify the ways of God to man in general, but has to reconcile the hidden fact that God rules with the manifest fact that Charles II rules and the saints do not.) Thus the *parlement*'s manifest sympathy for Jansenism is for Goldmann a sign of recognition by a segment of the middle class that in Jansenism their own fragmentary attitudes receive completer expression and endorsement than elsewhere.

Goldmann is at the opposite extreme from those self-styled Marxists who have tried to reduce the artist or the philosopher to a mere product of his social background. He sees that such a reduction fails to account precisely for what interests us in a writer's achievement, his distinctiveness. Goldmann's injunction is rather that we should understand the background through the writer, seeing in the coherence of great art or great philosophy something that is only implicit in the thought and action of ordinary men. So he invites us to understand Jansenism through Pascal, and the *noblesse de robe* through Jansenism. Moreover, the greatest writers both express and transcend their age. They show us the possibilities in the age of going beyond it, whereas lesser writers exhibit the limitations imposed upon them by the age.

It is not only Pascal whom Goldmann views in this light. He analyses Racine's tragedies in terms of the concept of the tragic vision, seeing a parallelism between the Jansenism of refusal of the world and the tragedies of refusal, *Andromaque* and *Britannicus*, while Pascal's attitude is paralleled in *Phèdre*. These parallelisms are brought out within a much more detailed classification of tragedy. The justification of this classification and the use of Lukács' artificial construct of the tragic vision can lie solely in whether it enables us to understand better not only the plays themselves, but also the author's relationship to them. And Goldmann follows Racine himself in seeing the heart of Jansenism in *Phèdre*. For it was in the preface to *Phèdre* that Racine hoped that his method in this play "would perhaps be a way of reconciling with tragedy a number of persons famous for both their piety and doctrine"—although he does so ostensibly for the platitudinous reason that in his play virtue and vice receive their deserts. Whereas in fact if Goldmann is right the greatness of Phèdre herself is that she cannot refuse the claims of the world as embodied in her own passion and her conception of Hippolytus but nor can she refuse to live with the eye of God upon her. Of Phèdre what Lukács wrote of the tragic hero holds:

> He hopes that a judgment by God will illuminate the different struggles which he sees in the world before him, and will reveal the ultimate truth. But the world around him still follows the same path, indifferent to both questions and answers. No word comes from either created or natural things, and the race is not to the swift nor battle to the strong. The clear voice of the judgment of God no longer sounds out above the march of human destiny, for the voice which once gave life to all has now fallen silent. Man must live alone and by himself. The voice of the judge has fallen silent forever, and this is why men will always be vanquished, doomed to destruction in victory even more than in defeat.

Tragic thought is not simply an episode in the past. Pascal, in Goldmann's view, is not only illuminated by Marx and Lukács, he is their ancestor. He anticpates their epistemology in two crucial respects. First of all, he understands that the knowledge of man himself depends on grasping the individual as part of a totality. Yet we cannot grasp the totality except insofar as we understand the individuals who comprise it. Marx wrote:

> A loom is a machine used for weaving. It is only under certain conditions that it becomes *capital*; isolated from these conditions it is as far from being capital as gold, in its natural state, is from being coin of the realm.

What are these conditions? They include both the existence of a whole system of economic activity and the informing of human activities and intentions by concepts which express the relationships characteristic of the system. We identify a loom as capital or gold as coin only when we have grasped a whole system of activities as a capitalist or monetary system. The individual object or action is identifiable only in the context of the totality; the totality is only identifiable as a set of relationships between individuals. Hence we must move from parts to whole and back from whole to parts.

Goethe, Hegel, and Marx all grasped versions of this truth about the human sciences. Pascal, as Goldmann interprets him, uses it against Descartes in the fragments about the whole and the parts and about figure and motion, which I quoted earlier. We can put the essence of his criticism by saying that, just as no amount of mechanical explanation of the working of a loom will tell us what weaving is, or how a loom becomes capital, so no amount of mechanical explanation of reflexes will tell us what human action is or how a man becomes in his actions like an angel or a beast. For that we need to understand human action as part of a total system in which certain norms are established. The difficulty is that men have false as well as true consciousness of the systems of which they form a part. They need a criterion for discriminating true from false, and they exhibit this need especially in trying to understand the over-all context of their actions. For Pascal this context is provided by God and his will; for Hegel and Marx by the history of society. For Pascal the contradictions involved in the task are ultimate and irresoluble; for Hegel and Marx they can be transcended in a future form of human community. But if tragic thought and dialectical thought differ in these crucial respects, they also resemble each other at key points. Both know that one cannot first understand the world and only then act in it. How one understands the world will depend in part on the decision implicit in one's already taken actions. The wager of action is unavoidable. Goldmann is willing even to use the word "faith" of the Marxist attitude, and he sees a real continuity between Augustinian theology and Marxism, despite their differences on such issues as the actual existence of God:

Subsequently Hegel, and especially Marx and Lukács, have been able to substitute for the wager on the paradoxical and mediatory God of Christianity the wager on a historical future and the human community. In doing so, however, they have not given up the main demands of tragic thought, that is to say a doctrine which explains the paradoxical nature of human reality, and hope in the eventual creation of values which endows this contradiction with meaning and which transforms ambiguity into a necessary element in a significant whole.

Not eternity but the future provides a context which gives meaning to individual parts in the present. The future which does this is as yet unmade; we wager on it not as spectators, but as actors pledged to bring it into being.

Thus if Goldmann presents us with a Marxist Pascal he also offers us a Pascalian Marx. In so doing he breaks, as the young Lukács broke before him, with the view of Marxism as a closed, mechanistic and deterministic system of thought, and he illuminates a variety of Marxist texts which both Marx's critics and his defenders too often neglect. He makes it possible to understand the horror with which the Stalinist Lukács must have come to regard his own youth.

Is what Goldmann says true? Partly this is an empirical question, to be answered by close historians of Jansenism and careful students of Pascal and Racine. Partly it is a question of how far the notion of "the tragic vision" is a useful construct. What does it help us to see to which we should otherwise be blind? But the implications of Goldmann's work extend far more widely than do these questions.

For by placing tragic thought, Cartesian rationalism, and Marxism in the way that he does he commits himself to schematic interpretation of the history of modern philosophy. This schematism is made explicit at a number of points in the book, but more especially in a brilliant excursus on the Faust legend and in several discussions of Kant, to whom Goldmann devoted an earlier book.[1] To put it very crudely, Goldmann sees Kant as standing at an extreme point in the development of the related rifts between fact and value and between virtue and happiness. For Kant the highest good is still virtue crowned with happiness; but virtue and happiness cannot be brought together within the world. It is only beyond the present world by a power outside it that they can be reconciled. Practical life is intolerable unless there is such a divine power, but theoretical inquiry cannot show either that there is or is not such a being. So for Kant moral rules are independent of how the world goes, to be obeyed whatever the consequences of obeying them; and yet there would be no point in obeying the rules unless the universe were of a certain kind. Thus Goldmann

[1] *La communauté humaine et l'univers chez Kant* (Paris: Presses Universitaires de France, 1948).

sees Kant, too, as holding together a tragic contradiction, and in so doing acting as Pascal's successor.

It is in his treatment of Kant that the striking differences between Goldmann and his Anglo-Saxon counterparts emerge. Moral philosophy in England is notably unhistorical. Books are too often written about "the" moral vocabulary apparently on the assumption that there is an unchanging structure of concepts. It is too often assumed, when moral philosophers apparently disagree about "good" and "ought," that they are holding rival and competing views of the same concepts, rather than elucidating very different concepts from very different historical periods. Goldmann's book is in this respect a model of how to write moral philosophy.

Moreover, in bringing out the links between Augustinianism and Marxism, for example—and they go far further than I have suggested in this review—Goldmann contributes to an urgent contemporary task, that of redrawing the lines of intellectual controversy. It has been becoming increasingly plain that whether a man calls himself a Christian, a Marxist, or a liberal, may be less important than what kind of Christian, Marxist, or liberal he is. I remarked earlier that Augustinians and Marxists do differ after all about the existence of God; but they agree that whether God exists or not is a crucial question. In so doing they unite against both Christians of the Tillich-Robinson kind and liberals of a certain kind who think religion a matter of "private" life. Equally that both Goldmann and Sartre call themselves Marxists does not obliterate the gulf that separates their views, let alone that which separates both from M. Garaudy[1] and the French Communist Party's intellectual enclave.

Finally, it is not of course true that the tragic is a category which can finally be transcended and left behind. It remains a possibility wherever the attempt is made to live within and to transcend a society. This attempt need not be tragic in its dimensions. Stendhal's heroes make it in quite a different way. But it remains a possibility:

> There are only three kinds of person: those who, having found God, seek Him; those who, not having found Him, spend their time seeking Him; and those who live without having found Him and without seeking for Him either. The first are both

---

[1] In spite of Roger Garaudy's later reversal of his Stalinist positions, I see no need to change what I wrote earlier.

blessed and reasonable, the last both mad and unhappy, and the second unhappy but reasonable (*fragment 257*).

This is an age when no one is blessed and reasonable and most are mad and unhappy. The task is to be unhappy but reasonable.

PART TWO

Philosophy and ideology:
Introduction to Part Two

The aspiration of Marxism was to provide a perspective in which the present might be understood as a transition from the enslavement of the past to the liberation of the future. This view of the present does of course appear in vulgarized form as a commonplace of the nineteenth century, not specific to Marxism. It reappears in psychoanalysis as a doctrine about individuals: "Where id was, there ego shall be." And it plainly has a Christian ancestry. But where Christianity saw this liberation as at the end of and transcending the history of this world, Marxism placed it within history and indeed within the foreseeable future. All three doctrines therefore characterize the present in terms of its relationship to past and future: as a time of redemption from sin, as a point where neurotic entanglements with the past give way before the constructive aspirations of the ego ideal, and as the period of the revolutionary passage from exploitation and unfreedom to socialism and then to Communism.

To characterize the present in these ways, to insist indeed that the present is only adequately described when it is characterized in these ways, is to use descriptions the application of which commits the user to certain evaluations. To say of a man that he is deeply neurotic, a sinner, or either exploited or an exploiter is not only to say what he is, but also to say what he ought to be. Just what is the relationship of this "is" to this "ought"? From Kant onward at least, there have been philosophers who have insisted that judgments of fact were one thing, judgments about what is right or good quite another thing, and that the latter could never be logically derived from the former. This view of morality as an autonomous sphere was certainly a faithful rendering of a view highly influential in the society which these philosophers belonged to. For, according to a view that was often tacitly presupposed by liberal individualism, questions of fact are settled independently of what anyone wants or chooses, but questions of value are settled only by the individual's choosing and standing by some particular set of principles. The individual confronts the objective facts with a freedom to make such evaluations as he will.

But is this view of man true? Or is it a view—true to some extent at least of liberal, individualist men—made true indeed by their believing it to be true? And does the corresponding philosophical view of the autonomy of morality and of the logical gulf between "is" and "ought" express what is true only of the scheme of ideas and beliefs which informed and informs liberal individualism, or does it rather express a truth about the nature of morality as such? It was against Kant's treatment of "is" and "ought" that the young Marx reacted as early as 1837; and certainly the truth of Kant's thesis is incompatible with the truth of Marx's mature doctrine. For according to Marxism, there are not neutral, objective facts on the one hand and individuals freely choosing their values on the other. It is rather the case that an individual with a given role has norms and ends such that when he accepts a given characterization of the facts, he also evaluates them in accordance with his class role. (Class role is of course never simply a matter of having a particular kind of occupation.) Hence, for Marxism the key descriptive expressions in our vocabulary are also evaluative. Nor is this merely a matter of such expressions being composites in which a descriptive component is joined to the expression of an evaluative choice. For in a Marxist view, values are not chosen, they are given; indeed, the view that values are not given but chosen is, in a Marxist view, one of the given evaluations of a liberal, individualist society. For it itself embodies an evaluative attitude.

By contrast, the view of social science implicit or explicit in the attitudes expressed by the end-of-ideology thesis is one that accepts the separation of fact and value, usually in a version derived from Max Weber. It follows that, underlying the confrontation of these two ideologies—Marxism and that which, as I argued earlier, is embodied in the end-of-ideology thesis—there is a crucial *philosophical* disagreement. Moreover, this same issue, and a number of other closely related philosophical issues, are raised by another problem that is central to the ideological themes discussed in the first part of this book. Marx originally indicted capitalist *values* as well as capitalist methods. His belief that any appeal to the exploiters on a moral basis was bound to embody the illusion of common standards of justice governing human behavior made him suspicious of all moralizing. But when Eduard Bernstein attempted to find a Kantian basis for socialism, the defenders of Marxist orthodoxy Karl Kautsky and Rosa Luxemburg were forced to reopen the question of the nature of the moral authority of the Marxist appeal to the working class. This question, as the experience of Luxemburg and of Lukács, of Trotsky and of Guevara shows, was never satisfactorily answered. Equally, those who broke with Marxism because of its moral failures, both under Stalin and in the post-Stalinist age, have been extremely unclear as to the kind of authority that their moral condemnation has possessed. To what were they appealing? Silone, for example, turned to so highly personal a Christian vision that it would be difficult to understand how this could provide a general and impersonal basis for the kind of moral dissidence that so many have underwritten. It does in fact seem to be the case that from the moral collapse of Marxism men can only turn back to clutch at fragments of that pre-Marxist moralizing which Marx criticized so radically and so effectively.

We therefore cannot escape asking the question: what is morality? and what is its power in the world? And this not only for the reasons I have already given. If we are to escape that "worship of the established fact" which is embodied in the end-of-ideology view of the world, if we are to criticize effectively the uncontrolled, destructive progress of advanced societies in the name of an alternative vision of human liberation—if, that is, we are to create a genuinely post-Marxist ideology of liberation, then we have to avoid the snares which Marxism did not, for all its great achievement, avoid. These snares were not only, of course, a matter of the nature of morality and the conditions under which morality can have power in the world; among the other snares was a lack of concern about philosophical truth, and such a concern is a necessary precondition of answering the questions about morality adequately and without illusion. Why is this so?

In *The German Ideology*, Marx and Engels remarked that "When reality is depicted, philosophy as an independent branch of activity loses its medium of existence"; and Marx elsewhere put this by saying that philosophy stands to a genuine understanding of reality as onanism does to real sexual activity. These aphorisms were, of course, aimed specifically at Hegelianism and Young Hegelianism, doctrines which absurdly inflated the claims of philosophy. But in discussing these pretensions, Marx and Engels proceeded to treat as unproblematic or as already resolved

questions and issues which later philosophy has illuminated—
but which even so have not been fully solved or resolved—but
from the study of which Marxism has insulated itself.

Two groups of questions in particular are crucial, and two non-
Marxist philosophical traditions have been important in contribut-
ing to the answers. The first group of questions will already be
clear. It concerns the nature of moral judgment. What do the key
evaluative words mean, words such as "good," "right," "virtue,"
"justice," "duty," "happiness," and the like? And to what kind
of standards with what kind of authority are we appealing when
we use them? Marxists have often shared with highly conservative
philosophers the view that a concern about the theory of meaning,
or about the nature of speech acts, is somehow a trivialization of
philosophy, a turning away from questions of substance. But it
has been precisely at the level of language that the moral inadequacies and corruptions of our age have been evident, and
certainly no less so by those with ideological stances than by others.
The key question for ideology—whether we (still) possess a
language in which we can say what we sometimes desperately want
to be able to say—cannot be answered until the philosophical
problems about meaning have been resolved.

The second group of questions concerns the explanation of
human action. If moral considerations are important, if socialism
is to have a human face, then we shall have to understand what
part reasoning and deliberation play in bringing about one sort of
action rather than another. Marx and Engels at the outset rightly
wished to draw a contrast between what really moved men to
act in certain ways and what the same men believed to have
moved them to act. This distinction is at the heart of the Marxist
theory of ideology. But Marx and Engels also asserted that men
could find reasons for action in the modern world which would not
only enable them to act effectively, but which would be such that
what they believed to be moving them to action would indeed
be what was in fact moving them to action. The empirical investigation of these questions cannot proceed successfully unless it is
preceded and accompanied by a philosophical account of the
relationship between the kind of explanation of human action in
terms of intentions, reasons, and purposes which is native to human
life itself and the kind of causal explanation which is familiar in the
natural sciences. Just these issues have been the focus of a good
deal of discussion by philosophers influenced by Wittgenstein,
Ryle, and Austin in the last two decades, and the questions in
moral philosophy which I have already instanced have provided a

similar focus. Since these discussions have at their best exhibited a care for rigor and for truth not always exhibited by those engaged in the ideological disputes of the age, it is all the more important that the bearing of these discussions on ideology should continuously be kept in mind. The investigations that form the subject matter of the second part of this book are expressions of this concern.

I spoke earlier of *two* philosophical schools whose importance had been overlooked by the Marxist tradition, and so far I have mentioned only one. The other is that part of the British idealist tradition which culminated in the work of R. G. Collingwood. I take it that Collingwood's outstanding merit was to have understood that we cannot investigate a philosophical subject matter adequately unless we take seriously the fact that such a subject matter always has a historical dimension. That dimension is missing in most work by philosophers within the analytical tradition.

I have reprinted the essays in this second part as they stood, without trying to produce a consistent and harmonious whole. They represent stages in a single inquiry, and I am well aware that they do not provide anything even approaching a unified and systematic treatment. But their fragmentary and tentative nature must not be allowed to detract from the importance of the questions that they raise not only for the professional philosopher, but also for all those who have a stake, whether they know it or not, in the outcome of the ideological debates.

12

What morality is not[1]

The central task to which contemporary moral philosophers have addressed themselves is that of listing the distinctive characteristics of moral utterances. In this essay I am concerned to propound an entirely negative thesis about these characteristics. It is widely held that it is of the essence of moral valuations that thcy arc universalizable and prescriptive. This is the contention which I wish to deny. I shall proceed by first examining the thesis that moral judgments are necessarily and essentially universalizable and then the thesis that their distinctive function is a prescriptive one. But as the argument proceeds I shall be unable to separate the discussion of the latter thesis from that of the former.

I

Are moral judgments essentially and necessarily universalizable? The contention that they are is expressed in its most illuminating form in R. M. Hare's paper on "Universalizability."[2] Hare borrows his terminology from E. Gellner's paper on "Logic and Ethics,"[3] where Gellner distinguishes what he calls U-type and E-type valuations. A U-type valuation is an application of "a rule wholly devoid of any personal reference, a rule containing merely predicates (descriptions) and logical terms."[4] An E-type valuation is one containing some uneliminable personal reference. Hare's thesis is that moral judgments are U-type valuations. To give a reason for an action is not necessarily to commit oneself to such a valuation "for I see no grounds in common language for

[1] Reprinted from *Philosophy*, 1957.
[2] *Proceedings of the Aristotelian Society* (1954–55), pp. 295–312.
[3] *Ibid.*, pp. 157–78.
[4] *Ibid.*, p. 163.

confining the word 'reason' to reasons involving U-type rules."[1]
But Hare goes on to say that his thesis "is analytic in virtue of the
meaning of the word 'moral.' "

What this amounts to is made very plain in an imaginary
conversation which Hare constructs between a "Kantian" and an
"Existentialist." This runs as follows:

E.: You oughtn't to do that.
K.: So you think that one oughtn't to do that kind of thing?
E.: I think nothing of the kind; I say only that *you* oughtn't
to do *that*.
K.: Don't you even imply that a person like me in circum-
stances of this kind oughtn't to do that kind of thing when the
other people involved are the sort of people that they are?
E.: No; I say only that *you* oughtn't to do *that*.
K.: Are you making a moral judgment?
E.: Yes.
K.: In that case I fail to understand your use of the word
"moral."

Hare's comment on this is: "Most of us would be as baffled as
the 'Kantian'; and indeed we should be hard put to it to think of
any use of the word 'ought,' moral or nonmoral, in which the
'Existentialist's' remarks would be comprehensible. Had the
'Existentialist' said 'Don't do that,' instead of 'You oughtn't to
do that,' the objections of the 'Kantian' could not have been made;
this illustrates one of the main differences between 'ought' and
ordinary imperatives."[2]

The crux then of Hare's position is the contention that whenever anyone says "I, you or he ought to do so-and-so," they are
thereby committing themselves to the maxim "One ought to do
so-and-so." This commitment is embodied in the meaning of the
word "ought" insofar as "ought" is used morally—and indeed,
Hare seems to say, in nonmoral uses of "ought" also. But is this
contention in fact correct? Consider the following example which
is borrowed from Sartre.[3] One of Sartre's pupils was confronted
during the war with the alternatives of leaving France to join de
Gaulle or of staying to look after his mother. His brother had been
killed in the German offensive in 1940 and his father was a
collaborator. These circumstances had left him with a strong
feeling that he was responsible as a patriot and they had left his

[1] *Ibid.*, p. 278.
[2] *Ibid.*, pp. 304–5.
[3] *L'Existentialisme est un Humanisme*, pp. 39–42.

mother in a state of almost complete dependence upon him. What should he do? Stay with his mother or escape to England? Sartre uses this problem in order to argue that there are no "objective" criteria by which such a choice may be made. Part of the force of his argument is this. Someone faced with such a decision might choose either to stay or to go without attempting to legislate for anyone else in a similar position. He might decide what to do without being willing to allow that anyone else who chose differently was blameworthy. He might legitimately announce his choice by saying, "I have decided that I ought to stay with my mother." If he did so, his use of "ought" would not express any appeal to a universalizable principle. It would not be a U-type valuation, but it would be a moral valuation.

Two points need to be made about this example. The first concerns the function of "I ought to do so-and-so" when it is used to announce a decision in a case like that of Sartre's pupil. Its use is plainly to commit oneself, to allow that if I do not do what I say I ought to do, then I am blameworthy. It is a per-formatory use of "I ought" in that its use makes one responsible for performing a particular action where before saying "I ought" one could not have been held responsible for performing that action rather than some alternative one. To note this is to bring out the oddity in Hare's treatment of the "Existentialist's" con-tribution to his dialogue. For in this nonuniversalizable sense of "ought" one could never say "You oughtn't" but only "I oughtn't." To say "You oughtn't" and suppose that you had used "ought" in this sense would be as odd as to say "You promise" and suppose that thereby one had committed someone else to a promise.

Secondly, it might be argued that the very possibility of a problem such as that of Sartre's pupil presupposes the acceptance of certain universalizable maxims as moral principles. If Sartre's pupil had not accepted the maxims "One ought to assist one's parents when they are in need" and "One ought to assist one's country when it is in need" there would have been no problem. What is important is that the clash between two principles need not be resolved by reformulating one of the principles or formulating a third one. Certainly this clash could be so resolved. Sartre's pupil might have acted on the maxim "Duties to one's parents always have precedence over duties to one's country." Had he done so he would have legislated not only for his own but for all relevantly similar situations. But in order to make his own decision he does not need to so legislate. Now it seems to be a consequence of Hare's position that if the decision between principles is itself to be a moral decision it *must* itself rest upon the adoption of a universalizable maxim. This, in the light of Sartre's example, could only be defended by an a priori restriction on the use of the word "moral." Such a restriction, however, would not be merely a restriction upon our use of a word. For to adopt Hare's use of "moral" would be to permit only one way of settling conflicts of principle (that of formulating a new principle or reformulating an old one) to be counted as genuinely a moral solution to a moral problem, while another way—that of the nonuniversalizable decision à la Sartre—would be ruled out from the sphere of morality. To do this is plainly to do more than to offer a descriptive analysis of the meaning of "moral." It is to draw a line around one area of moral utterance and behavior and restrict the term to that area.

What one can conclude from this is twofold. First, not all, but only some, moral valuations are universalizable. What leads Hare to insist that all are is his exclusive concentration on moral rules. For rules, whether moral or nonmoral, are normally universal in scope anyway, just because they are rules. As Mr. Isaiah Berlin has written in another context, "In so far as rules are general instructions to act or refrain from acting in certain ways, in specified circumstances, enjoined upon persons of a specified kind, they enjoin uniform behavior in identical cases."[1] If this is so, then there is nothing specific to moral valuation in universalizability and in so far as moral valuations are not expressions of rules they are not universalizable. Secondly, the exceptions are not simply cases analogous to that of Sartre's pupil. A whole range of cases can be envisaged where moral valuations are not universalizable. At the one extreme would be those instances where in adopting a moral position someone consciously refrains from legislating for others, although they might have done so; where a man says, for example, "I ought to abstain from participation in war, but I cannot criticize or condemn responsible nonpacifists," but might have said, "One ought to abstain from participation in war." In such a case whether to make a universal or a merely personal judgment is itself a moral problem. The fact that a man might on moral grounds refuse to legislate for anyone other than himself (perhaps on the grounds that to do so would be moral arrogance) would by itself be enough to show that not all moral valuation is universalizable. Or rather that once again this thesis can only be maintained by an a priori and quite unjustifiable restriction upon the word "moral." In other words, a man might conduct his moral

[1] "Equality," in *Proceedings of the Aristotelian Society* (1955–56).

life without the concept of "duty" and substitute for it the concept of "my duty." But such a private morality would still be a morality.

More commonly, however, nonuniversalizable judgments occur when a man finds that the concept of "duty ' has limits which render it useless in certain situations of moral perplexity. Such is the example of Sartre's pupil. And such are the cases at the other end of our scale where moral valuations must be nonuniversalizable, where it is logically impossible to universalize. This is the case with what the theologians call "works of supererogation." A work of supererogation is by definition not numbered among the normal duties of life. Those duties—such things as keeping one's promises and paying one's debts—are partly characterized by the fact that the maxims which enjoin them are universalizable. But there are a great many acts of moral worth which do not come within their scope: one may be virtuous in the sense in which virtue is demanded of everyone without being morally heroic. A moral hero, such as Captain Oates, is one who does more than duty demands. In the universalizable sense of "ought" it does not therefore make sense to assert that Captain Oates did what he ought to have done. To say of a man that he did his duty in performing a work of supererogation is to contradict oneself. Yet a man may set himself the task of performing a work of supererogation and commit himself to it so that he will blame himself if he fails without finding such a failure in the case of others blameworthy. Such a man might legitimately say, "I have taken so-and-so as what I ought to do." And here his valuation cannot, logically cannot, be universalized.

II

Crucial to the argument so far that universalizability is not a necessary characteristic of all moral valuation has been the distinction between first-person and third-person uses of moral valuation. Before the force of this distinction can be fully understood, however, it is necessary to inquire what the function of moral valuation may be. The argument of this section will be that there are a great variety of uses to which moral utterance may be put, none of which can claim the title of "the" function of moral valuation. It will be useful to list some of the tasks which even so familiar a form of moral judgment as "X ought to do Y" may be set.

1.   *The expression of indignation or other violent or mild emotion.*

This is characteristically a function of third-person uses. "He ought to put his foot down," we may say angrily, although we might hesitate to advise him by saying, "You ought to put your foot down," and if we did so we would be advising as well as, or even rather than, expressing our emotion. Clearly, of course, we might say "He ought to put his foot down" without any kind of emotion, and here we would presumably be prescribing a course of action. If we did this we would be committing ourselves to the advice "You ought to put your foot down" even if we never did in fact utter this advice. This brings out already how the same form of words may be put to quite different use in moral utterance. Those emotive theorists who said that the function of moral utterance was to evince emotion would therefore have been correct if they had substituted the indefinite for the definite article.

2.   *The expression of commands or exhortations.* This is of course a second-person use. As Stevenson pointed out, we may often say (to a child, for example) "You ought not to do that," meaning simply "Don't do that."[1] We may, of course, and often do so use "ought" that "You ought" has more than, or other than, imperatival force, but we need not do so. Hare in his dialogue allows that the "Existentialist" would have spoken correctly had he said "Don't do that" instead of "You oughtn't to do that." But he does not consider the possibility that the substitution of "ought" for an imperative might be something other than a universalizing of the imperative. Yet clearly in ordinary usage the use of "ought" might simply be an indication of the importance attached to the imperative, as it could be in the case of the command to the child.

3.   *The appraisal of actions.* We can appraise equally the past, present, and future actions of ourselves and others, whether in their absence or to their faces. This is therefore one of the most general uses of "ought" whether in tense or in person. When "ought" is used for purposes of appraisal, it differs from "good" in that comparatives and superlatives are not available. "He did what he ought to have done" or "He failed to do what he ought to have done" are the only two verdicts available. So that appraisal by use of "ought" is appraisal that implies a single standard. If you made this use central to your moral utterance you would produce a morality akin to that of the Stoics, where to fall from good in the slightest degree is to fall into evil. ("A man drowns in six inches of water as easily as in six feet.") At this point it is important to note that this use of "ought" is logically independent of the imperatival use. That is, there is no inconsistency in saying

[1] *Ethics and Language*, p. 21.

"You ought to do this, but don't." Those philosophers who have insisted on analysing moral utterance in terms of imperatives would be forced to interpret this as meaning "Do this (Let anyone in this sort of situation do this kind of thing), but don't," which would be as nonsensical as any utterance of the form p. $\sim$ p. But where the "ought" expresses an appraisal there is no inconsistency. For however morally reprehensible it may be, there is no inconsistency in pointing out what the moral appraisal of an action would be and then suggesting that one act otherwise. Some writers have attempted to argue against this by interpreting "You ought to do this, but don't," as meaning "In this society most people would consider that you ought to do this, but I think you ought to do that." But while this might be what would be meant, it need not be. A man might commit himself to a certain moral appraisal but not use it as a guide for action—"This in the light of morality is how your action would be appraised: but don't follow the guidance of morality."

4. *The giving of advice.* This is a genuinely prescriptive function of moral utterance. It is also one in which genuinely universalizable maxims are employed. For when we advise someone to undertake a certain course of action we do so in virtue of certain characteristics of their situation and certain characteristics of the recommended course of action. But while this might seem to be a use of "ought" which accords admirably with Hare's analysis, there is one point that stands out for notice; namely, that the giving of advice is always a question of second-person utterance. So that while "You ought to do so-and-so" may express a universalizable prescription when it is offered as advice, clearly "I ought to do so-and-so" cannot function in the same way. For one cannot advise oneself.

5. *Persuasion.* So much has been said so well on this subject by Stevenson that the only necessary comment is to point out that the present list of ways in which "ought" can be used merely brings out the error of offering an analysis of "ought" which restricts it to one of its possible uses.

6. *The expression of one's own principles.* This is the most characteristic first-person use of "ought." But I do not think many people say "I ought to do so-and-so" very often, and when they do, it is usually, I suspect, "I ought to do so-and-so, *but . . .*" or "I don't know what I ought to do over so-and-so." In other words "I ought" is used to express doubt and perplexity as well as and indeed perhaps as much as to give voice to moral assurance. This point will need to be developed later.

III

This incomplete catalogue of uses of "ought" in simple sentences such as "X ought to do Y" has one main point: moral philosophy to date has been insufficiently lexicographical. Even a partial enumeration of the differences already noted between first-, second-, and third-person uses of "ought" (of which that between a particular first- and a particular third-person use noted in the discussion of Sartre's example now turns out to be only a particular case) should make us conscious of the need for a far wider range of patterns of analysis than any contemporary writer has so far offered. But, instead of enlarging on this topic here, a possible reply to the arguments that universalizability is not a necessary attribute of moral valuation of the form "X ought to do Y", and that such valuations do not necessarily have a prescriptive function, must be considered. Against these contentions the following counterargument might be brought.

The essence of moral judgments it might be said is their impersonality. When we judge morally it is at the heart of the matter that we "do not make exceptions in our own favor" (Kant), that the moral agent must "depart from his private and particular situation" (Hume). When the moral agent judges an action he judges therefore what anyone should do in that or relevantly similar situations. When he appraises the action of another he thereby commits himself to saying what anyone and a fortiori he himself ought to have done. When he decides how to act he thereby commits himself to an appraisal of any similar action by anyone else. Thus appraisal, advice, and practical decisions are inexorably linked together. But of these three, practical decisions have the primacy; to appraise someone else's action is to say how he ought to have acted and to give advice is to tell someone else how to act. Moral language, or at least "ought", is employed par excellence in guiding action. In this form the argument brings out the interconnection of the claim that moral judgments are essentially universalizable and the claim that they are essentially practical and prescriptive. Its force is further brought out by noting a consequence which Hare has drawn from the conclusions of this argument. Hare argues that to say that a man holds a moral principle is to say that he at least sometimes acts on it. A man who claims to believe in keeping promises but habitually breaks them does not in fact hold the principle that one ought to keep promises, according to Hare. Those who have objected to this contention have usually pointed to the problem of ἀκρασία, have argued that if Hare were right we would not have the case of the man whose practice is radically inconsistent with his principles.[1] But this objection takes no cognizance of the way in which the notion of consistency is built into this argument at the theoretical level.

Take the example of a man who appraises actions by one standard and guides his own conduct by another. This differs from the case of the man who is guilty of weakness of will, for such a man's conduct is consistent with his principles, or rather with that set of his principles which he uses to guide his conduct. He merely has two sets of principles. This is sometimes condemned by invoking the maxim "Practice what you preach" which is also, of course, used to condemn weakness of will. We condemn such a man because and if we disapprove of inconsistency between appraisals and principles of conduct. But while such inconsistency may be morally objectionable, it is not—and the fact that it can be comprehended to such a degree as to be found morally objectionable shows that it is not—unintelligible. Yet in the argument outlined above this is what it must be. For if the meaning of the appraisal "He ought to have done Y" is even partly "I ought to have done Y in those circumstances" (interpreted as "That is the maxim that would have governed my conduct" not "That is the maxim by which I would have appraised my conduct") then the man who asserts that he appraises by one set of principles but acts by another speaks unintelligibly. In other words, the view that I am criticizing makes consistency between appraisals and principles of conduct a logical requirement. That principles should be so consistent is built into the meaning of moral words such as "ought." But the demand for consistency is in fact a moral not a logical requirement. We blame a man for moral inconsistency perhaps, but we do not find what he says meaningless. Appraisals and principles of conduct are logically independent, although in a liberal morality they are required to be morally interdependent. And now we can understand why universalizability is given such a central place by those philosophers whose analyses are directed upon the concepts of liberal morality. For the requirement that everyone shall be judged by the same standard (the moral counterpart of the political principle that everyone is to count as one and nobody as more than one) in the sense that everyone shall judge everyone else by the standard by which he judges himself is so basic to liberal morality that it is

[1] E.g., P. L. Gardiner, "On Assenting to a Moral Principle," *Proceedings of the Aristotelian Society*, (1954-55).

converted from a requirement of morality into a requirement of logic. It is not part of the meaning of "morality" *tout court* that moral valuations are universalizable, but liberals tend to use the word "morality" in such a way that this is made part of its meaning. It is worth noting a consequence of this transition from morality to logic, of a kind not unfamiliar in moral argument. If we so characterize moral judgments that we mean by a "moral judgment" an impersonal one, we make it impossible to approve or disapprove morally of impersonality in judging. For if part of the meaning of "ought," for example, is such that to say "X ought" is to say "X would not be making an exception in his own favor if he . . ." or "X would be departing from his private and particular situation if he . . ." then to say "X ought not to make an exception in his own favor" is to utter an empty tautology. This is in essence the same argument as that which Moore used against naturalism, an argument which, as Professor Prior has shown, was anticipated in many ways by Cudworth and Adam Smith. But as Prior has also shown, Moore's argument is not conclusive.[1] A tough-minded naturalist can save his position "by admitting that the assertion that, say, pleasure and nothing but pleasure is good, *is* for him a mere truism; and that if Ethics be the attempt to determine what is in fact good, then the statement that what is pleasant is good is not, strictly speaking, an ethical statement, but only a way of indicating just what study is to go under the name of 'Ethics'—the study of what is actually pleasant, without any pretence of maintaining that the pleasure has any 'goodness' beyond its pleasantness."[2] Similarly an upholder of the universalizability view of morality could accept the consequence that it is a mere truism to say "X ought not to make exceptions in his own favor" and contend that all he meant to achieve by this truism was the definition of the field of morality. But if he made this his contention a further consequence would follow (and a similar consequence would follow for Prior's tough-minded naturalist); namely, that he would have to abandon any claim to be offering us a neutral logical analysis of moral language. For plainly ordinary moral agents do disapprove of making exceptions in one's own favor in nontruistic fashion (just as they hold that pleasure is good in similar fashion). To assert that universalizability is of the essence of moral valuation is not to tell us what "morality" means or how moral words are used. It is to prescribe a meaning for

[1] *Logic and the Basis of Ethics* (London and New York: Oxford University Press, 1949), Ch. 1 and passim.
[2] *Op. cit.,* p. 9.

"morality" and other moral words and implicitly it is to prescribe a morality.

Finally, one more feature of the prescriptive theory of moral valuation must be examined briefly. A maxim may be said to prescribe or to guide conduct in one of two ways. Clearly we might describe conduct that accorded with a maxim as guided by it and speak of it as the conduct prescribed by the maxim, if we were willing to adduce the maxim to justify the conduct. A man who habitually kept his promises might when challenged on a particular occasion as to why he had put himself out to meet a friend or to pay a debt avow "One ought to keep one's promises." It would be natural to describe the man's conduct as guided by the maxim. But this is not to say that up to the point where justification was demanded the maxim ever entered his thoughts, at least since the time that he learned it as a child. And thus the maxim guides conduct in a sense quite different from that in which a maxim may be said to guide conduct if we explicitly consult it when perplexed as to what we ought to do. Most of the actions discussed in moral philosophy textbooks—promise-keeping, truth-telling and the like—are in practice carried out without any sort of conscious reference to maxims. So that in the more explicit sense of "guide," where part of what we mean by "guide" is "to give guidance," "to tell us what to do," the relevant maxims do not guide us when we keep promises or tell the truth. They do not guide us because we do not need to be guided. We know what to do. We tell the truth and keep promises most of the time because it does not occur to us to do otherwise. When we are tempted not to do these things from some motive of self-indulgence, it would still not be true to say that if we resist the temptation, the maxim guided our conduct. What guided our conduct was our decision to abide by the conduct prescribed by the maxim. So that in this sense "X ought to do Y" prescribes a certain line of conduct but it does not guide us or tell us what to do. That this is so is even more obvious when we consider those cases where we have already noted a common use of "ought," cases of moral perplexity. When Huckleberry Finn wrestles with the problem of whether to return Jim, Miss Watson's slave, he is not guided by the maxims of his morality, for his whole problem is whether to abide by those maxims or not. The maxims tell him that property is sacred and that Jim is merely property. Nor is Huck guided by a new set of maxims, perhaps the anti-slavery maxim that "One ought to treat no human being as a slave." For Huck retains the same general attitudes that he was brought up with. (When someone inquires if anyone has been injured in a steamboat accident, he says "No'm, killed a nigger.") In fact in deciding not to inform on Jim he feels wicked and thinks of himself as wicked. He thinks of himself in fact as making an exception in his own favor, of favoring his own friend at the expense of morality. He finds his way morally by means of an only half-articulate sympathy. But he does not find it by universalizable maxims or indeed by maxims at all.

When you leave the ground of conventional morality, you leave the guidance of maxims behind. Yet it is just here that one needs guidance. Where men pass from one set of maxims to another, or act morally without maxims, there is an area where the logician and the linguistic analyst are necessarily helpless. For they are not presented with the kind of material which they need for analysis. Only the phenomenologist can help us here and the kind of phenomenology we need is that supplied by the novelist. It is because the moral philosophers of existentialism have been primarily concerned with this kind of situation that they have so often resorted to the novel. For all that can be done is to exhibit the passage of the moral agent through perplexity. To offer us a maxim on which or in accordance with which the moral agent finally acted is to tell us what the resolution of perplexity was but not how the perplexity was resolved. In this clear-cut sense then the maxims of morality do not guide us, nor do they prescribe conduct to us. And to describe the function of moral valuation in general or of "ought" in particular as prescriptive is highly misleading unless this is made clear. The catalogue of possible uses of "ought" needs to be supplemented by a catalogue of those moral purposes for which "ought" and words like it and sometimes any words at all can be of little or no use.

One last point relating moral perplexity to the claims made for moral judgment as prescriptive and universalizable: here, as everywhere in moral philosophy, much depends on the choice of examples. Where there is real moral perplexity it is often in a highly complex situation, and sometimes a situation so complex that the question "What ought I to do?" can only be translated trivially into "What ought someone like me to do in this kind of situation?" This is important because this translation is often not trivial at all. When I am puzzled it is often useful to pick out the morally relevant features of the situation and of my position in it and, having isolated them from the particular situation, I am in a better position to solve my problem. But, where a situation is too complex, phrases like "someone like me" or "this kind of situation" become vacuous. For I am the only person sufficiently "like me" to be morally relevant and no situation could be sufficiently like "this kind of situation" without being precisely this situation. But what situation could be complex in this way? The situation of Françoise in Simone de Beauvoir's *L'Invitée* or that of Mathieu in Sartre's *Les Chemins de la Liberté* are examples that spring to mind, for part of their problem is to decide which features of their situation are relevant; part of their problem is to discover precisely what their problem is. And this brings out the point that it is because Sartre and Simone de Beauvoir are concerned with morality of this kind and in this way that they present and can only present their insights in the form of novels rather than of logical analyses.

13

Hume on "is" and "ought"[1]

I

Sometimes in the history of philosophy the defense of a particular philosophical position and the interpretation of a particular philosopher become closely identified. This has notoriously happened more than once in the case of Plato, and lately in moral philosophy it seems to me to have happened in the case of Hume. At the center of recent ethical discussion the question of the relationship between factual assertions and moral judgments has continually recurred, and the nature of that relationship has usually been discussed in terms of an unequivocally sharp distinction between them. In the course of the posing of this question, the last paragraph of Book III, Part i, Section 1, of Hume's *Treatise* has been cited over and over again. This passage is either quoted in full or at least referred to—and with approval—by R. M. Hare,[2] A. N. Prior,[3] P. H. Nowell-Smith,[4] and a number of other writers. Not all contemporary writers, of course, treat Hume in the same way; a footnote to Stuart Hampshire's paper, "Some Fallacies in Moral Philosophy,"[5] provides an important exception to the general rule. But very often indeed Hume's contribution to ethics is treated as if it depended largely on this one passage, and this passage is accorded an interpretation which has acquired almost the status of an orthodoxy. Hare has even spoken of "Hume's Law."[6]

[1] Reprinted from *The Philosophical Review*, 1959.
[2] *The Language of Morals* (London and New York: Oxford University Press, 1952), pp. 29 and 44.
[3] *Logic and the Basis of Ethics* (London and New York: Oxford University Press, 1949), pp. 32–33.
[4] *Ethics* (London and Baltimore: Penguin Books, 1954), pp. 36–38.
[5] *Mind*, LVIII (1949), p. 466.
[6] *Proceedings of the Aristotelian Society* (1954–55), p. 303.

What Hume says is:

> In every system of morality which I have hitherto met with, I have always remark'd, that the author proceeds for some time in the ordinary way of reasoning, and establishes the being of a God, or makes observations concerning human affairs; when of a sudden I am surpriz'd to find, that instead of the usual copulations of propositions, *is*, and *is not*, I meet with no proposition that is not connected with an *ought*, or an *ought not*. This change is imperceptible; but is, however, of the last consequence. For as this *ought* or *ought not*, expresses some new relation or affirmation, 'tis necessary that it should be observ'd and explain'd; and at the same time that a reason should be given, for what seems altogether inconceivable, how this new relation can be a deduction from others, which are entirely different from it. But as authors do not commonly use this precaution, I shall presume to recommend it to the readers; and am persuaded that this small attention wou'd subvert all the vulgar systems of morality, and let us see, that the distinction of vice and virtue is not founded merely on the relations of objects, nor is perceiv'd by reason.[1]

The standard interpretation of this passage takes Hume to be asserting here that no set of nonmoral premises can entail a moral conclusion. It is further concluded that Hume therefore is a prime opponent of what Prior has called "the attempt to find a 'foundation' for morality that is not already moral." Hume becomes in this light an exponent of the autonomy of morality and in this at least akin to Kant. In this essay I want to show that this interpretation is inadequate and misleading. But I am not concerned with this only as a matter of historical interpretation. The thread of argument which I shall try to pursue will be as follows. First, I shall argue that the immense respect accorded to Hume thus interpreted is puzzling, since it is radically inconsistent with the disapproval with which contemporary logicians are apt to view certain of Hume's arguments about induction. Secondly, I shall try to show that if the current interpretation of Hume's views on "is" and "ought" is correct, then the first breach of Hume's law was committed by Hume; that is, the development of Hume's own moral theory does not square with what he is taken to assert about "is" and "ought." Thirdly, I shall offer evidence that the current interpretation of Hume is incorrect.

---

[1] Selby-Bigge, p. 469.

Finally, I shall try to indicate what light the reinterpretation of Hume can throw upon current controversies in moral philosophy.

II

To approach the matter obliquely, how can we pass from "is" to "ought"? In Chapter iv of *The Language of Morals*, Hare asserts that a practical conclusion and a fortiori a moral conclusion is reached syllogistically, the minor premise stating "what we should in fact be doing if we did one or other of the alternatives open to us" and the major premise stating a principle of conduct. This suggests an answer to our question. If you wish to pass from a factual statement to a moral statement, treat the moral statement as the conclusion to a syllogism and the factual statement as a minor premise. Then to make the transition all that is needed is to supply another moral statement as a major premise. And in a footnote to Chapter iii of *Ethics* we find Nowell-Smith doing just this. He quotes the following passage from Bishop R. C. Mortimer: "The first foundation is the doctrine of God the Creator. God made us and all the world. Because of that He has an absolute claim on our obedience. We do not exist in our own right, but only as His creatures, who ought therefore to do and be what He desires."[1] On this Nowell-Smith comments: "This argument requires the premise that a creature ought to obey his creator, which is itself a moral judgment. So that Christian ethics is not founded solely on the doctrine that God created us:"[2] That is, he argues that the inference, "God created us, therefore we ought to obey him," is defective unless and until it is supplied with a major premise, "We ought to obey our creator."

I can only make sense of this position by supposing that underlying it there is an assumption that arguments must be either deductive or defective. But this is the very assumption which underlies Hume's skepticism about induction. And this skepticism is commonly treated as resting upon, and certainly does rest upon, a misconceived demand, a demand which P. F. Strawson has called "the demand that induction shall be shown to be really a kind of deduction."[3] This is certainly an accurate way of characterizing Hume's transition from the premise that "there

[1] *Christian Ethics* (London: Black, 1950), p. 7.

[2] *Op. cit.*, p. 51.

[3] *Introduction to Logical Theory* (London: Methuen; New York: Barnes & Noble, 1952), p. 250.

can be no *demonstrative* arguments to prove, that those instances of which we have had no experience resemble those of which we have had experience" to the conclusion that "it is impossible for us to satisfy ourselves by our reason, why we should extend that experience beyond those particular instances which have fallen under our observation."[1] Part of Hume's own point is that to render inductive arguments deductive is a useless procedure. We can pass from "The kettle has been on the fire for ten minutes" to "So it will be boiling by now" (Strawson's example) by way of writing in some such major premise as "Whenever kettles have been on the fire for ten minutes, they boil." But if our problem is that of justifying induction, then this major premise itself embodies an inductive assertion that stands in need of justification. For the transition which constitutes the problem has been justified in the passage from minor premise to conclusion only at the cost of reappearing, as question-beggingly as ever, within the major premise. To fall back on some yet more general assertion as a premise from which "Whenever kettles have been on the fire for ten minutes they boil" could be derived would merely remove the problem one stage farther and would be to embark on a regress, possibly infinite and certainly pointless.

If then it is pointless to present inductive arguments as deductive, what special reason is there in the case of moral arguments for attempting to present them as deductive? If men arguing about morality, as Bishop Mortimer is arguing, pass from "God made us" to "We ought to obey God," why should we assume that the transition must be an entailment? I suspect that our inclination to do this may be that we fear the alternative. Hare suggests that the alternative to his view is "that although, in the strict sense of the word, I have indeed shown that moral judgments and imperatives cannot be *entailed* by factual premises, yet there is some looser relation than entailment which holds between them." I agree with Hare in finding the doctrine of what he calls "loose" forms of inference objectionable; although I cannot indeed find this doctrine present in, for example, Professor S. E. Toulmin's *The Place of Reason in Ethics* which Hare purports to be criticizing. And certainly entailment relations must have a place in moral argument, as they do in scientific argument. But since there are important steps in scientific argument which are not entailments, it might be thought that to insist that the relation between factual statements and moral conclusions be deductive or nonexistent

---

[1] *Treatise*, I, iii, 6; (Selby-Bigge, pp. 89 and 91).

would be likely to hinder us in elucidating the character of moral arguments.

How does this bear on the interpretation of Hume? It might be held that, since Hume holds in some passages on induction at least that arguments are deductive or defective, we could reasonably expect him to maintain that since factual premises cannot entail moral conclusions—as they certainly cannot—there can be no connections between factual statements and moral judgments (other perhaps than psychological connections). But at this point all I am suggesting is that our contemporary disapproval of Hume on induction makes our contemporary approval of what we take to be Hume on facts and norms seem odd. It is only now that I want to ask whether—just as Hume's attitude to induction is much more complex than appears in his more sceptical moments and is therefore liable to misinterpretation—his remarks on "is" and "ought" are not only liable to receive but have actually received a wrong interpretation.

III

The approach will still be oblique. What I want to suggest next is that if Hume does affirm the impossibility of deriving an "ought" from an "is" then he is the first to perform this particular impossibility. But before I proceed to do this, one general remark is worth making. It would be very odd if Hume did affirm the logical irrelevance of facts to moral judgments, for the whole difference in atmosphere—and it is very marked—between his discussion of morality and those of, for example, Hare and Nowell-Smith springs from his interest in the facts of morality. His work is full of anthropological and sociological remarks, remarks sometimes ascribed by commentators to the confusion between logic and psychology with which Hume is so often credited. Whether Hume is in general guilty of this confusion is outside the scope of this essay to discuss. But so far as his moral theory is concerned, the sociological comments have a necessary place in the whole structure of argument.

Consider, for example, Hume's account of justice. To call an act "just" or "unjust" is to say that it falls under a rule. A single act of justice may well be contrary to either private or public interest or both.

But however single acts of justice may be contrary, either to public or to private interest, 'tis certain, that the whole plan or scheme is highly conducive, or indeed absolutely requisite both to the support of society, and the well-being of every individual. 'Tis impossible to separate the good from the ill. Property must be stable, and must be fix'd by general rules. Tho' in one instance the public be a sufferer, this momentary ill is amply compensated by the steady prosecution of the rule, and by the peace and order, which it establishes in society.[1]

Is Hume making a moral point or is he asserting a causal sociological connection or is he making a logical point? Is he saying that it is logically appropriate to justify the rules of justice in terms of interest or that to observe such rules does as a matter of fact conduce to public interest or that such rules are in fact justified because they conduce to public interest? All three. For Hume is asserting both that the logically appropriate way of justifying the rules of justice is an appeal to public interest and that in fact public interest is served by them so that the rules are justified. And that Hume is clearly both justifying the rules and affirming the validity of this type of justification cannot be doubted in the light of the passage which follows.

And even every individual person must find himself a gainer on balancing the account; since, without justice, society must immediately dissolve, and everyone must fall into that savage and solitary condition, which is infinitely worse than the worst situation that can possibly be suppos'd in society.

Moreover, this type of argument is not confined to the *Treatise*; elsewhere also Hume makes it clear that he believes that factual considerations can justify or fail to justify moral rules. Such considerations are largely appealed to by Hume in his arguments in the essay "Of Suicide" that suicide is morally permissible.

To return to the justification of justice: Hume clearly affirms that the justification of the rules of justice lies in the fact that their observance is to everyone's long-term interest; that we ought to obey the rules because there is no one who does not gain more than he loses by such obedience. But this is to derive an "ought" from an "is." If Hare, Nowell-Smith, and Prior have interpreted Hume correctly, Hume is contravening his own prohibition. Someone might argue, however, that Hume only appears to contravene it. For, if we ignore the suggestion made earlier in this essay that the attempt to present moral arguments as entailments

---

[1] *Ibid.*, III, ii, 2; Selby-Bigge, p. 497.

may be misconceived, we may suppose that Hume's argument is defective in the way that Bishop Mortimer's is and attempt to repair it in the way Nowell-Smith repairs the other. Then the transition from the minor premise "Obedience to this rule would be to everyone's long-term interest," to the conclusion "We ought to obey this rule" would be made by means of the major premise "We ought to do whatever is to everyone's long-term interest." But if this is the defense of Hume, if Hume needs defense at this point, then he is indefensible. For the locution offered as a candidate for a major premise, "We ought to do what is to everyone's long-term interest," cannot function as such a premise for Hume since in his terms it could not be a moral principle at all but at best a kind of compressed definition. That is, the notion of "ought" is for Hume only explicable in terms of the notion of a consensus of interest. To say that we ought to do something is to affirm that there is a commonly accepted rule; and the existence of such a rule presupposes a consensus of opinion as to where our common interests lie. An obligation is constituted in part by such a consensus, and the concept of "ought" is logically dependent on the concept of a common interest and can only be explained in terms of it. To say that we ought to do what is to the common interest would therefore be either to utter an aphoristic and misleading truism or else to use the term "ought" in a sense quite other than that understood by Hume. Thus the locution "We ought to do what is to everyone's long-term interest" could not lay down a moral principle which might figure as a major premise in the type of syllogism which Hare describes.

The view which Hume is propounding can perhaps be illuminated by a comparison with the position of J. S. Mill. On the interpretation of Mill's ethics for which Professor J. O. Urmson has convincingly argued,[1] Mill did not commit the naturalistic fallacy of deriving the principle that "We ought to pursue the greatest happiness of the greatest number" from some statement about what we ourselves or all men desire. He did not commit this fallacy for he did not derive his principle at all. For Mill, "We ought to pursue the greatest happiness of the greatest number" is the supreme moral principle. The difference between Mill's utilitarianism and Hume's lies in this: that if we take some such statement as "We ought to do whatever is to the advantage of most people," this for Mill would be a moral principle which it would be morally wrong to deny, but which it would make sense to deny. Whereas for Hume to deny this statement would be

[1] *Philosophical Quarterly*, III (1953), 33.

senseless, for it would detach "ought" from the notion of a consensus of interest and so evacuate it of meaning. Roughly speaking, for Mill such a principle would be a contingent moral truth; for Hume it would be a necessary truth underlying morality.

Moreover, Hume and Mill can be usefully contrasted in another respect. Mill's basic principle is a moral affirmation independent of the facts: so long as some course of action will produce more happiness for more people than alternative courses will, it provides at least some sort of effective moral criterion. But at any rate, so far as that part of his doctrine which refers to justice is concerned, it is quite otherwise with Hume. We have moral rules because we have common interests. Should someone succeed in showing us that the facts are different from what we conceive them to be so that we have no common interests, then our moral rules would lose their justification. Indeed the initial move of Marx's moral theory can perhaps be best understood as a denial of the facts which Hume holds to constitute the justification for social morality, Marx's denial that there are common interests shared by the whole of society in respect of, for instance, the distribution of property meets Hume on his own ground. (We may note in passing that the change from Hume's characterization of morality in terms of content, with its explicit reference to the facts about society, to the attempt by later writers to characterize morality purely in terms of the form of moral judgments is what Marxists would see as the significant change in philosophical ethics. Since I would agree with Marxists in thinking this change a change for the worse —for reasons which I shall indicate later in the argument—I have been tempted to retitle this essay "Against Bourgeois Formalism in Ethics.")

One last point on the contrast between Hume and Mill: since Mill's basic principle in ethics is a moral principle, but Hume's is a definition of morality, they demand different types of defense. How does Hume defend his view of the derivation of morality from interest? By appeal to the facts. How do we in fact induce someone to do what is just? How do we in fact justify just actions on our own part? In observing what answers we have to give to questions like these, Hume believes that his analysis is justified.[1]

IV

What I have so far argued is that Hume himself derives "ought"

[1] *Op. cit.*, Selby-Bigge, p. 498.

from "is" in his account of justice. Is he then inconsistent with his own doctrine in that famous passage? Someone might try to save Hume's consistency by pointing out that the derivation of "ought" from "is" in the section on justice is not an entailment and that all Hume is denying is that "is" statements can entail "ought" statements, and that this is quite correct. But to say this would be to misunderstand the passage. For I now want to argue that in fact Hume's positive suggestions on moral theory are actually an answer to a question posed in the "is" and "ought" passage, and that that passage has nothing to do with the point about entailment at all. The arguments here are twofold.

First, Hume does not actually say that one cannot pass from an "is" to an "ought" but only that it "seems altogether inconceivable" how this can be done. We have all been brought up to believe in Hume's irony so thoroughly that it may occasionally be necessary to remind ourselves that Hume need not necessarily mean more or other than he says. Indeed the rhetorical and slightly ironical tone of the passage renders it all the more ambiguous. When Hume asks how what seems altogether inconceivable may be brought about, he may be taken to be suggesting either that it simply cannot be brought about or that it cannot be brought about in the way in which "every system of morality which I have hitherto met with" has brought it about. In any case it would be odd if Hume thought that "observations concerning human affairs" necessarily could not lead on to moral judgments since such observations are constantly so used by Hume himself.

Secondly, the force of the passage as it is commonly taken depends on what seems to be its manifest truth: "is" cannot entail "ought." But the notion of entailment is read into the passage. The word Hume uses is "deduction." *We* might well use this word as a synonym for entailment, and even as early as Richard Price's moral writings it is certainly so used. But is it used thus by Hume? The first interesting feature of Hume's use of the word is its extreme rarity in his writings. When he speaks of what we should call "deductive arguments" he always uses the term "demonstrative arguments." The word "deduction" and its cognates have no entry in Selby-Bigge's indexes at all, so that its isolated occurrence in this passage at least stands in need of interpretation. The entries under "deduction" and "deduce" in the Oxford English Dictionary make it quite clear that in ordinary eighteenth-century use these were likely to be synonyms rather for "inference" and "infer" than for "entailment" and "entail." Was this Hume's usage? In the essay entitled "That Politics may be Reduced to a

Science," Hume writes, "So great is the force of laws, and of particular forms of government, and so little dependence have they on the humors and tempers of men, that consequences almost as general and certain may sometimes be deduced from them as any which the mathematical sciences afford us."[1] Clearly, to read "be entailed by" for "deduced from" in this passage would be very odd. The reference to mathematics might indeed mislead us momentarily into supposing Hume to be speaking of "entailment." But the very first example in which Hume draws a deduction makes it clear how he is using the term. From the example of the Roman republic which gave the whole legislative power to the people without allowing a negative voice either to the nobility or the consuls and so ended up in anarchy, Hume concludes in general terms that "Such are the effects of democracy without a representative." That is, Hume uses past political instances to support political generalizations in an ordinary inductive argument, and he uses the term "deduce" in speaking of this type of argument. "Deduction" therefore must mean "inference" and cannot mean "entailment."

Hume, then, in the celebrated passage does not mention entailment. What he does is to ask how and if moral rules may be inferred from factual statements, and in the rest of Book III of the *Treatise* he provides an answer to his own question.

V

There are, of course, two distinct issues raised by this essay so far. There is the historical question of what Hume is actually asserting in the passage under discussion and there is the philosophical question of whether what he does assert is true and important. I do not want to entangle these two issues overmuch, but it may at this point actually assist in elucidating what Hume means to consider briefly the philosophical issues raised by the difference between what he actually does say and what he is customarily alleged to say. Hume is customarily alleged to be making a purely formal point about "ought" and "is," and the kind of approach to ethics which makes such formal analyses central tends to lead to one disconcerting result. The connection between morality and happiness is made to appear purely contingent and accidental. "One ought to . . ." is treated as a formula

[1] Essay III in Hume, *Theory of Politics*, ed. by F. Watkins (London and Camden, N.J.: Thomas Nelson, 1951), p. 136.

where the blank space might be filled in by almost any verb which would make grammatical sense. "One ought occasionally to kill someone" or "One ought to say what is not true" are not examples of moral precepts for more than the reason that they are at odds with the precepts by which most of us have decided to abide. Yet if ethics is a purely formal study, any example ought to serve. If a philosopher feels that the connection between morality and happiness is somehow a necessary one, he is likely to commit, or at least be accused of, the naturalistic fallacy of defining moral words in factual terms. It is obvious why philosophers should seem to be faced with this alternative of committing the naturalistic fallacy or else making the connection between morality and happiness contingent and accidental. This alternative is rooted in the belief that the connections between moral utterances and factual statements must be entailments or nothing. And this belief arises out of accepting formal calculi as models of argument and then looking for entailment relations in nonformal discourse.

To assert that it is of the first importance for ethics to see that the question of the connection between morality and happiness is a crucial one is not, of course, to allow that Hume's treatment of it is satisfactory. But at least Hume did see the need to make the connection, whereas the "is" and "ought" passage has been interpreted in such a way as to obscure this need.

Secondly, the reinterpretation of this passage of Hume allows us to take up the whole question of practical reasoning in a more fruitful way than the formalist tradition in ethics allows. If anyone says that we cannot make valid inferences from an "is" to an "ought," I should be disposed to offer him the following counter-example: "If I stick a knife in Smith, they will send me to jail; but I do not want to go to jail; so I ought not to (had better not) stick a knife in him." The reply to this may be that there is no doubt that this is a valid inference (I do not see how this could be denied) but that it is a perfectly ordinary entailment relying upon the suppressed major premise "If it is both the case that if I do x, the outcome will be y, then if I don't want y to happen, I ought not to do x." This will certainly make the argument in question an entailment; but there seem to me three good reasons for not treating the argument in this way. First, inductive arguments could be rendered deductive in this way, but, as we have already noted, only a superstitious devotee of entailment could possibly want to present them as such. What additional reason could there be in the case of moral arguments that is lacking in the case of inductive arguments? Moreover, a reason akin to that which we have for

5

not proceeding in this way with inductive arguments can be adduced in this use also, namely that we may have made our argument into an entailment by adding a major premise; but we have reproduced the argument in its nonentailment form as that premise, and anything questionable in the original argument remains just as questionable inside the major premise. That premise itself is an argument and one that is not an entailment; to make it an entailment will be to add a further premise which will reproduce the same difficulty. So whether my inference stands or falls, it does not stand or fall as an entailment with a suppressed premise. But there is a third and even more important reason for not treating the transition made in such an inference as an entailment. To do so is to obscure the way in which the transition within the argument is in fact made. For the transition from "is" to "ought" is made in this inference by the notion of "wanting." And this is no accident. Aristotle's examples of practical syllogisms typically have a premise which includes some such terms as "suits" or "pleases." We could give a long list of the concepts which can form such bridge notions between "is" and "ought": wanting, needing, desiring, pleasure, happiness, health—and these are only a few. I think there is a strong case for saying that moral notions are unintelligible apart from concepts such as these. The philosopher who has obscured the issue here is Kant, whose classification of imperatives into categorical and hypothetical removes at one blow any link between what is good and right and what we need and desire. Here it is outside my scope to argue against Kant; all I want to do is to prevent Hume from being classified with him on this issue.

For we are now in a position to clarify what Hume is actually saying in the "is" and "ought" passage. He is first urging us to take note of the key point where we do pass from "is" to "ought" and arguing that this is a difficult transition. In the next part of the *Treatise* he shows us how it can be made; clearly in the passage itself he is concerned to warn us against those who make this transition in an illegitimate way. Against whom is Hume warning us?

Hume himself identifies the position he is criticizing by saying that attention to the point he is making "wou'd subvert all the vulgar systems of morality." To what does he refer by using this phrase? The ordinary eighteenth-century use of "vulgar" rules out any reference to other philosophers and more particularly to Wollaston. Hume must be referring to the commonly accepted systems of morality. Nor is there any ground for supposing Hume to depart from ordinary eighteenth-century usage on this point. Elsewhere in the *Treatise*[1] there is a passage in which he uses interchangeably the expressions "the vulgar" and "the generality of mankind." So it is against ordinary morality that Hume is crusading. And for the eighteenth century, ordinary morality is religious morality. Hume is in fact repudiating a religious foundation for morality and putting in its place a foundation in human needs, interests, desires, and happiness.

Can this interpretation be further supported? The only way of supporting it would be to show that there were specific religious moral views against which Hume had reason to write and which contain arguments answering to the description he gives in the "is" and "ought" passage. Now this can be shown. Hume was brought up in a Presbyterian household and himself suffered a Presbyterian upbringing. Boswell records Hume as follows: "I asked him if he was not religious when he was young. He said he was, and he used to read *The Whole Duty of Man*; that he made an abstract from the Catalogue of vices at the end of it, and examined himself by this, leaving out Murder and Theft and such vices as he had no chance of committing, having no inclination to commit them."[2] *The Whole Duty of Man* was probably written by Richard Allestree, and it was at once a typical and a popular work of Protestant piety, and it abounds in arguments of the type under discussion. Consider, for example, the following: "whoever is in distress for any thing, wherewith I can supply him, that distress of his makes it a duty on me so to supply him and this in all kinds of events. Now the ground of its being a duty is that God hath given Men abilities not only for their own use, but for the advantage and benefit of others, and therefore what is thus given for their use, becomes a debt to them whenever their need requires it. . . ."[3] This is precisely an argument which runs from "the being of a God" or "observations concerning human affairs" into affirmations of duty. And it runs into the difficulty which Hume discusses in the section preceding the "is" and "ought" passage, that what is merely matter of fact cannot provide us with a reason for acting—unless it be a matter of those facts which Hume calls the passions; that is, of our needs, desires, and the like. Interestingly enough, there are other passages where Allestree provides his arguments with a backing which

[1] I, iv, 2.

[2] Boswell, "An Account of My Last Interview with David Hume, Esq.," reprinted in Hume, *Dialogues Concerning Natural Religion*, ed. by N. K. Smith (second ed., Indianapolis: Bobbs-Merrill, 1948).

[3] Sunday XIII: Sec. 30.

refers to just this kind of matter. "A second Motive to our care of any thing is the USEFULNESS of it to us, or the great Mischief we shall have by the loss of it. . . . 'Tis true we cannot lose our Souls, in one sense, that is so lose them that they cease to Be; but we may lose them in another. . . . In a word, we may lose them in Hell. . . ."[1] That is, we pass from what God commands to what we ought to do by means of the fear of Hell. That this can provide a motive Hume denies in the essay "Of Suicide": obviously in fact, though he does not say so very straightforwardly, because he believes that there is no such place.

The interpretation of the "is" and "ought" passage which I am offering can now be stated compendiously. Hume is not in this passage asserting the autonomy of morals—for he did not believe in it; and he is not making a point about entailment—for he does not mention it. He is asserting that the question of how the factual basis of morality is related to morality is a crucial logical issue, reflection on which will enable one to realize how there are ways in which this transition can be made and ways in which it cannot. One has to go beyond the passage itself to see what these are; but if one does so, it is plain that we can connect the facts of the situation with what we ought to do only by means of one of those concepts which Hume treats under the heading of the passions and which I have indicated by examples such as wanting, needing, and the like. Hume is not, as Prior seems to indicate, trying to say that morality lacks a basis; he is trying to point out the nature of that basis.

VI

The argument of this essay is incomplete in three different ways. First, it is of certain interest to relate Hume's argument to contemporary controversies. On this I will note only as a matter of academic interest that there is at least one recent argument in which Hume has been recruited on the wrong side. In the discussion on moral argument between Hare and Toulmin,[2] Hare has invoked the name of Hume on the side of his contention that factual statements can appear in moral arguments only as minor premises under the aegis of major premises which are statements of moral principle and against Toulmin's contention that moral arguments are nondeductive. But if I have reread Hume on "is"

[1] Preface.
[2] *The Language of Morals*, p. 45; *Philosophical Quarterly*, I (1950–51), p. 372; and *Philosophy*, XXXI (1956), p. 65.

and "ought" correctly, then the difference between what Hume has been thought to assert and what Hume really asserted is very much the difference between Hare and Toulmin. And Hume is in fact as decisively on Toulmin's side as he has been supposed to be on Hare's.

Secondly, the proper elucidation of this passage would require that its interpretation be linked to an interpretation of Hume's moral philosophy as a whole. Here I will only say that such a thesis of Hume's as that if all factual disagreement were resolved, no moral disagreements would remain, falls into place in the general structure of Hume's ethics if this interpretation of the "is" and "ought" passage is accepted; but on the standard interpretation it remains an odd and inexplicable belief of Hume's. But to pursue this and a large variety of related topics would be to pass beyond the scope of this essay.

Finally, however, I want to suggest that part of the importance of the interpretation of Hume which I have offered in this essay lies in the way that it enables us to place Hume's ethics in general and the "is" and "ought" passage in particular in the far wider context of the history of ethics. For I think that Hume stands at a turning point in that history and that the accepted interpretation of the "is" and "ought" passage has obscured his role. What I mean by this I can indicate only in a highly schematic and speculative way. Any attempt to write the history of ethics in a paragraph is bound to have a *1066 and All That* quality about it. But even if the paragraph that follows is a caricature it may assist in an understanding of that which it caricatures.

One way of seeing the history of ethics is this. The Greek moral tradition asserted—no doubt with many reservations at times—an essential connection between "good" and "good for," between virtue and desire. One cannot, for Aristotle, do ethics without doing moral psychology; one cannot understand what a virtue is without understanding it as something a man could possess and as something related to human happiness. Morality, to be intelligible, must be understood as grounded in human nature. The Middle Ages preserves this way of looking at ethics. Certainly there is a new element of divine commandment to be reckoned with. But the God who commands you also created you and His commandments are such as it befits your nature to obey. So an Aristotelian moral psychology and a Christian view of the moral law are synthesized even if somewhat unsatisfactorily in Thomist ethics. But the Protestant Reformation changes this. First, because human beings are totally corrupt their nature cannot be a foundation for true morality. And next because men cannot judge God, we obey God's commandments not because God is good but simply because He is God. So the moral law is a collection of arbitrary fiats unconnected with anything we may want or desire. Miss G. E. M. Anscombe has recently suggested that the notion of a morality of law was effectively dropped by the Reformers;[1] I should have thought that there were good grounds for asserting that a morality of law-and-nothing-else was introduced by them. Against the Protestants Hume reasserted the founding of morality on human nature. The attempt to make Hume a defender of the autonomy of ethics is likely to conceal his difference from Kant, whose moral philosophy is, from one point of view, the natural outcome of the Protestant position. And the virtue of Hume's ethics, like that of Aristotle and unlike that of Kant, is that it seeks to preserve morality as something psychologically intelligible. For the tradition which upholds the autonomy of ethics from Kant to Moore to Hare, moral principles are somehow self-explicable; they are logically independent of any assertions about human nature. Hume has been too often presented recently as an adherent of this tradition. Whether we see him as such or whether we see him as the last representative of another and older tradition hinges largely on how we take what he says about "is" and "ought."

[1] "Modern Moral Philosophy," *Philosophy*, XXXIII (1958), pp. 1–19.

14

Imperatives, reasons for action, and morals[1]

The thesis that moral utterances are somehow or other essentially imperatival, or at least that they resemble imperatives in some important way, is interesting not only because of the possibility that it may throw light on the nature of moral utterances, but also because the project of explaining moral concepts with the aid of a grammatical category, that of the imperative, obviously could have consequences for our understanding of the possible relationship between the study of language and philosophy. It is partly because this essay is skeptical in intention that I do not pay regard to the very different versions of the thesis that have been advanced. Instead, what I have done initially is to examine first the nature of the imperative mood, to see whether any kind of utterance is necessarily expressed by means of it, and then the relation between imperatives and reasons for action, in order to understand the possible role of imperatives in practical discourse. It is only finally and briefly that some considerations about moral discourse obtrude themselves.

I

Jespersen says that "The imperative is used in requests, which according to circumstances may range from brusque commands to humble entreaties, the tone generally serving as a key to the exact meaning."[2] Hare says that "An indicative sentence is used for

[1] Reprinted from *The Journal of Philosophy*, 1965.
[2] Otto Jespersen, *Essentials of English Grammar* (London: Allen & Unwin; New York: Holt, Rinehart and Winston, 1933), p. 294. In *A Modern English Grammar on Historical Principles* (Heidelberg: C. Winter, 7 vols., 1909–49; London: Allen & Unwin, 1927–50) Jespersen adds wishes and permissions to requests.

telling someone that something is the case; an imperative is not— it is used for telling someone to make something the case."[1] This concurrence of grammarian and philosopher, however, still leaves one in some doubt. Both seem to assert that the class of imperative sentences may be segregated by identifying their use or function. But when Fanny Farmer says, "Take six eggs," she certainly neither commands nor entreats and does not even request; and when in giving an order an officer says, "The following will report at the Guard Room at 18.00 hours: Smith, Jones, Robinson," an indicative is being used to tell someone to do something. These elementary examples throw an important initial doubt on whether Jespersen and Hare have characterized the relationship between grammatical form and linguistic function correctly. In order to strengthen this doubt I want to inquire how, in trying to understand the unfamiliar language of an alien culture, we might discover whether that language contained imperative sentences and how to identify them.

The first point to be noted—from the earlier examples—is that imperative sentences may be used to serve more than one purpose. They are of course commonly used to tell some specific person to do something; but they are also commonly used to tell anyone *how* to do something. That the same form should serve both purposes is easily intelligible; for a set of instructions in a cookbook or a carpentry manual, when recited by a mistress to her servant or by a master carpenter to an apprentice on a specific occasion as directions for the performance of a specific task, becomes a set of orders or requests. It remains true that the existence of the single grammatical form in virtue of which this is possible is a contingent feature of English, Latin, and other languages. So the first precaution to be taken in examining an unfamiliar language would be to inquire whether the two functions of *telling* someone *to do something* and of *telling how to do something* are served by a single form.

A second preliminary point is that, if attention were concentrated on *telling to*, we should have to be careful to distinguish between imperative sentences and sentences not of imperative form which are expressions of desires or wishes, translatable as "I want you to do ..." or "Would that you would do. ..." Both classes of sentence would be employed in utterances in which the naming of an action to some specified person or range of persons would often be followed by the performance of the action by those to whom utterance was addressed, and the action would be performed

[1] R. M. Hare, *The Language of Morals* (London and New York: Oxford University Press, 1952), p. 5.

precisely because of what had just been said. But the reason for the performance of the action would be quite different in the one case from the other. "I did it because you wanted me to" is quite different from "I did it because you told me to." None the less, those imperatives which are used to express requests are often interchangeable with expressions of a want. "I would like a lemonade, please" can be interchanged with "Get me a lemonade, please," and the latter can thus function as an expression of a want. This again is easily intelligible, for "The primitive sign of wanting is *trying to get*,"[1] and the utterance of an imperative as either command or request is one form of *trying to get*. But it follows that the segregation of genuinely imperative sentences from sentences of the form "I want . . ." is all the more difficult. Nonetheless, this segregation is essential, both for the reason already given—that the imperative usually affords the person to whom it is uttered a different kind of reason for action from that afforded by the expression of a desire—and also because the imperative, when it *is* used to tell someone to do something, need not in any way express the particular desire or wish of the speaker. The bored officer on parade may in fact hope that when he issues the command "Present arms!" all the troops will fall off their horses.

It follows from all this that the isolation of an imperatival form in a language would be the isolation of a form available for a given and quite wide range of functions, but that these functions do not have any obvious unity, although each is related intelligibly to at least one of the others. From this it seems to follow both that we can have no a priori reason for expecting the occurrence of such a grammatical form in any other language and also that in our own language we cannot use the imperatival form to pick out a homogeneous and well-defined class of utterances. It will be at the very least highly misleading to begin with the concept of an imperative and then to explain the nature of, for example, moral injunctions or some other use of language by comparing them to imperatives. For *all* that is clearly segregated by the concept of an imperative is a certain grammatical form. To emphasize this point, it is perhaps worth while to examine a little further the relations between *telling to*, *telling how*, and *telling that*.

The introduction of *telling how* would itself be sufficient to destroy any neat pairing off of imperatives with *telling to* and indicatives with *telling that*. The instructions by means of which someone is told how to bake a cake or make a cupboard may equally

[1] G. E. M. Anscombe, *Intention* (Oxford: Basil Blackwell; Ithaca, N.Y.: Cornell University Press, 1957), p. 68.

well be expressed by imperatives or by indicatives; and, if expressed by the latter, the instructions will take the form of statements which are true or false about causes and effects. In this case *telling how* and *telling that* would coincide, just as, in the case where instructions are given to a specific person both to make and how to make something, *telling to* and *telling how* may coincide. What makes a particular utterance a case of *telling to* but not of *telling how*, or of *telling to* and of *telling how*, or of *telling to* but not of *telling that*, and so on is, therefore, not only a matter of the sense and reference of what is said, but also a matter of who is talking to whom with what intention and in what manner. Sometimes the sense and reference of the words alone without knowledge of the context would enable us to identify correctly the purpose being served by the words; sometimes the same words with the same sense and reference will be used for quite different purposes, and what the purposes are will be correctly identifiable only by identifying the nature and context of the utterance. And what holds of sense and reference in this argument is also true of grammatical form.

Moreover, so far I have used the expression "telling someone to do something" as though it required no further explanation. But I may tell someone to do something by way of warning, advising, threatening, or ordering; and I may ask someone to do something by way of requesting, beseeching, or praying. In all of these cases I may use an imperative. But could I use an imperative to tell or to ask someone to do something which did not fall under any of these headings or under any similar heading? Can I intelligibly say, "I didn't warn, advise, threaten, or order him to do it; I just told him to do it"? Certainly there are cases where we can be clear about someone else that he is telling someone to do something, but where we are in no position to provide any further description of what he is doing in so telling. But could there be cases where no further description of the relevant type was applicable? Consider what has to be stripped away to leave us with such a case.

If I advise, warn, or threaten you, I back up my imperative implicitly or explicitly by giving you reasons for action; and it is the character of the reasons that makes of the imperative a piece of advice rather than a warning or a warning rather than a threat. The tone of voice or the choice of words may convey that what is being uttered is a threat, but what makes a threat a threat is the implicit or explicit answers offered to the questions "And what if I do not?" and "And what if I do?" addressed to the utterer of the imperative. If I order or command you, what makes the imperative an order or command is—in the standard case—the position of the person who utters the imperative in some hierarchy of rank relative to the person to whom the imperative is addressed. This has to be qualified in at least two ways. First of all, not every imperative uttered by a superior to an inferior is thereby constituted an order. The requests or threats made in a private capacity by superior to inferior do not count as orders because not made in due form. What due form is varies with the type of hierarchy; in most armies an imperative can be made into an order just by saying "This is an order." Secondly, we characterize certain imperatives as orders because the person who issues them behaves as if he were a superior addressing an inferior when in fact he is not. So we may speak of one person as ordering another about when neither is a member of any hierarchy.

When an order is issued, the person to whom it is issued is thereby given a reason and perhaps reasons for action. What the reasons are depends upon what he believes the consequences of disobeying the order may be and also upon what he believes the point of giving and obeying orders of the relevant kind is. Thus, in the case of orders and commands as well as in the case of warnings, pieces of advice, and threats, what gives the imperative its character as an utterance is the kind of reason that might be given by the speaker for uttering the imperative and the kind of reason that might be given by the hearer for acting on it. Therefore, to strip away all character from the utterance other than that which the bare imperative has by itself, to try and leave us with a bare case of *telling to*, would be to leave us with an imperative which is un-backed, either implicitly or explicitly, by reasons offered by the speaker and which affords to the hearer no reason at all for acting upon it.

Now, clearly, there *could* be such a form of utterance. Two men quite unacquainted with each other are sitting on the same park bench. The one says, "Pick up that cigarette end." How is the other to take this? Suppose that he asks, "Are you asking me, threatening me, or what?" and receives the reply, "I am just telling you to." What is he or are we to make of this? We can certainly understand the meaning of what is said, but could we understand the nature of his utterance?

Having suggested the difficulty of giving a clear answer to this question, I am now in a position to suggest some initial conclusions. I began with the thesis that imperatives and indicatives are con-trasted forms, each of which is used to serve a specific function, respectively, that of telling someone to do something and that of telling someone that something is the case. Against this thesis I have argued, first, that the imperative as a grammatical form is used for a variety of purposes and, secondly, that, although imperatives are used to tell people to perform actions, telling someone to do something is characteristically not just issuing an imperative, but issuing an imperative backed up by the giving of a certain kind of reason for action. The character of the imperatival injunction derives from the character of this backing. Since the expression of the reasons for action will be in indicative form, the relation between such indicative expressions and such imperative expressions becomes crucial to the discussion. But the argument so far has shown that to concentrate on grammatical form alone would in any case be misleading.

II

Philosophical inquiries into the relation of imperatives to reasoning have tended to concentrate on the deductive relationships into which imperative sentences may enter and have been conducted with an eye to the alleged large dichotomies of fact and value, describing and prescribing, and so on. Less ambitiously, I want to make some more elementary points about the relationship between imperatival injunctions and the reasons for action from which they derive their specific character as threats, warnings, and the like on the one hand and orders and commands on the other. The first is that someone to whom an injunction in the form of a warning or a threat is addressed may take up three attitudes toward it: he may accept it, either by doing as he is enjoined to do or by taking precautions against the consequences of not so doing; he may refuse to believe the statement that asserts the possibility or probability of such consequences and, therefore, not act as he is enjoined to do; or again, he may believe the statement and yet think that it does not adequately warrant obedience to the injunction. It is upon the first and third cases that I wish to concentrate attention in order to ask what may be the difference between a warranted and an unwarranted injunction. Suppose a man threatened with dire consequences if he does not take one course of action is advised by a friend to take another incompatible course of action. The blackmailer says, "Forge the check," saying or implying "or else I will ruin your reputation." The friend says, "Don't forge the check. You will always regret it." (Note incidentally that in this example the imperatives are being used in an attempt to persuade. Imperatives need not so be used. A man who seeks to advise need not be seeking to persuade. This is a matter of his intentions and not of the grammatical form of his utterance.) If the man addressed could be sure either that he would not regret his action or that the blackmailer could not ruin him, he would have no reason to do other than he was enjoined, in the former case by the blackmailer, in the latter by the friend. And if he did do other than he was enjoined, his action would be irrational in the sense that it ran counter to the only reason he had for acting in one way rather than another. "I have reasons only for doing X and not Y, but I am going to do Y and not X" is the paradigmatic avowal of irrationalism in this case. To this there is a counterpart in the issuing of imperatives.

"You have reasons only for doing X and not Y, but do Y and not X" breaks no linguistic canons and is not inconsistent in the sense of containing or entailing any contradictions, but it is irrational in that it urges irrationalism in the sense defined above. As such its utterance would be self-defeating, for it not only provides no reasons for acting on it, but even provides reasons for not acting on it. Thus the connection between an imperative and the reason that backs it up is intelligible in terms of the connection between an action and the reason that backs it up, and not in terms of any direct logical link between imperative sentence and the sentence expressing the reason. Now to return to the situation where an agent is considering rival and incompatible injunctions, each backed up by a reason which he takes seriously. He will not act irrationally in choosing to have regard to one consideration rather than the other, provided of course that his wants, needs, purposes, and projects are not frustrated rather than advanced by the consideration to which he chooses to have regard; but his so choosing will precisely be an index of his preferring one kind of consideration before another.

In a parallel way the man who issues an imperative and backs it up with a reason is committing himself not to the view that the reason he cites entails the imperative, but to the view that the reason he is giving outweighs any other reason so far on the scene. "Do X, although there are stronger reasons for doing not X but Y" is self-defeating. It follows that the force of an imperative, deriving as it does entirely from the reason that backs up the imperative, is never clear until we know what reasons might be offered to the agent for disregarding the imperative. Since in principle there may always be more relevant reasons to be considered than have been considered so far, any injunction is liable to be disregarded, not because the reasons which back it up are not good reasons or do not seem good reasons, but because there may always be reasons which outweigh them for that particular agent. We ought, therefore, to note that not only does it always make sense to say that "There is such and such a good reason for doing X and not Y, but do Y and not X" but that to say this does not imply any doubt either about the truth of what is alleged as a good reason for doing X and not Y or about its standing as a good reason. All that it implies is a belief that there are or may be countervailing reasons.

It is clear that this last discussion is irrelevant to the relation between those imperatival injunctions which express orders or commands and the reasons there may be for regarding or disregarding them. For it is of the nature of an order or command that it makes a claim upon those to whom it is addressed precisely as an order or command, and that is to say, in a way that makes the existence of good reasons for regarding or disregarding it irrelevant. The force of a threat varies with the power that backs it up; the force of a command varies with the authority of the man who utters it. The man who issues the command may have good or bad or no reasons for issuing it; the man who obeys it may have good or bad or no reasons for obeying it. But the command has its character as a command quite independently of these reasons. Hence, commands in this respect are different from threats, warnings, and pieces of advice. It is legitimate, indeed necessary, to say of commands that they too are imperatival injunctions backed up by reasons for action; but the key reason for acting in response to a command addressed to me is simply that it is a command addressed to me (supposing me to be subject to the authority of whoever issues it).

Putting commands on one side, therefore, I want to draw some obvious conclusions from what has been said about those imperatival injunctions which constitute pieces of advice. Among the statements by which I may back up imperatival injunctions in such a way as to give advice will be found more than one type of "ought" statement. There are, for example, statements of the form "You ought to go to bed with so high a temperature," which typically back up imperatival injunctions but which may be outweighed as reasons by such statements as "But that article has to be finished by tomorrow." Someone who in the light of such a consideration disregards the injunction "So go to bed" can be quite consistent in admitting that he ought to go to bed. That is, in the case of this type of "ought" statement, I may, without inconsistency or lack of sincere belief in and assent to the statement which provides the reason for the injunction, disregard the consequent injunction.

In parallel fashion, someone who issues an injunction may say, without inconsistency or irrationality or lack of sincere belief in the "ought" statement, "You ought to do X and not Y, but do Y and not X." But what type of "ought" statement is in question? The meaning of "ought" in "You ought to go to bed with so high a temperature" can be understood by treating the statement as equivalent to "If you do not go to bed, you will fare badly."

Consider now another type of "ought" statement, of which an example is "You ought to pay your taxes before January 1st," where the point of "ought" is to refer us to some established and recognized rule, in this case a legal statute, and where "you ought" may be expanded into "you are obliged to," an expression that would make nonsense in the previous type of case. Clearly, this type of statement, too, may be offered as a reason backing up an imperatival injunction. And, just as in all other such cases, it may be outweighed by counterreasons, so that someone who sincerely believes such a statement to be true may without inconsistency disregard it in his actions, and someone who issues an imperatival injunction may say without inconsistency or irrationality, "You ought to pay your taxes before January 1st, but don't"—provided only that he can or hopes to be able to cite some other reason that will outweigh it.

III

We are now in a position to summarize some of the difficulties that stand in the way of the protagonists of any theory purporting to assimilate moral utterances to imperatives. First of all, since it was made clear that the imperatival form does not of itself segregate any well-defined class of utterances, it is clear that some better defined class of utterances that can be expressed by means of imperatives would have to be picked out to provide a comparison with moral utterances. Secondly, it was also made clear that, where the class of utterances that can be characterized as instances of *telling to* rather than of *telling that* or of *telling how* are concerned, we must ask for some further characterization beyond that of *telling to*. Now what has been said about commands and orders makes it highly implausible that moral utterances could be illuminated by comparison with them; it is, therefore, all the more plausible that, if moral utterances are a form of or resemble imperatival injunctions, the class of imperatival injunctions to be examined is that which includes threats, warnings, and pieces of advice. But the account of this class of injunctions which has already been given would appear to make *any* assimilation of moral utterances to imperatives highly implausible, since that account at least *suggests* that in moral discourse perfectly ordinary and genuine imperatives may play a part and that the distinguishing moral components of moral utterance will be found in the statement of the reasons backing up the imperatival injunction and not in the imperative itself. For just this was found to be the case with the two types of "ought" statements so far briefly examined.

To this it may be replied that neither of these "oughts" is the *moral* "ought." The first might be ruled out on the ground that it is the "ought" of hypothetical and prudential injunctions rather than that of moral injunctions, the second on the grounds that it is the "ought" of legally and socially established codes, not the "ought" of individual moral principle. The moral "ought" is, therefore, to be sought elsewhere, and, when it is found, it will turn out that "You ought to do X and not Y, but do Y and not X"—is not a possible piece of advice if the "ought" is the moral "ought." For the moral "ought" will have an imperatival character, such that anyone who assents to a moral injunction assents to the corresponding imperative. Indeed it has been held that to assent sincerely to a moral injunction entails not only assenting to the corresponding imperative but also acting on it when occasion requires; and yet clearly, in the view that I have outlined, I may sincerely assent to and believe the statement that you ought to do something but yet tell you by means of an imperatival injunction to do something else, and I may even sincerely assent to and believe the statement that I ought to do something but find reasons for doing something else.

It remains, therefore, to hunt out the moral "ought" and see if it has a different relation to the imperative mood. Now it might appear that this was bound to be a hopeless quest. For the first type of "ought" was in fact that characteristic of those teleological moralities in which the criterion of what a man ought to do is what will enable him to fare well or badly, and some concept of what it is for a man to fare well or badly underpins the morality. So the heirs of Aristotle. And the second type of "ought" is characteristic of these moralities in which belief in a divine law is fundamental, and moral rules have a status similar to the status of legal statutes. So the heirs of the Stoics and the Torah. Since these "oughts" are therefore at home in moralities of such importance, how could some other "ought" claim the title of "the" moral "ought"? But to pursue this line of argument might be to miss the point.

Suppose a society in which there was a moral ethos of either the Aristotelian or the Judaeo-Christian kind or perhaps some synthesis of the two. The uses of "ought" in such a society would be as I have outlined, and its relation to imperatival injunctions would also be as I have outlined. But now suppose also that belief in the divine law declines and that the formerly shared conception of what human well-being consisted in is no longer shared. None the less, people continue to use the word "ought," but in new contexts. Sometimes, indeed, they ask skeptically whether they ought to obey the divine law or whether one ought to preserve former conceptions of human well-being. The "ought" of these inquiries clearly cannot be either of the "oughts" previously current. When "ought" is now used to reinforce an imperatival injunction, it will add little but emotive force. When used by itself: "You ought to do X and not Y," what force is there left for it to have but an imperatival force?

In such a situation emotivist and prescriptivist theories, indeed any theory of a kind which assimilated "ought" to imperatival injunctions, would tend to flourish. Nor would these theories be wholly incorrect; for they would be describing correctly the role in language which a certain class of sentences had assumed when cut off from the background of beliefs necessary for them to be understood as they had been in the past. Moreover, such theories might well, if they enjoyed a vogue, help to propagate the linguistic usages of which they furnished an analysis. But we should expect, with such a degree of innovation, considerable linguistic strain. The framework of our language would, one would expect, be such that the claim that the form, "You ought to do X and not Y, but do Y and not X," does not make sense or indicates insincerity or embodies a contradiction would be implausible in all sorts of ways. None the less, the inclination to make this claim, in order to explain correctly how "ought" was now often being used, would be widespread.

Just this may well be our situation. It is at least a plausible hypothesis. If it is correct, then simply to conclude that the case for assimilating moral utterances to imperatives could not be made out would be to ignore changes that social history has brought about in the linguistic relationships. And this would reinforce the suggestion, which has been apparent throughout this essay, that to attempt to characterize a given class of utterances by means of an appeal to grammatical form is one of the less happy ways of making use of linguistic classifications in the course of philosophical inquiry.

15

"Ought"

I

Not only the suggestion that different societies have had widely different moral beliefs, but also the more radical suggestion that the conceptual schemes embodied in their moralities have differed widely, would appear as a banal truism to any anthropologist. From Vico to Karl Marx, moral philosophers too appeared willing to entertain this prosaic suggestion. But the notion of a single, unvarying conceptual structure for morality dies hard; and from the eighteenth century to this day, the English utilitarians and idealists, logical empiricists and analytical philosophers, have all been willing to discuss moral philosophy on the assumption that there was something to be called *"the* moral consciousness" or, in a later idiom, *"the* language of morals." The questions *"Whose* moral consciousness?" or *"Which* language?" have rarely, if ever, been raised. Both a cause and a consequence of this situation is the extremely short method with examples adopted by many writers. Since the question "But is this how anyone in particular really talks, and if so who?" is not considered relevant, since we are ostensibly concerned with what can or what cannot be said and not with what is as a matter of fact said, a self-indulgent imaginative liberty is sometimes allowed to reign. Moral philosophers are often able to discern and to decry this liberty in their immediate predecessors: it is not unfashionable to pillory the abstract and misleading character of Ross's use of perplexity over a promise to return a book which I have borrowed as a paradigmatic example of a moral dilemma or of Moore's famous choice between two uninhabited worlds. But if the abbreviation of their own examples by moral philosophers is a liberty, the short shrift which they administer to the examples of others is more a form of intellectual violence. I want to try and avoid such extreme methods in a consideration of two recent attempts to characterize what have come to be called evaluative expressions. I say "what have come to be called" evaluative expressions because how one identifies or segregates the relevant class of expressions is partially, at least, dependent upon which philosophical theory one holds. The two theories with which I am concerned are versions of prescriptivism and naturalism. My procedure will be as follows. First I shall set out the rival contentions. Then I shall argue that it is not only a matter of observed fact that neither party to the dispute is able to produce conviction in the other—which it certainly is—so that the argument appears interminable and unsettlable, but also that each party seems able to accommodate, to its own satisfaction at least, every objection that can be brought against it by the other. Lastly I shall try to inquire how we can escape from this highly unsatisfactory situation.

II

By prescriptivism I understand the following set of positions:

1. That the utterance of a moral judgment commits the utterer to the utterance of a corresponding imperatival injunction in such a way that "You ought to do this, but don't" or "I ought to do this, but don't" (addressed to me) are inconsistent expressions. In cases where "You ought to do this, but don't" is not to be construed as inconsistent, then the "ought" is some secondary, derivative, perhaps inverted-commas use of "ought," perhaps with the meaning "People in general think you ought, but don't."

2. That no moral, indeed no prescriptive, use of "ought" can appear in a categorical judgment that is the conclusion of a valid argument, if the premises of that argument are all factual assertions. For such an argument to be valid, at least one of the premises must contain a prescriptive "ought." No "ought" from "is."

3. That the only limitations upon our choice of moral principles are those of syntactical form and of consistency; we cannot choose a moral principle which we should not be prepared to apply equally to others and to ourselves in relevantly similar circumstances; and that in moral justification our chain of reasoning will bring us at last to a set of first principles; these cannot be supported further by reasons, but must be adhered to by choice.

4. That to call something good may often be to apply conventionally accepted criteria for the goodness of whatever it is that is called good. But it is also—except in inverted-commas cases—to

endorse the criteria, if they are conventional, and this endorsement expresses the agent's own choice of criteria.

5.   That in ordinary language there are many expressions in which, either in certain contexts or always, a prescriptive or evaluative and a descriptive component are welded together. The use of these creates an illusion that the applicability of a particular description entails the making of a particular evaluative judgment. But, in fact, it is always possible to separate the two components; their relationship is purely contingent, external, and conventional.

By naturalism, I understand the following set of positions:

1.   That evaluative conclusions may be validly derived from factual premises by virtue of the criteria for the correct application of certain evaluative expressions; that such criteria are factual and that the relevant class of expressions includes the virtue words. From the fact that you acted in such and such a way it follows that you are courageous, and in being courageous you behaved as a man ought to behave.

2.   That the chain of justifications for holding that someone ought to do something will lead back, not to an ultimate assertion of principle resting upon a choice which can have no further justification, but to an assertion that behavior of the kind in question is a realization of or is productive of some recognized human good, such as health and pleasure.

3.   That the class of such goods can be delimited; that the criteria for something's being a good are independent of the agent's choices, and that therefore what I ought to do does not depend on my choices, although what I am going to do may so depend.

4.   That the question of what I ought (in the fullest moral sense) to do can be raised and settled by me without the question of what I am going to do being so raised, let alone settled.

5.   That factual or descriptive and evaluative or prescriptive are not mutually exclusive predicates of judgments, and that a judgment which is both factual and evaluative is not a judgment which combines two separable components; to say that it is evaluative is to speak about the point of making it, while to say that it is factual is to speak about how its truth or falsity is to be determined.

The strategies and counter-strategies used by each of these parties against the other are parallel ones, and their ritual procedures might be set out as follows. First, a counter-example is cited by one party; secondly, the other produces its own account of the counter-example; thirdly, the first party points out that some crucial distinction is omitted by this account; fourthly, the other

"Ought" 139

party either accepts this omission with all its consequences, or gives its own quite different account of the distinction. Now an unlimited willingness to accept the consequences of their own point of view, which characterizes the leading protagonists on both sides, leads to an increasing doubt on the part of an observer as to what the subject matter of this controversy in fact is. I propose to follow through the course of two of these ritual engagements to illustrate this point, one starting-point being taken from each side of the controversy. But it may help to exhibit the inaccessibility of each party to the other's polemics, if I follow through two arguments in which essentially the same issue is at stake. We can put this issue as follows. The individual agent comes upon the moral scene with a set of wants and interests. He finds the members of his society speaking an evaluative language such that the normal usage is expressive of certain established standards. Naturalist and prescriptivist are both prepared to agree that every established society will speak a moral and evaluative language which does express the conventionally accepted standards. What they disagree about is whether this is purely a contingent union of disparate elements, so that the key terms could be purged of their descriptive meaning and so of their particular adherence to a particular way of life, or whether it is impossible at the most fundamental level to perform this task. Can the individual agent construct a set of moral standards that are genuinely his own, or can he only appeal to something that may be called a standard, if he agrees to speak the language that he finds? In another idiom, do we make or do we discover our values?

The central naturalist charge against prescriptivism in this area of the controversy is that the prescriptivist cannot in important cases distinguish evaluative judgments from the expression of private wants and preferences. The central prescriptivist charge against naturalism is that the naturalist cannot give any account of evaluative innovation, that yet the possibility of such innovation is always present. The naturalist, to spell it out more fully, asserts that we cannot but consider certain dispositions virtues. To this the prescriptivist may reply that a situation in which the meanings of the moral expressions in our language guarantee that the standards by which we decide what is or is not a virtue are unalterable is a *1984* situation; and moral language does not have to be like *Newspeak* nor is it commonly like *Newspeak*. The naturalist reply in turn will be that any *particular* moral scheme may be criticized or transcended by reference to universal human goods, such as happiness. To this the prescriptivist will rejoin that if "happiness" is invoked in this way it is as a prescriptive and not as a descriptive term, and that the agent has a choice of whether to invoke happiness in this way or not. And so on.

Or to begin the argument from the other side, the prescriptivist asserts that for our ultimate principles we can give no justificatory reasons which are other than a specification of what it would be to live by such principles. To this the naturalist replies that if this is so, the distinction between the assertion of a moral principle and the expression of a private want or preference is obliterated. The prescriptivist will deny this on the grounds that the expression of a want or preference is not universalizable; even if the agent does as a matter of contingent fact want both himself to do such-and-such *and* everyone else in relevantly similar circumstances to do such-and-such, this is not the same as being logically committed, by one's adherence to the view that one ought oneself to do such-and-such, to the view that so ought everyone else in relevantly similar circumstances. The naturalist may admit *this* distinction but will insist that there is another distinction between the assertion of a moral principle and the expression of a want or preference which the prescriptivist has obliterated. The prescriptivist will reply that this further distinction—that between reason-supported assertions and non-reason-supported assertions perhaps —can be made in every case except that of fundamental moral principles. And so on. *Ad nauseam.*

I do not doubt that both prescriptivists and naturalists will be extremely dissatisfied with this portrayal; and there has been no lack of peacemakers attempting to patch up things between them. But I would like to suggest that no conclusive argument is found at any point in these exchanges; conclusive, that is, in terms other than those of the party that propounds them. And this raises the interesting question: what are they arguing about? What is the subject matter of the dispute? Ostensibly the language of morals, or moral concepts. But moral utterance and moral practice might be thought to pre-exist philosophical theorizing about morality, to provide an independent subject matter, so that philosophical theories would be tested by comparing them with the facts of moral utterance and practice. To which the reply may be twofold: first, that some past philosophical theorizing has played at least some part in shaping later moral concepts, so that moral utterance is not entirely innocent of philosophical preconceptions; and secondly that in order to pick out *moral* utterance and practice (as contrasted with legal or scientific, say) or in order to pick out *evaluative* utterance and practice (as contrasted with predictive, say), one already has to have a criterion and such a criterion will imply more or less of a theory. The first point one may concede at once. The force of the second may be brought out by considering a parallel case.

Clearly, in picking out the *legal* rules of a particular community from its other rules we need to approach the social facts with a criterion; and this criterion will be more or less theory-laden. When legal theorists, for example, began to examine law in certain primitive societies, some of them concluded from the fact that certain factors hitherto considered essential factors of any legal system whatsoever were absent from the institutional arrangements of these societies that such societies possessed no law at all. This conclusion, however, totally obscured the genuine continuity between the sanction-backed public rules of these societies and the later legal codes which had sometimes grown out of them. This fact provided grounds for concluding not that such primitive societies had no legal system, but that the definition of law and the corresponding theories of law needed to be amended to accommodate the new facts. This example shows plainly that we are not necessarily the prisoners of our criteria or theories, even in cases where we cannot segregate the relevant class of facts without some initial minimal theoretical commitment.

It follows that if the argument between prescriptivism and naturalism is not to be an empty and pointless contest, which has by the very virtuosity of the contestants in the performance of the task of redescription been deprived of that independent subject matter, the characterization of which was the sole point of the whole enterprise, one prerequisite is that as far as possible both theories are matched against the facts, so far as these can be independently delineated, and the tendency to redescribe the facts in accordance with the requirements of the rival theories must be curbed as far as possible. It is not too difficult to see how this might be done. It is by approaching the linguistic facts at first as much as possible in the mode of the lexicographer rather than of the philosopher; by next setting the linguistic facts in their social contexts; and finally by asking whether this does not enable us to discriminate, in relation to the theories of both prescriptivism and naturalism, the types of moral situation of which each doctrine is the natural and convincing explanation and analysis from the types of moral situation which one or the other doctrine has to distort. In so doing we shall treat these doctrines as hypotheses, which invoke a stylized model of argument to explain the actual patterns of moral speech and controversy.

The examples which I shall take are all stages in the history of the word "ought" and of words in other languages translatable into English as "ought".

III

"Ought" and "should" are sometimes used interchangeably in contemporary English. But "should" often has a subjunctive role which "ought" never has. ("If you should not hear from me. . . .") Both "ought" and "should" can be used to give advice on any topic whatsoever; both are sometimes used in such a way that moral injunctions or advice are distinguished from either prudence or expediency. "You ought to do so-and-so; how you would fare if you did is another matter." This use of "ought" or "should" is the latest in time to emerge. What precedes it is the general advice-giving "ought" of hypothetical imperatives, whether of skill or of prudence. If we work backward in time we shall find that "*the* moral 'ought' " which is used to express the claims of Duty (in the singular and with a capital letter), although it appears prominently in the utterances of Kant, the Duke of Wellington, George Eliot, and Mr. Gladstone (who wrote of "The two great ideas of the divine will, and of the Ought, or duty . . ."), does not seem to appear before the eighteenth century.

If we are to properly distinguish the categorical "ought" of final moral appeal from the "ought" of hypothetically expressed general advice-giving, it must be done by citing more than the logical distinction between categorical and hypothetical judgments. For the general advice-giving "ought" may of course be used in categorical expressions of advice: not, "You ought if . . ." but "You ought, since. . . ." What distinguishes the "ought" of final moral appeal is that it can be used without reason-giving of any kind, that its force does not depend upon the force of some attached condition, whether fulfilled or unfulfilled, neither "if" nor "since," but "Why ought you?" . . . "You just ought."

The general advice-giving "ought" is in use from the high Middle Ages onward. It has to be distinguished from the use in which "ought" is equated with, indeed is the same word as, "owe." This "ought" is used both of owing money, and also of owing services by virtue of occupational status or kinship. "A man ought to be . . ." can mean "A man is owed the position of being. . . ." (So Wyntoun writes that "Robert the Brus, Erle of Karagh, aucht to succeed to be kynrike.") The earliest recorded use of "ought" ("ahte") in English translates "debebat" (in the sense of "owe" in the Vulgate) by "ahte to zeldanne." We thus discover three stages in the use of "ought": a first in which "ought" and "owe" are indistinguishable; a second in which "ought" has become an auxiliary verb, useable with an infinitive to give advice; and a third in which the use of "ought" has become unconditional. We can now place expressions from other languages commonly translated into English as "ought" in terms of these three stages.

The Greek δεῖν and its cognates can be used to express both the first and the second stage, both what it is incumbent upon a man to do as a such-and-such, and what a man ought to do if he wants such-and-such; but not the third stage. The Icelandic "skyldr" (ancestor of "should") never seems to go beyond the first stage. It would seem therefore most illuminating to look at the Icelandic and Greek social contexts for these linguistic facts, in order to observe first the use of an "ought" that never goes beyond the first stage and then the use of an "ought" that never goes beyond the second.

IV

In the society of the Norse sagas, the rules defining social roles and the obligations attaching to them include the rules of vendetta. Obligation is tied to kinship so closely that a near kinsman is a "skyldr fraendi"; and "o-skyldr," which might be naturally, if clumsily, translated as "not connected to one by way of obligation," means "unrelated." In the saga of Gisli the Soursop, Vestein is killed either by Thorkell or by Thorkell's emissary, and Thorkell is killed in turn by Vestein's sons. Bork then says, "More I should take up Thorkell's case than anyone else since he was my brother-in-law." It follows from the facts that Thorkell has been killed and that Bork is Thorkell's close kinsman, that Bork ought to avenge Thorkell's death. What gives the rules by virtue of which Bork cannot avoid this conclusion their authority is simply the recognition of these rules by the entire community. Which rules the community so recognizes and what these rules prescribe are questions of fact. If we pursue the chain of reasoning by which a moral conclusion is justified in such a society, it will run as follows: You ought to kill so-and-so. Why? Because he killed so-and-so, who is your nearest kinsman. Why because he killed my nearest kinsman, ought I to kill him? The rules so prescribe. Here the chain of justifications terminates. There is no way for me to ask why I ought to obey the rules. Notice that each "Why?" is answered by a factual assertion.

It would be equally distorting to try to give either a prescriptivist or a naturalistic account of this morality. Suppose, for instance, that a prescriptivist were to argue that as a matter of contingent fact agents in such a society may infer the conclusion "I ought to do such-and-such" from the premise "The rules prescribe such-and-such" and so appear to derive an "ought" from an "is"; but that they can do so only by virtue of tacitly presupposing some unstated major premise, such as: "We ought always to do what the rules prescribe." The historical facts about Icelandic society have to be interpreted in the light of our a priori understanding of the forms of valid arguments. But the prescriptivist who tries to argue in this way is forced to misrepresent the conceptual scheme of Icelandic morality. For on his own terms, if the transition from "The rules prescribe such-and-such" to "So I ought to do such-and-such" is to be legitimated by the addition of a major premise to the effect that "We ought always to do what the rules prescribe," the "ought" in the conclusion has to be the same "ought" as the "ought" in the major premise. Now the "ought" in the conclusion has its force only by virtue of its use involving an appeal to the established rules; but this feature must be missing from the "ought" in the newly supplied major premise, since this "ought" cannot derive any force from the very rules which it is being used to enjoin us to obey. Thus the prescriptivist's attempt to bridge what he sees as a logical gap fails. What was mistaken in his attempt from the outset was his belief that there is a gap here waiting to be bridged. Why there is not we can best understand by considering how "skyldr" ties together "ought" and "owe." For the saga use of "skyldr" is parallel to our use of "owe."

Whether I owe you money or not, how much I owe you, and when the debt falls due for payment are questions of fact settled by discovering the truth about antecedent transactions between us, whether you lent me money and so forth. The institutional framework of rules governing monetary transactions in general and borrowing and lending in particular is such that given that I received \$5 under certain conditions I now owe you \$5; just so in the saga, given that the sons of Vestein killed Thorkell under certain conditions, Bork now owes Thorkell's kinsmen their death. Bork can of course ask: "Given that I ought to kill the sons of Vestein, shall I do it?" But when all the facts are settled, he cannot still ask: "But ought I to do it?" For that he ought to do it is just one of the facts, in the only sense and use of "ought" available to him.

But now the prescriptivist might retort that Bork's "ought" has just been compared to "owe," and that although it may be a question of fact whether I owe you $5, the question of whether I *ought* to pay what I owe can always be raised, and that this question is not a question of fact. But the prescriptivist's ability and our ability to raise this question depends upon the availability of an "ought" that is just not present in the language spoken by Bork. What is required for that "ought" to be available is that a new use be introduced, and that is to say, in this case, a new social practice. Now it is clearly logically possible that at any time someone may innovate radically. But the fact that this is always logically possible does not entail that such an ability to innovate was in fact present. Such an ability requires a detachment from the established institutional rules which has yet to come on the scene, which itself has certain social preconditions.

If the prescriptivist cannot make the "ought" expressed by the saga's "skyldr" conform to his pattern of analysis, it is of course also true that the naturalist cannot hope to succeed in this project either. For the termination of the chain of justifications in the sagas is simply the assertion of the relevant rules; there is no citing of some human good which will be procured by whatever action is in question. Indeed, the fact that obedience to the rules will produce disaster for a man is sometimes noted in the sagas, not merely by the narrator, but by the agent himself. And this contributes not at all to showing that the agent therefore ought not to do what the rules prescribe. In a precisely similar way, you may show me that if I pay my debts the results will be disastrous for me or my creditors or both; but this does not show in any way that I do not after all owe them money. Thus, this first use of "ought" gives aid and comfort neither to prescriptivist nor to naturalist.

It is of course open to either or both to say that this is a special type of case, which we *only* recognize as morality and which we *only* characterize by translating its key expressions with words like "ought," because it can be and was as a matter of history later on transformed into the kind of moral scheme which fits the prescriptivist or naturalist pattern. But this, although perhaps true, does not affect any of the preceding arguments.

V

Consider now a quite different type of example. In Xenophon's *Oeconomicus*, Socrates reports a conversation with an ideal Athenian gentleman, Ischomachus, who is in high repute as καλὸς κἀγαθός and who is deeply concerned about knowing ἃ δεῖ ποιειν (what he ought to do). It becomes clear that he is considered an ideal character because he occupies himself in promoting his health and strength, his military skills, and his private fortune. He does what he ought because he pursues these ends, and these ends stand in no further need of justification. This account of Ischomachus reminds us of Hume: "Ask a man *why he uses exercise*; he will answer *because he desires to keep his health*. If you then inquire, *why he desires health*, he will readily reply, *because sickness is painful*. If you push your inquiries further and desire a reason *why he hates pain*, it is impossible he can ever give any. This is an ultimate end and is never referred to any other object."[1] The chain of justifications ends with the citation of a good beyond which it would not be possible to go. What a man ought to do, then, is what he ought to do if he is to achieve certain desired ends. The "ought" of the morality of the *Oeconomicus* appears to be no other than the ordinary general advice-giving "ought" of the second stage in the development of "ought" in English. The naturalist could have no objection to assenting to this; the prescriptivist, however, would be forced to assert that we could only hold that we *ought* (in any full and proper *moral* use of "ought") to do what will as a matter of fact produce health and other such goods, if we also believe that we ought to pursue health and other such goods. And that whether I believe that or not, or whether Ischomachus believes that or not, must depend upon the ultimate moral principles chosen by myself or by Ischomachus. To this the naturalist may rightly reply that the answer to the question of whether health, for example, is a good cannot depend upon the agent's choice of principles or criteria or anything else. What makes health a good is that it is a characteristic object of human desire; and a society in which health was not so desired would scarcely be a human society. In the face of this contention prescriptivists are, I think, faced with a choice of alternative strategies. An unreformed prescriptivist may make the barren and boring rejoinder that even if health is so desired, I still have to decide

[1] *Inquiry*, I, 5.

whether I hold that I and others ought to fulfill this desire. This rejoinder is barren and boring because in the vocabulary available to Ischomachus the question of whether I ought to pursue health could only *be* the question of whether health was among the goods; no other "ought" is available. A reformed prescriptivist might admit this, however, and recommence the argument by pointing out that in the relatively narrow circles in which Ischomachus moved a short and succinct list of human goods is taken for granted. But what when a wider perspective opens, what when competing sets of goods confront the agent with alternative and incompatible goods? The reformed prescriptivist, that is, abandons any part of his original view which entails the consequence upon which so much scorn has been lavished, that anything at all could be a good. He allows that only that which is a characteristic object of desire can be a good, and perhaps leaves open the question of the range of possible objects of desire. Instead he fastens attention upon a situation where there are competing sets of goods. In such a situation the agent who is able to assert both that "You ought to do X if you want A" and "You ought to do Y if you want B," still has to inquire, "But which goods *ought* I to pursue, A or B?" Ischomachus may argue from "is" to "ought" by saying that "Health is a good for man, horse-riding will make me healthy, so I ought to ride," but this apparent naturalistic pattern of argument is only possible for Ischomachus because he accepts without question one out of all the possible sets of competing goods.

To this it may be conceded that such an argument from "is" to "ought" only has practical force or consequence for a man who recognizes health as good for him; but this is to allow that, given the accepted set of objects of desire in a society such as that of an Athenian gentleman, moral discourse and argument will be precisely as naturalism portrays them. Yet the reformed prescriptivist has made it possible to begin to see more clearly what a moral scheme amenable to prescriptivist analysis would be like. Suppose a morally pluralist society in which there are two or more competing moral schemes, with alternative and incompatible goods; in such a society a man might ask—would sometimes be unable to avoid asking—which of these moralities he ought to live by. A naturalist might suggest to him that although he cannot avoid asking "Which of these moralities *shall* I live by?" since he is not asking what a given established set of rules prescribed with Bork, nor what will produce one or more out of a given set of desirable ends with Ischomachus, he cannot ask "What *ought* I to do?" To this the prescriptivist might for the moment simply note that as a matter of fact "ought" is used in this way on occasion; and a third example may clarify how, as a matter of history, this came to be the case.

VI

Question XI: How we ought to aid our parents when in want . . .

Question XVI: What reward is proposed by God for obedience to parents . . .

Question XX: With what punishments children are visited who are neglectful of this commandment . . .[1]

Consider the "ought" of Christian theism. The theistic moral scheme of Christianity perhaps provides both an example of a moral scheme only amenable to a naturalistic analysis and also a background which explains some of the characteristics of those post-theistic moralities which are most obviously amenable to prescriptivist analysis. We can distinguish three layers in the theistic moral scheme. The first is the thesis that God created men with a determinate human nature, so that only certain ends are genuinely desired by them. At this level theism provides metaphysical underpinning for some form of teleological morality in which moral precepts are of the form already noticed in the Greek example, "You ought to do so-and-so, if and since you want such-and-such." Unlike most other such forms of morality it is not necessary to the theistic moral scheme that there shall be a lack of awareness of alternative moralities. What matters is simply the belief that God alone is in a position to know what will satisfy human nature—for He created it.

The second layer in theistic morality is suggested by Hobbes' answer to the question why we dignify the prudential precepts of reason with the name of moral "laws." The answer, says Hobbes, is: because they are commandments of God. As divine commandments, the precepts of morality are given an additional sanction. The first and best reason for obeying the precepts is that by so doing you avoid the fate of those who gain the whole world but lose their own souls; however, for those who do not see the point of giving up the whole world, there is the sanction of eternal rewards and eternal punishments.

To say that you ought to do so-and-so is therefore both to give

[1] Catechism of Conc. Trent. Pt. iii.

advice and to refer to the force of a body of rules established in the cosmos by God, with the status of law. Doing what the rules prescribe and doing what will secure your happiness do in fact coincide. But in the course of Christian history two other elements entered. The first was an increasing conviction among theologians (most radical perhaps among Protestants but also influential among Catholics) that the corruption of human nature is such that men cannot perceive what their human nature really wants or needs at all. What God prescribes will in the end satisfy their wants, but from a human point of view the Divine Will appears and must appear as a series of incomprehensible and inscrutable fiats. In consequence, from Occam onward the question "Why ought I to do what God commands?" becomes more and more difficult to answer. The Thomist answer, the Christian version of the Greek answer—"Because this will satisfy your most fundamental desires as a man"—is no longer available to those sensitive to their cultural situation; for the gap between the observed facts about what men want and the allegedly revealed propositions as to what God prescribes for them is now only to be bridged by faith.

The question "Why ought I to do what God commands?" is first raised in the modern literature by that great heroic innovator, Milton's Satan. When Satan raises the question of "Why ought we to obey God?" it is not merely a prudential inquiry; he is an angel of principle. No reason can be found, he in effect argues, why I should obey any law that I do not utter to myself. But the "ought" of theism survived his and other doubts about God's commandments. Theistic characteristics still cling—in a somewhat paradoxical way—to the "ought" that is historically used to pose the moral doubts about theism. Now if an "ought," the use of which presupposes theistic beliefs, is in fact used to question the standpoint of theism, we would expect an internal incoherence in this use of "ought" to be manifest. For it could at least be plausibly maintained that such an "ought" would have to fulfill the following apparently inconsistent requirements: (1) its theistic character entails that it must involve an appeal to a law, that is, to a set of established and identifiable rules; (2) its Occamist and post-Reformation inheritance entails that this appeal to a law must not be confused with any formulation of prudential recipes about what will serve our happiness; (3) it must be available for use in asking whether any authority whatsoever, including divine authority, ought to be obeyed; (4) it must be a law which we utter to ourselves; (5) obedience to this law presupposes that although in trying to obey it we are not using our happiness in any way as a

goal determining what we ought to do, none the less to do what the
law prescribes must be crowned by happiness, if the whole enterprise is not to be pointless.

The incoherence of these requirements is clear: it centers
upon the notion of something which has the authority of a law and
yet which no one utters to us except ourselves. But clearly some
such incoherence in the use and sense of "ought" might well be
produced in the course of the secularization of a Christian morality,
especially of a Protestant morality. And this suggests that we should
give more credence than we are accustomed to do to Kant's claim
that his moral theory expresses articulately the presuppositions
latent in ordinary moral discourse. (Kant himself was ambivalent
about this view of his enterprise: compare the title of the first
part of the *Grundlegung* with the complaint that the assorted moral
principles of his age comprised a "mishmash" and that the
philosopher has to introduce a superior principle of unity.)

Neither Satan nor Kant can claim to be the first prescriptivist;
but in their joint insistence on autonomy they helped to father
the categorical "ought" of nineteenth-century invocations of
Duty, an "ought" which furnished an ultimate ending for the
chain of moral justifications and so is the immediate ancestor of
the "ought" of prescriptivism. This "ought" is criterionless:
the philosopher who throws most light on it is perhaps Sidgwick,
who has earned abuse from Miss Anscombe precisely because of
his fidelity in analysing a use of "ought" peculiar to his own age.
Sidgwick would dearly have liked to be able to reduce all categorical
imperatives to hypothetical imperatives; but he had to report in
the end an ineliminable categorical element in moral discourse,
that which drives him to the use of the word "intuition." It has
been insufficiently remarked that the use of "ought" statements to
make categorical moral judgments not supported by further
reasoning does not originate with philosophical theorizing, but is
a feature of ordinary non-philosophical moral discourse in the last
two hundred years; theories such as intuitionism, emotivism, and
prescriptivism can all be viewed as attempts to provide a philosophical account of a use of language which is best explained as a
survival from a theistic age. The breakdown of the framework of
theistic belief has left behind a family of concepts which now, as it
were, have to find a status in isolation from the context in which
they originated. But if this were the whole story, the problem of
their status would not be so acute as it is.

VII

It is a banal commonplace that the breakdown of the theistic framework produced a morally plural society; and in such a society prescriptivism comes into its own. The reformed prescriptivist whom I characterized earlier no longer insists that anything can be a good or any principle a moral principle. Instead, he points out, when one has listed the recognized and recognizable human goods one is faced with a large and indefinite variety of competing alternatives. The admission that pain is an evil is equally consistent with the morality of the sagas or the Spartans, in which its point is to provide occasions for manifesting fortitude and courage; the morality of the Christians in which it is to be alleviated wherever possible; and the morality of de Sade in which the infliction of pain is an expression of the agent's liberty and autonomy. How does one choose between these moralities? There is no way of taking the admitted list of human goods and finding criteria for judging between such moralities; for in the competition between moralities goods are matched against goods, and there is no superior criterion of judgment. In the modern world the sphere of morality is essentially the sphere of tragedy as Hegel defined it. Consider, to take a quite different type of example, some features of Kierkegaard's argument in *Either/Or*.

In *Either/Or* Kierkegaard exhibited the necessity for a criterion-less choice between two ways of life: the aesthetic, in which the good of pleasure is allowed an overriding character, and the ethical, in which the goods of a dutiful life are allowed an overriding character. Suppose I try to find some criterion which will enable me to decide between these two on impersonal grounds, some criterion which will liberate me from the subjectivity of criterion-less choice. If I ask: "Which life will satisfy my wants?" then I have already in choosing this criterion chosen the aesthetic. If I ask: "Which life ought I to pursue?" then the "ought" is the "ought" of Duty, and I have already chosen the ethical life. Considerations such as these led Kierkegaard to conclude that one can do no more than offer rival descriptions of the two lives; the reader is then left to choose, and the moral to be drawn is that no description can possibly determine his choice.

His choice may of course be expressed simply by "I shall choose such-and-such"; but there is a modern use of "ought" according

6

to which he might express a choice that he recommends to every-one and which expresses his commitment to recommend it to everyone by saying, "So I ought to choose so-and-so." This "ought" is the "ought" of the prescriptivist analysis. In other words, the argument that prescriptivism is always a correct account of moral language because it is found to be a correct account of these peculiarly modern situations of radical choice is one that I have rejected throughout this essay; but this does not entail that it is an incorrect account of these choice situations. For in such situations ultimate moral principles do have to be chosen; no description of the alternatives confronting us logically entails any conclusion about what we ought to do or to choose, and perhaps it is even the case that the only available criterion of whether we have adopted one particular alternative is its embodi-ment in our actions in the form of obedience to self-addressed im-perative injunctions. All that has been abandoned to naturalism as regards this type of example is the claim that anything what-soever could be a good.

VIII

It is perhaps possible that there should exist a society in which all "oughts" were of the first kind which I examined, that exemplified in the saga's "skyldr"; but almost certainly there never was. It is clear that even if there was not in the language of the sagas a single-word equivalent to the "ought" in "If you want this, you ought to do that," what is expressed by this sentence is also expressible by "If you want this, do that." And it is difficult to envisage a form of society without a use for that type of sentence; difficult, although perhaps not impossible. It is not only clear that there could be, but clear that there have been societies with "oughts" only of the first and second, or only of the second kind. England in the Middle Ages appears to be one. The specific notion of a duty or duties or of an obligation or obligations may in such a society give goods for uttering injunctions which makes use of this "ought," but it is not specifically tied to notions of this kind. Such societies have moralities of which naturalism provides an adequate account. It is only perhaps in modern society that we have "oughts" of all three stages marked by the dictionary. The fact that this is so, and the further fact that this is not ade-quately recognized by moral philosophers, is responsible for some recent controversies in which general theses derived from prescriptivism or naturalism have been tested against examples, without inquiry ever being made as to the character of the examples, that is, as to which stage in the history of "ought" they exemplify. Consider in this respect John Searle's "How to derive 'Ought' from 'Is'" and Max Black's "The Gap between 'Is' and 'Should'."[1]

Searle constructs an argument in which we pass through a series of statements each of which he contends to be factual by means of a series of logical transitions each of which he contends to be an entailment from "Jones uttered the words : I hereby promise to . . ." to "Jones placed himself under an obligation to . . ." to "Jones ought to. . . ." Searle's prescriptivist critics have argued either that there is a suppressed premise, embodied in the institutional rules governing *promising*, to the effect that everyone ought to keep their promises, or else that one of his inferences is illegitimate. But what they (and perhaps Searle himself) have not understood is that *promising* is an institution in our society comparable to vendetta in Icelandic society, in which the established rules are such that if you make a promise to someone, you ought to do whatever it is, in this sense, that you owe it to him. That, "If you have made a promise, you ought to keep it," is guaranteed only when the use of "ought" is of this kind, an "ought" of the first type. I can always ask, using either the advice-giving sense of "ought" or the prescriptive "ought", whether I ought to keep this particular promise or any promise at all, and I can do this in cases where there is no question of conflict of obligations. Searle's critics would be quite right in contending that from the fact that I made a promise it does not follow—if "ought" is used in either of these two latter ways—that I ought to keep it. Searle would be quite right in contending that if "ought" is used as it was when it was the same word as "owe," then it does follow from the fact that I made a promise that I ought to keep it and no additional major premise is necessary. But the argument of Searle's critics never in fact meets Searle's argument, because the presence of these two radically different "oughts" in the language is not allowed for by either party.

Equally, Max Black's naturalism leaves prescriptivism fundamentally untouched and for a similar reason. Black argues that an argument from the premise that a given course of action would cause pain, while some alternative course of action would be identical in every way but that it would not cause pain, to the conclusion that therefore we ought to pursue the latter rather than the former course is a valid deductive argument in which the transition from

[1] Both in *The Philosophical Review*, 1964.

"is" to "should" or "ought" is made legitimately. An unreformed prescriptivist would presumably and unfortunately invoke the suppressed major premise gambit (Hare's paper on *Pain and Evil*, suggests that he might follow that course); but a reformed prescriptivist would simply point out that although it is undeniable that pain is an evil and that the gratuitous infliction of pain is an evil, and that it is this which warrants Black's argument, it is only in the rarest of contexts that gratuitous pain is and could be a matter for moral judgment. We teach children to infer from "That would be gratuitous infliction of pain" to "So I ought not to do it." But the moment the infliction of pain is a possibility in a context where, say, Christian, Nietzschean, and Sadean moralists were at odds, questions of fundamental choice would arise which could in no way be settled by an appeal to the legitimacy of that inference. It is not surprising that some would-be naturalists have tried to assimilate all evils to pain, all goods to pleasure, and the logical character of the concept of pleasure to that of pain. For it is just in such narrow contexts of child morality that the naturalist account is adequate. It only fails when we pass outside. Hence I conclude that just as Searle and his critics did not distinguish the first type of use of "ought" from the second and third, so Black does not distinguish the second, or naturalist use, from the third, or prescriptivist. The nursery, like classical Greece or medieval Europe, is one of the natural homes of naturalism. But societies change and people grow up.

IX

Two main theses have now emerged from my argument: the first that naturalism and prescriptivism are most plausibly understood not as rival accounts of the whole field of moral or even of evaluative discourse, but as accounts of different types of moral and evaluative discourse. These types of discourse I have tried to discriminate in terms of three uses of "ought" which recur successively in the history of that word in the English language and English-speaking society. But I have also maintained that all three uses of "ought" occur in current English and I want now to consider this fact. Just as prescriptivism, in order that it could be understood as a correct account of those fundamental moral choices on which existentialist moral philosophers have laid so much emphasis, had to be amended, so naturalism, in order that it can be understood as a correct account of those situations in which, because of the existing social framework and vocabulary, fundamental choice cannot arise, must also be amended. For naturalists advance against prescriptivists, as I have already remarked, the argument that it must *always* be possible to discriminate between moral judgments on the one hand and expressions of personal preference on the other. And they complain that upon a prescriptivist analysis, as equally upon an emotivist, this distinction disappears. What is not clear, however, is the nature and grounds of the contention that it must *always* be possible to discriminate in principle—not necessarily always in practice, of course, in particular cases—between moral judgments and expressions of personal preference. For the a priori claim that this distinction must always be applicable fails with precisely those uses of "ought" which are correctly characterized by prescriptivists. That is, it is not the prescriptivist who in his theoretical account obliterates a distinction implied in all the ordinary uses of "ought" by moral agents and moral critics. It is rather that in certain types of situations—those of fundamental choice—the use of "ought" by such agents and critics is such that this distinction can no longer be applied. Is such a use of "ought" necessarily unintelligible or incoherent? I have suggested that it is partially intelligible as a survival, first of all from those immediately post-theistic humanists for whom Duty was still the ghost of the divine commandments sitting crowned upon the grave thereof, and secondly from Christian theism. But it is also intelligible in the sense that its use is rule-governed and embodied in contemporary social practice. A reformed naturalism therefore would have to allow, if it aspired to be a description of the language we have, that although the distinction between moral judgment and personal preference holds in all those contexts of which naturalism is the correct account, it does not hold for every intelligible use of "ought." But the naturalist point, once it is understood not to impugn the correctness of the prescriptivist account of fundamental choice, still has force in another direction.

The use of "ought" in moral injunctions—just because it has the past history it has—always suggests an appeal to some criterion, whether a socially established rule or a precept about how some desired good is to be obtained. When in modern society an "ought" finally emerges such that the injunctions which it is used to formulate have no greater authority than is conferred upon them by the speaker's own choices, even if there are no conceptual grounds for accusing the speaker of unintelligibility, there are certainly grounds for accusing him of trading upon the prestige which belongs to other present, and even more to past, uses of "ought"; so that his "ought" has the semblance of an appeal to an impersonal criterion, while it is in fact only the mask for his personal preferences. In a morally pluralist society such as ours moreover it is at points where much is at stake—in certain fundamental choices—that this modern use of "ought" is most likely to involve deception and self-deception. Understanding this use of "ought" in the light of prescriptivism therefore might comprehensibly lead to the conclusion that in the cases where prescriptivism is correct, no honest man would want to continue to use "ought." For the good of truthfulness is not one which we are free either to regard or to discard. But to pursue the implications of this conclusion would take me beyond moral philosophy.

16

Some more about "ought"

In his paper "Does Moral Philosophy Rest On A Mistake?" published in 1912, H. A. Prichard either explicitly makes or clearly assumes four main points about the word "ought" and its uses. The first point—and the order in which I put them is not the same as Prichard's—is that there is a proper linguistic form for judgments expressing the idea that he takes to be conveyed by the word "ought." "The word 'ought,'" he asserts, "refers to actions and to actions alone. The proper language is never 'So and so ought to be,' but 'I ought to do so and so.' Even if we are sometimes moved to say that the world or something in it is not what it ought to be, what we really mean is that God or some human being has not made something what he ought to have made it" (p. 4).

Secondly, Prichard declares that "An 'ought,' if it is to be derived at all, can only be derived from another 'ought'" (p. 4). The example given is that from the premise that certain medicines will heal our disease we cannot derive the conclusion that we ought to take those medicines. Thirdly, Prichard makes it clear that he regards the word "obligation" as the abstract noun corresponding to the verb "ought." He passes from the one to the other in a way which makes it clear that he believes that "I ought to do so and so" means the same as "I have an obligation to do so and so." Moreover it may be true of me—as indeed it seems it must on occasion be true of me, if this equivalence of meaning is to be preserved—that I have an obligation, without my having an obligation to any particular person.

Fourthly, in connection with both "ought" and "obligation" Prichard makes it clear that what it is the case that I ought to do is both logically and causally independent of what it is the case that I want or of what will make me happy or of what will be good for me or for others or for both or of what will be productive of good and so be an exercise of a virtue. Prichard does not therefore conclude that morality has two parts, one concerned with what he calls obligation and one concerned with what he calls the virtues. He concludes instead that the pursuit of the virtues has no part in morality and reserves the word "morality" strictly for the realm of obligation.

A first response to these four points, made or presumed as they are so brusquely—and it is indeed Prichard's central point in writing his paper that on these matters philosophical argument is redundant and out of place—might well be that Prichard has simply himself made a series of mistakes. First of all, it is just not true that whenever we use the word "ought" in a categorical assertion we mean or even imply that someone ought to do or ought to have done something. "The weather ought to be better tomorrow," or "The solution ought to be a prime number," commit me to judgment on neither men nor God if it goes on raining or the solution to my algebraic problem is "14." Secondly, it is equally false that we cannot derive categorical conclusions containing the word "ought" from premises that do not contain it. There are valid arguments of many different kinds which exemplify this point. From the premises that "If you stick a knife in him, you will go to prison" and "You do not want to go to prison," it certainly follows that "You ought not to stick a knife in him." From the premise that "He is a sea captain," it certainly follows that "He ought to do whatever a sea captain ought to do."

Thirdly, although the word "obligation" has come to be used as the abstract noun corresponding to the verb "ought," this is not its only or its primary use. The concept of an obligation is originally a narrower and more specialized concept; an obligation derives from a promise or a contract. Thus an obligation is always an obligation to some particular person or persons. This narrower concept of obligation may be contrasted with a corresponding concept of duty. A duty arises from a status or an office, not from a promise or a contract. As a father I have a duty to my children; as an employer I have obligations toward my servants. But Prichard in his other writings uses the notion of duty precisely as he uses that of obligation. In his paper on "Moral Obligation," written a quarter of a century after "Is Moral Philosophy Based Upon A Mistake?" he not only asserts that "we, in our ordinary unreflective state of mind, regard statements of the form 'X ought to do so and so,' 'X has the duty of doing so and so,' and 'X is morally bound to do so and so' as equivalent in meaning," but also that he regards "X has a moral obligation to do so and so" as equivalent in meaning, too. He does, however, make one crucial point that is missing in the earlier paper. For he distinguishes between a moral sense of "ought" and a non-moral sense, and in so doing provides himself with an answer to the counter-examples which I produced to his first two points. It is quite clear that Prichard would in fact have said that the "ought" in these examples was used in a non-moral sense. But now let us look at the position to which he is committed in consequence. For Prichard "X has an obligation to do so and so" and "X has a duty to do so and so" cannot and do not represent two different types of ground or reason which may be offered to support the conclusion that "X ought to do so and so"; nor could it be the case in Prichard's view that one man might argue for the conclusion that "X ought to do so and so" on the ground that it would make X happy and another man might argue for the conclusion that "X ought to do so and so" on the ground that X has an obligation to do so and so and these two men might be offering different reasons in support of the same conclusion. They would in fact be coming to two different conclusions. That this would be Prichard's view is made clear in his discussion of Kant on categorical and hypothetical imperatives where Prichard insists that "the distinction . . . is really not . . . one between two statements containing the word 'ought' made on different grounds, but one between two statements in which 'ought' has a completely different meaning" (p. 91).

Thus Prichard's original insistence that morality is limited to the realm of obligation has now become the claim that there is a distinctive sense which "ought" has when it is used to express the distinctive demand that morality makes of us. The characterization of this demand in Prichard has a certain circular quality. Prichard speaks of a feeling of imperativeness, but he never characterizes this imperativeness except as that which obligation makes us feel. What morality *is not* is clear: everything done from desire, or for an end, is not done from a sense of obligation and is not matter for morality. The contrast is therefore between a set of obligations which constitute morality and the rest of human life, especially our desires and our pursuit of happiness, and for the expression of this contrast a special moral sense or use—let us say, neutrally, a special type of occurrence—of "ought" is required.

My question now is: "Is there—or as it will turn out, more appropriately, was there—such a type of occurrence of 'ought'?" How are we to decide whether a given word has more than one sense or use? I wish to answer this question without fatally entangling myself in the thickets of contemporary linguistics and it is partly in order to achieve this that I have used the weak expression "type of occurrence"; but this wish is perhaps bound to be idle. But what I can do is to provide a case where the distinction to be made will provide us with at least provisional criteria for distinguishing different types of occurrences of the same word and then see whether in this particular sense of "type of occurrence" there is a special moral type of occurrence of "ought." To provide my initial exemplar I turn to the earlier history of the word "ought" and its cognates: δεῖν in Greek, *debere* in Latin and *ahte* in Anglo-Saxon and Middle English all mean both what we mean by "ought" and what we mean by "owe." But there comes a time in the history of each language when "ought" and "owe" are discriminated. Even when the same word is used, as *debere* continues to be used in Latin, for example, the question "Do I owe this to X?" is discriminated from the question "Ought I to give this to X?" in such a way that "I ought to give to X what I owe to X" becomes non-tautological. Can I therefore take it that the successful discrimination of two types of occurrence of a verb has been achieved if in the use of a sentence where the verb is used twice the statement made has a form that would normally be tautological, and yet the statement in question is clearly not tautological? The answer is clearly "no"; this cannot be a sufficient condition for the achievement of the discrimination of two senses, since we can produce clear counter-examples. Pontius Pilate's "What I have written, I have written" is non-tautological, but this in no way suggests that there are two senses of the verb "to write." It might then be suggested that what we need to do is to add a second condition, namely that if one use of the verb in question is negated, then a contradiction is not produced. For a contradiction would have been produced if Pilate had asserted "What I have written, I have not written," thus showing that the non-tautological repetition is a type of emphatic locution and does not involve two senses. But there could, I think, be no plausible counter-examples to the claim that where two verbs are used in a sentence the form of which would normally ensure that any statement it was used to make would be tautological, *and* the statement thus made is clearly not tautological, *and* in addition one at least of the verbs can be negated without the statement being thereby transformed into a contradiction, two types of occurrence are involved. So similarly "I ought to give what I owe" is non-tautological, even in languages where the same word might recur; "It is not the case that I ought to give what I owe" is certainly not a contradiction. What use can we make of this tentative finding to evaluate Prichard's claim about "ought?"

The attitude that I want to take to Prichard's claim involves applying to the interpretation of Prichard an argument that R. G. Collingwood originally deployed against Prichard's interpretation of Plato. Collingwood rightly objected to Prichard's attempt to show that he, Prichard, was right and that Plato was grossly mistaken in what Prichard took to be their rival accounts of morality. For, argued Collingwood, what Plato was talking about was just not the same as what Prichard was talking about: "a Greek word like δεῖ cannot be legitimately translated by using the word 'ought' *if* [my italics] that word carries with it the notion of what is sometimes [i.e., by Prichard] called 'moral obligation.' " Was there any Greek word or phrase to express that notion? The "realists" (Prichard and his school) said there was; but they stultified themselves by adding that the "theories of moral obligation" expounded by Greek writers differed from modern theories such as Kant's about the same thing. How did they know that the Greek and the Kantian theories were about the same thing? Oh, because δεῖ (or whatever word it was) is the Greek for "ought." "It was like," Collingwood went on, "having a nightmare about a man who had got it into his head that τριήρης was the Greek for 'steamer,' and when it was pointed out to him that descriptions of triremes in Greek writers were at any rate not very good descriptions of steamers, replied triumphantly, 'That is just what I say. These Greek philosophers ... were truly muddle-headed and their theory of steamers is all wrong.' " In order not to make about Prichard the mistake which Prichard made about Plato and Aristotle, we have to ask what Prichard was talking about and whether we can locate his subject matter historically. I would like to offer historical evidence on two points.

The first concerns the homogenization of the ordinary moral vocabulary. It is not only in the writings of philosophers from Kant to Prichard, but in the writings of politicians and novelists too that we can perceive the loss of any feeling for the more specific meanings of words such as "duty" and "obligation." "Duty" becomes not the singular of "duties" but a noun that is distinguished from that singular by not having a plural. There are of course philosophers such as Green and Bradley who resist this trend, but the Duke of Wellington, George Eliot, and Mr. Gladstone are all on Prichard's side. Moreover it is precisely these who homogenize the moral vocabulary who find themselves confronted with a single, simple contrast between the demands of morality and those of the ends of life and the claims of desire.

"There is not much happiness for any of us in this life, but we can all of us ride straight ahead and do our duty," said the Duke of Wellington and W. S. Gilbert's *Pirates of Penzance*, subtitled *The Slave To Duty*, is precisely a joke about how the concept of duty has got out of hand in this respect. We recognize Prichard's "feeling of imperativeness" when George Eliot in her famous talk with F. W. H. Myers in the garden of Trinity College, Cambridge, spoke of " . . . how peremptory and absolute" are the demands of duty. (Myers gives "Duty" a capital letter in his account.) But what then of the word "ought"? Do we find a special sense of it?

The Oxford English Dictionary asserts that there is. But almost every example that it cites is far from conclusive, and some certainly not to the point at all.

At least an indication that we do find such a sense is provided by Gladstone's capitalization of "Ought," strongly reminiscent of Myer's capitalization of "Duty," when he speaks of the "Ought" that constitutes morality. But we have other sources here. One is the Victorian novel. Consider the following passages of dialogue from *Is He Popenjoy?* (1878) by Anthony Trollope. The first was:

" . . . I think one should always promise to do everything that is asked. Nobody would be fool enough to expect you to keep your word afterwards and you'd give a lot of pleasure."

"I think promises ought to be kept, Captain de Baron."

"I can't agree to that. That's bondage, and it puts an embargo on the pleasant way of living that I like. I hate all kinds of strictness, and duty, and self-denying, and that kind of thing. It's rubbish . . ." (pp. 120–21).

It is certainly the case that a passage like this is in no way conclusive in suggesting that "ought" is being used in a special moral sense. But there is at least one relevant point about such a passage. Not only is "ought" used in such a passage in conjunction with the notion of duty, but it is not used, and I think it is never used, in either the novels of Trollope or indeed in those of George Eliot, in such a way that a premise about what will make someone happy supports a conclusion about what one ought to do. Ordinary Victorian conversation, insofar as Trollope and George Eliot record it, is Prichardian and neither Platonic, nor Aristotelian, nor

Benthamite. Indeed I have only found one use of "ought" so far in either novelist which is not in a moral context. I have already said that I do not take this to be conclusive. For the Prichardian claim, as I am now interpreting it, is that moral considerations are not just one ground for which conclusions about what agents ought to do can be devised, but that there is a specifically moral sense of "ought" and the passages cited from Trollope and George Eliot do not force us to take the Prichardian view although I think that they strongly suggest it. Consider, however, a second passage from *Is He Popenjoy?*

> "I'm quite sure Lord George Germain never in his life did anything that he ought not to do. That's his fault. Don't you like men who do what they ought not to do?"

> "No," said Mary, "I don't. Everybody always ought to do what they ought to do . . . ." (p. 81).

The first speaker contrasts liking people with judging whether they do what they ought to do; the second speaker, Lady Germain, accepts the distinction in order to deny that if the criterion were liking then men ought not (that is, had better not, if they want to be liked) to do what they ought to do. The addition of the word "always" makes it even clearer that "Everybody always ought to do what they ought to do" is used by Trollope and his character to deny that sometimes people ought not to do what they ought to do. The intelligibility of this denial entails that the test which I specified earlier for deciding whether in one particular type of sentence two senses or uses—two types of occurrence—of a word do or do not occur has in fact been applied. For this denial would result in a contradiction unless two senses or uses of "ought" were being used in the sentence "Everybody always ought to do what they ought to do." It is the second "ought" which is clearly the moral "ought" of which Prichard speaks.

Before I pass on to discuss this question further, I ought perhaps to say a little more about my attempted manoeuver to avoid entanglement with linguistics. I have cited one example of a case in the history of "ought" where we might be strongly tempted to say that two *senses* of "ought" were involved: that in which "I ought" has to be discriminated from "I owe" and that in which the moral or Prichardian "ought" has to be discriminated from the ordinary advice-giving or prudential "ought." The reason why we perhaps ought to resist this temptation is that in contemporary linguistics strong grounds are alleged for only in the last analysis explaining differences in the meaning of two statements expressed by the same sentence by adducing different senses of the same word. One alternative possibility in the present case would be to understand the second Prichardian "ought" in "Everybody always ought to do what they ought to do" as a type of occurrence of "ought" in which there is a systematic deletion, explicable possibly in terms of maxims governing conversational proprieties. My difficulty with this suggestion is in knowing how to characterize the deletion in question. If it is suggested that what has been deleted is some such phrase that would give us a rewriting of "Everybody always ought to do what they ought to do" as "Everybody always ought to do what the rules of morality prescribe that they ought to do," then we should have to ask what is meant in this context by the rules of morality. If my cultural analysis is correct, then these rules can only be expressed for Prichard and his cultural allies by using the very "ought" that we are trying to analyse. Hence we shall be involved in useless circularity. But there may well be some other characterization of the difference between the two "oughts" in Trollope's sentence in terms of a deletion, and my argument certainly should not be taken to imply that this is not so. For my immediate purposes, the difference between one type of occurrence of "ought" and another has now been adequately characterized, and it is in any case clear to me that in one ordinary language sense of "meaning," differences in what I have called type of occurrence are called differences in meaning. I shall therefore continue for my own purpose to use the words "meaning" and "sense" in this way without (in another sense of "sense") much sense of shame.

I therefore provisionally conclude that in the main Prichard is not giving us an incorrect account of the use and meaning of a word "ought" with the use and meaning of which we are all familiar, but a correct account of one use and one meaning of "ought" with which many of us at least—and there will be variations here perhaps with age, social class, and place of upbringing—are unfamiliar. I also think it possible that there was a tendency in the mid and late nineteenth century and early twentieth century, at least in certain social groups in England, for this "ought" of which Prichard speaks to become the dominant or even the only use of "ought" so that where the general advice-giving "ought" which I have paraphrased by "had better" would have been used in other milieus various equivalent locutions are used. If this were so, it might explain why in 1912 Prichard thinks that in giving his account he is simply explaining the meaning and use of "ought" as such, whereas in 1937 he is more modestly discriminating and explaining one meaning and use of "ought" as contrasted with others.

One final historical remark: the moral "ought" explicated by Prichard is not to be found before the late eighteenth century, just as it is in the latter part of the eighteenth century that "duty" and "obligation" begin to discard their more distinctive meanings (although they never do this entirely) and in consequence it ceases to be the case that premises about duty, premises about obligation, and premises about happiness may all lead to one and the same conclusion about what men ought to do in one and the same sense of "ought." Insofar as morality is defined as Prichard defined it, morality, like the railway and the polka, is an innovation of the nineteenth century; and like the railway and the polka its appearance or survival is perhaps intelligible only against a particular cultural background.

For if we now take Prichard's characterization with some seriousness we must surely become extremely puzzled in yet another way. Consider three characteristics of the use of the Prichardian "ought." First, when I tell someone or say to myself that he or I ought to do so and so, in this sense of "ought" I am not just—or perhaps at all—telling someone or myself to do something even if a recognition that I ought so to do involves me in a feeling of imperativeness. I am, it seems clearly, in Prichard's view offering a particular type of reason for doing whatever it is. Secondly, however, this reason cannot itself be supported by further reasons, unless the sentences which express them also contain the Prichardian "ought." Thus the kind of explication of a type of statement which is given by considering what types of reason might be offered either for asserting or for denying it must be completely lacking. The only answer we are given by Prichard to the question of how we can know that it is or is not the case that we ought in the Prichardian sense to do so and so is that "the only remedy lies in actually getting into a situation which occasions the obligation, or—if our imagination be strong enough—in imagining ourselves in that situation, and then letting our moral capacities of thinking at this work." The example that Prichard has just given is that of a "doubt whether we ought, for example, to pay our debts" and Prichard must therefore mean that the way to settle this doubt is to imagine that we are in debt or, if our imaginations are not strong enough, actually to get into debt. This is bizarre, but the bizarrerie perhaps belongs to the whole notion of what Prichard calls "the immediacy of our apprehension" of what we ought to do. He also uses the expression "self-evidence" of this alleged apprehension.

Thirdly, it is clear that so far as the meaning of the key expressions, "ought," "obligation," "duty," and the like is concerned, as they are understood by Prichard, no subjectivist account can be correct. For in saying that I ought to do I in no way express my own choice, preference, feelings, or attitudes; for only I know what I ought in this sense to do, these all still remain to be determined. That this is so is clear from the whole tenor of Prichard's discussion; and it is equally clear in Trollope and George Eliot. For Trollope the demands of "ought" are counterposed to those of "liking"; and for George Eliot the problem is how to relate the demands of right action to the realm of feelings left out of the definition of right action in the moral scheme of some of these characters whom she represents in order to criticize. "But yet sometimes when I have done wrong," says Maggie Tulliver to her brother, "it is because I have had feelings that you would be the better for, if you had them." The demands of morality are in no way expressions of personal preference.

These three characteristics of the moral "ought" ought to puzzle us in much the way that Captain Cook and his sailors were puzzled when they first encountered the word "taboo". For they found that to say that a class of actions was taboo was apparently not to just say that actions of that particular kind were prohibited, but to point to some particular kind of reason for the prohibition. Yet since no further reason could be given for giving this reason, the nature or the reason being adduced for the prohibition remained completely obscure. Had the eighteenth-century inhabitants of Polynesia had philosophers among them, Captain Cook's seamen would doubtless have learnt that a taboo, if it can be derived at all, can only be derived from another taboo, or that taboos are matter for the immediacy of our apprehension, or even, if things had gone far enough, that "taboo" is the name of a non-natural quality. But Polynesia is not Oxford or Cambridge, nor the eighteenth century the twentieth. Yet I find no reason to treat either time or place differently from the other, and consequently find no reason to suppose that my investigation of Prichard's claims and of the social background of those claims ought to differ radically from an anthropologist's or an anthropologically minded historian's investigation of eighteenth-century Polynesia. We should all of us, I think, be a little surprised if an elucidation of the concept of taboo were to be a central feature of a book called *The Language of Morals*, as a book by one of Prichard's successors is entitled, or of one called *Moral Obligation*, as Prichard's collected papers were entitled by another of his successors. There are a variety of moral schemes in different times and places for the philosopher to investigate and some sense of this variety may be necessary if we are not to treat our local moral schemes as timeless and universal conceptions, something that we should rightly judge an absurdity in Polynesians, although it is not in fact Polynesians who need this reminder. Suppose that we do in fact treat the Prichardian "ought" as the anthropologist treats the Polynesian "taboo," what would be the outcome?

We make a social practice intelligible by placing it in some context where the point and purpose of doing things in one way rather than another is exhibited by showing the connection between that social practice and some wider institutional arrangements of which it is a part. So the passing of a verdict has to be understood in the context of a legal system, and the concept of a home run has to be understood in the context of baseball. When we cannot make a practice intelligible by supplying such a context, there are two possibilities. The first is that we have not been adequately perceptive or understanding in our investigation of that particular social order; the other is that the practice just is, as it stands, unintelligible. One hypothesis which we may advance as a result of coming to the latter conclusion, a hypothesis which has the additional merit, if it is independently supported, of supporting the latter conclusion, is that the practice in question is a survival. That is to say, we explain the practice in its present form by supposing that it is the historical product of an earlier practice which existed in a social context that has now been removed and of the consequences of the removal of that context. What do I mean by a context? A set of beliefs expressed in institutionalized social practice. Hence what I want to maintain is that the use of the Prichardian moral "ought" can perhaps only be made intelligible as a social practice by supposing it to be a survival from a lost context of beliefs, just as the eighteenth-century Polynesian use of "taboo" can perhaps only be made intelligible by supposing it to be a survival from a lost context of beliefs.

Consider two earlier forms of moral scheme. The first is that embodied in Humean utilitarianism. Hume takes it that when one asserts for anyone that he ought to do so and so, one is appealing to a standard of justice or of obligation or of virtue—one is expressing the sentiment of adherence to that standard and appealing to the sentiment of adherence in others—which standard is to be justified by showing us that it gives us all what we want. What we want is a matter of our passions and the passions which compose human nature are a determinate set. Moreover not only is this so, but the passions are such that if any two men have the same rational powers and the same information, then they will agree on what it is that ought to be done. This happy coincidence secured by the contingent facts of human psychology, this pre-established having of the emotions and of the desires, is the presupposition of Hume's moral scheme. Now there seem to me strong reasons for believing that Hume, unlike later utilitarians, gives us a true report of the passions, but not of the passions as they are biologically, not of some basic human nature, but of the passions as they were ordered in one particular cultural and social order. That order was shattered and fragmented by the impact of those changes which at the level of high art are the Romantic movement. With that movement the presupposition of any moral scheme of the type represented by Hume is removed; the passions and the sentiments confront the established rules and ends in such a way as to constitute a set of problems for morality rather than its foundation. It is upon this that Kant, who is essentially a post-*Sorrows of Werther* moralist, remarks; it is this that Jane Austen confronts in the character of Marianne in *Sense and Sensibility*. There is no longer a determinate set of passions, let alone a pre-established harmony in our desires. If therefore men are to continue to assert that they ought to do what they formerly asserted that they ought to do, it will have to be on some new basis or in some new way.

As with the emotions formerly presupposed, so also with the theology formerly presupposed. That Christian scheme according to which God created man so that he had a determinate human nature, the desires of which would be frustrated if he did not follow the precepts of morality, and according to which what God commands is what will in the end satisfy that nature, was destroyed by the Protestant insistence that human nature is so depraved that the commandments of God must appear to us as arbitrary fiats. The chaos of Romantic emotion and the arbitrariness of Protestant moral theology have one classic imaginative representation in James Hogg's *Memoirs of a Justified Sinner*. It is only, be it noted, in post-Protestant cultures that the moral "ought" ever appears. And it appears precisely in the period when the judgment that men ought to do so and so can no longer be supported by appeal to the nature that God created and the purposes toward which the commandments of God are directed.

Detached from a theological scheme and a scheme of the

emotions, both of which were embodied in the vocabulary and in the norms which defined the transactions of daily life, what should we expect to happen to the use of "ought"? There are clearly a number of possible outcomes. But clearly one might be that men would go on saying that one ought to do so and so, expecting their utterance to be endowed with the same locutionary and allocutionary force—or lack of it—as before, but unable now when pressed to offer the same or any other justification. What had formerly been a conclusion from premises, resting on certain presuppositions which made the necessary inferences possible, will now become a type of statement which can be derived from nothing other than a more general statement of the same type. "An 'ought', if it is to be derived at all, can only be derived from another 'ought.'" Deprived of its rationale, the use of this "ought" would necessarily be unsusceptible of further explication, and the continuance of its use would be in a real sense superstitious. But this judgment perhaps sounds unnecessarily harsh. Yet consider how the moral or Prichardian "ought" was in fact used. The central features of its use can be brought out by comparing the following three imaginary dialogues:

1. A. Sir, return to me that copy of Warburton's sermons.
   B. Why?
   A. Sir, you have promised to return it and therefore you ought to return it.
   B. But why should I keep promises?
   A. Sir, promise-keeping, as Mr. Hume has shown in his *Treatise*, is an institution invented to produce benefits for beings who desire, as you desire and I desire, to rely on our expectations of each other.
   B. Sir, your appeal to the passions has enslaved my reason. Here is your book.

2. A. Sir, return to me that copy of *The Language of Morals*.
   B. Why?
   A. I choose to ask for this, I do ask for it. Give it to me. Let anyone who has borrowed a book give it to its owner.
   B. Why should your preferences interest me?

3. A. Sir, return to me that copy of *Moral Obligation*.
   B. Why?
   A. You ought to return what you have borrowed.

B.   Why?

A.   I can give you no further answer. For I am using the distinctively moral "ought." You just ought, and if you cannot see this, I cannot help you.

In the first of these dialogues the force of "You ought" is entirely derived from the force of the impersonal standard of utility, understood as Hume understood it. There is a genuine backing of the injunction to act in a certain way, by the giving of a reason. In the second dialogue, there is no such backing of the injunction at all; the injunction is presented as the expression of the naked will of the speaker and unless the hearer has some reason to regard the will of the speaker—because, for example, he hates or loves, has hopes of or fears of the speaker—he has been afforded no reason at all for doing what he has been enjoined to do. But that this is so has been made entirely clear by the speaker's use of imperatival form and of expressions which are plainly no more than expressions of personal preference and choice.

In the third dialogue however matters are very different. The use of "ought" makes it sound as if the situation is the same as in the first dialogue, as though there is the giving of a reason for following the injunction to action, by means of an appeal to an impersonal standard. But the inability to back up this use of "ought" by any further reason-giving renders this appearance entirely deceptive. The hearer has in fact been given no more reason to follow the injunction than he was in the second dialogue, but the appeal to naked will has been clothed with the semblance but not the reality of reason-giving by the use of the Prichardian "ought." It is considerations such as these that suggest that the use of such a word as "superstition" may not be out of place. This is not a matter of the intentions of particular individuals. Where a particular use of the word "ought" is an established social practice a particular individual may well use it without the intention of exercising bluff or deception upon his hearers. But his hearers will in fact be bluffed or deceived, whatever the speaker intends, just insofar as they attach a seriousness and a force to what he says which they would not attach to the utterance of imperatives or expressions of personal preference and choice.

That this is so throws light on the theory of moral utterance that immediately succeeded Prichard's intuitionism. Emotivism has always been an implausible theory about the *meaning* of moral words and sentences. "Good," "right," and "ought" involve an appeal to some standard which expressions of preference or choice or imperatival expressions do not involve; and as R. M. Hare pointed out, statements containing evaluative expressions have or can have logical relation to each other and to other statements which expressions genuinely used as expressions of feeling ("What a splendid day!" or "Hurrah for the red, white and blue!") do not and cannot have. Hence Stevenson was in error when he represented his analyses as offering even rough and approximate equivalences of meaning between classes of expression. But Stevenson's version of Emotivism can be more fruitfully understood in another way. For the account of the Prichardian or distinctly moral "ought" which I have given would lead us to conclude that when this "ought" was being used, agents who believed themselves to be doing other and more than expressing their own feelings and attitudes were in fact doing no other and no more than that. In a precisely similar way religious language when it survives into a non-religious and irreligious culture may change its use without changing its meaning. There have been times and places when a man who said "God give me patience!" would necessarily have been uttering a prayer; but a man in our culture who says "God give me patience!" may not be praying— for the practice of prayer presupposes a context of belief which is often now lacking—but expressing his feelings of exasperation. The words have not changed their meaning; but the expression has changed its use. Emotivism understood as a theory of use, and not as a theory of meaning at all, turns out to be true not of morality in general, but rather of what morality came to be at a particular period of time. To put the point in another idiom, Prichard presents us with the self-image of one particular morality, taken at its own face value. He never pierces below the ideological surface. Stevenson does just this. But Stevenson, like Prichard, accepts too much from the morality itself. He takes it, for example, to be a characterization of morality as such, that disagreement may always be interminable, whereas this is a characterization only of moralities which are detached from any background of beliefs, whether theological or naturalistic, which supply established and ultimate criteria. Stevenson, like Prichard, lacks any sense of the historical dimension of morality. Hence his theory is not a true theory of moral utterance, but a true theory of intuitionist moral utterance, if we understand by intuitionism not merely the doctrine of a group of philosophers, but the doctrine of a social milieu.

The Prichardian or distinctively moral "ought" was a ghost and it is a ghost that still walks in certain quarters, although more and more obviously, like other ghosts, a survival. Yet so long as it survives, morality involves a degree of bluff and deception that can only have the effect of engendering cynicism whenever it is once more expressed. This paper is therefore not only an attempt at analysis; it is also hopefully an exorcism.

17

Pleasure as a reason for action[1]

It is often said nowadays that to understand pleasure we must understand it as affording us a reason for or an explanation of action. It is only from the standpoint of the agent that we can avoid being misled. Both Professor Nowell-Smith[2] and Mr. Manser[3] have argued along these lines; and Dr. Kenny[4] has written that "pleasure is always a reason for action" and has elucidated what he means by a footnote: "I do not mean that a thing's being pleasant is always a sufficient reason for doing it; there may be strong reasons for abstaining. I mean merely that it is always silly to ask a man why he wants pleasure." When I first saw this point made, I had the perhaps not uncommon philosophical experience of immediately finding it both lucid and convincing, but then afterwards gradually becoming less and less clear about the source of my conviction. The reasons for my obfuscation are as follows. In one crucial sense anything can afford an agent with a reason for action. It depends upon what the agent wants and upon the projects in which he is engaged. Moreover, without having any strong reasons for abstaining from what will give me pleasure, I may not be at all moved by the prospect of pleasure. As I write this essay I can list a dozen activities or experiences which would afford me pleasure. I have no strong reason for abstaining; I do not particularly enjoy writing essays; I am not writing with a great sense of urgency; I have the time and the money to indulge myself. Yet I do not rush to open a Guinness or Mr. P. G. Wodehouse's new novel. So that far from its being silly to ask me why I do not apparently

---

[1] Reprinted from *The Monist*, Vol. 49, No. 2 (1965) with permission of The Open Court Publishing Co., La Salle, Illinois.

[2] P. H. Nowell-Smith, *Ethics* (London and Baltimore: Penguin Books, 1954), p. 132.

[3] A. Manser, "Pleasure," *Proceedings of the Aristotelian Society*, 1958.

[4] A. Kenny, *Action, Emotion and Will* (London: Routledge & Kegan Paul; New York: Humanities Press, 1963), p. 134.

want pleasure at the moment, it is a question that I find forced upon me. But if this question makes sense, there is at least a problem as to why "it is always silly to ask a man if he wants pleasure." For one might expect the two questions to stand or fall together. This is the problem to which I address myself in this essay. But in order to do so I must first take up certain points from recent discussions which are in danger of preventing a solution.

I

There are two classical treatments of pleasure, the Benthamite[1] and the Aristotelian.[2] If I deal with them in that rather than in the chronological order, it is because in recent philosophical writing about pleasure, the Benthamite view has provided the target for attack, the Aristotelian view the weapons. It seems clear that Bentham treated both "pleasure" and "pain" as the names of sensations. These sensations are distinct existences which may, and on occasion do, exist without being accompanied by any act of will. It is not entirely clear whether Bentham himself thought the connection between pleasure and pain on the one hand, and acts of will and actions on the other, to be purely contingent or not. For one thing it is "the idea of pleasure" rather than the sensation which has an effect on the will, according to Bentham. But Bentham certainly appears to believe, first, that in all cases where I take pleasure in or enjoy something, what constitutes the pleasure or enjoyment is an accompanying sensation, which exists over and above the object of pleasure or enjoyment; and, second, that when I do something for pleasure or enjoyment and achieve it, the pleasure or enjoyment is a sensation separately identifiable from the means by which I procure the sensation. Bentham gives fifty-eight synonyms for "pleasure"; his use of the notion of synonymity reinforces the view that he takes there to be a single, simple concept of pleasure, so that "enjoyment" for example means precisely what "pleasure" means and names precisely what "pleasure" names.

In Aristotle's view, which is far less tidy than Bentham's, pleasure is analysed at one point in terms of unimpeded activity and at another in terms of its resemblances and differences to an

---

[1] J. Bentham, *Principles of Morals and Legislation* (New York: Hafner, 1948), Chapter 4 and elsewhere.

[2] Aristotle, *Nicomachean Ethics* (London and New York: Heinemann and Putnam (Loeb), 1926), Book VII and Book X.

end. Both analyses derive from Aristotle's belief that, if I do something because I enjoy doing it, my action is not a means to a separately identifiable end, my enjoyment. He therefore finds himself at one stage arguing that to enjoy doing what one is doing is simply to do whatever it is without hindrance; and at another that, although pleasure is a reason for acting and that to get pleasure from doing something is a criterion of success in action, we cannot identify any specific type of action in terms of its being a means to pleasure. I have used the words pleasure and enjoyment indifferently to convey Aristotle's views; he himself uses the single word ἡδονή and appears to believe that he is dealing with a single concept.

In recent discussions the Aristotelian stress upon pleasure as not separately identifiable from the enjoyed activity has been forcefully deployed against the Benthamite view. None the less, the discussion has had three unsatisfactory features. First of all, too often pleasure, enjoyment, liking, happiness, and the rest have been treated as if Bentham and Aristotle were right in seeing a single concept here. Secondly, if pleasure is not separately identifiable as an end-state to which actions are a means, a short sharp refutation of hedonism is obviously available. But too short and too sharp a refutation. Clearly hedonism does treat pleasure as an end and equally clearly as an end among other alternative and rival ends. For hedonism bids us to pursue pleasure rather than other goals. But in the Aristotelian view pleasure supervenes upon activity successfully carried through; it cannot be the end of activity. And moreover in the Aristotelian view since pleasure is specified in terms of successful activity and not vice versa, pleasure cannot be a criterion for choosing among ends. Pleasure supervenes on every achieved end. It follows that hedonism makes no sense. Yet hedonism is in fact fully intelligible as a set of recommended moral choices. And it is so, first, because the hedonist uses the word "pleasure" in a sense which needs to be discriminated from other senses of that word—as neither the Aristotelian view nor the Benthamite does discriminate it; and, secondly, because in treating pleasure in his sense as an end, the hedonist treats pleasure as intrinsically bound up with certain activities and certain experiences rather than others—whereas in both the Aristotelian and the Benthamite view pleasures can, logically, be had from *any* activity. Now perhaps any activity or experience can be enjoyed in some sense; but only some give pleasure in the hedonist's sense.

It may be objected that I am unjustifiably restricting the use of the word "hedonist," for the word has been used to characterize the views of both of those who hold that as a matter of fact we all do pursue pleasure or happiness, these terms being used indifferently (so the Abbé Brémond called the Jansenists "panhedonists") and of those who hold that we ought to pursue pleasure rather than other possible ends. It is as a mere matter of convenience that I invoke the latter rather than the former use, my model for a hedonist being Norman Douglas rather than the Abbé de Saint-Cyran. I am interested in the word "pleasure" as it is used in connection with beer and pickles, oysters and champagne, racecourses, dogtracks, and what Lord Denning in his report called "popsies." There is, then, something of an initial difference of interest from those philosophers who have treated as paradigm cases of pleasure digging, going for walks, fishing, and even writing philosophical papers. This difference of interest is connected not only with a belief that a family of interconnected concepts has been misunderstood by treating them as if they were all one and the same concept, but also with a concern that the role of the senses and of sensations in pleasure has received insufficient attention.

This is the third defective feature of contemporary discussions. Convinced, and rightly convinced, that Bentham was mistaken in identifying pleasure with a sensation, philosophers have tended to neglect both sensations and the senses and to concentrate on enjoyable activities. I can thus redefine the goal of this essay in terms of these two points: to discriminate different concepts of pleasure and enjoyment, with a view to clarifying the role of the senses and of sensations in pleasure, and at the same time to make clear in what different senses pleasure can be a reason for action.

II

First of all, then, to remark some of the variety of concepts:
1. "Heureux qui, comme Ulysse . . ." (du Bellay); "O happy is the man who hears instruction's warning voice" (Ps. i, Scots metrical version). The use of "happy" to express a verdict on a man's life depends upon a sense of "happy" in which a man may truly be called happy who has suffered a great deal, as well as a man who has prospered.
2. I may be called happy in the above sense, because during my life I have enjoyed myself on many occasions. But, in giving this supporting reason for the verdict, I am using "enjoy" to mean something other than "be happy." I can enjoy a game, a holiday,

a friend's company, digging, editing a Greek text. My motive in doing these things need not be a wish for enjoyment for me to enjoy whatever it is; I may play games or dig for the sake of my health and edit a text because I need to earn money, and yet enjoy what I do. Whether I enjoy what I do or not is a question that others may answer by observing whether or not I try to prolong the activity, appear absorbed in it, yawn, and so on. But my own testimony is highly important, although not necessarily always conclusive.

3. An activity, a sensation, a sight or sound, a work of art, a taste, a smell may be called pleasant or unpleasant, enjoyable or unenjoyable. In so characterizing it, I do not commit myself to having enjoyed it or found it pleasant on any particular occasion. It may well be that it takes experience to find it pleasant, or it equally may well be that familiarity dulls the pleasure. ". . . 'I add to them, in the laying out of grounds, a third and distinct character, which I call *unexpectedness.*' 'Pray, sir,' said Mr. Milestone, 'by what name do you distinguish this character when a person walks around the grounds for the second time?' " (Peacock).

Moreover, when I call something pleasant or enjoyable, although I may not be able to give reasons for my characterization, it always makes sense to ask for them. I may call a drink pleasant because it is refreshing, a holiday enjoyable because it combined sun and sea with the opportunity to look at paintings. If I call something pleasant or enjoyable I am saying, or at least giving my hearers to understand, that the standard criteria for that sort of thing's being an enjoyable one have been satisfied, at least where there are such criteria. And commonly there are.

4. Pleasure as a distinct object of pursuit might be said to consist in the enjoyable qualities of those activities, sensations, tastes, and the like, which are, and can only be, sought for the sake of the pleasure found in them. And certainly even if I not only enjoy nursing the sick or working on an automobile production line, but do these things because I enjoy them, I cannot be said to be devoting myself to pleasure in this sense. Yet to say this would be to attend to one end of a spectrum only, a spectrum which must be defined partly in terms of this end of the scale and partly in terms of the contrast between activities which can only be carried on for the sake of pleasure and activities which could in no sense be said to be pursued only for pleasure's sake, even when we enjoy them. For there are many activities which carried on in one type of context could only be done for pleasure, but which in another type of context could be carried on for other reasons. Such is fishing. And

there are activities which embody values so central to human life that although they are highly productive of pleasure, they could not be undertaken without some attention to those values and so could not be done purely for pleasure. Such is mountaineering. But there are at the opposite end of the spectrum from that of which I first spoke, when the activities to which I wanted to draw attention were eating and drinking what is not designed to prevent hunger and thirst, the enjoyment of tastes and smells, sensual pleasure, and all those items to which the OED may be taken to be referring when it gives as its second definition of "Pleasure": "In bad sense: Sensuous enjoyment as a chief object of life or end in itself."

The most important ground on which I have distinguished between these four concepts is the difference in each case in what would make statements embodying them true or false. This attention to truth-conditions, rather than to syntactical distinctions or idiomatic nuances, is necessary because the words used to express these concepts are, in contemporary English as contrasted with the English of earlier generations, often interchangeable. There are indeed idiomatic points to be made of philosophical interest: tastes, smells, and sensations are usually said to be pleasant or pleasurable, activities to be enjoyable. In this way different parts of the spectrum of pleasure are distinguished in ordinary usage. But for most idioms that make use of some form of "enjoy" and its cognates there is an equivalent idiom using "please" or "pleasure." It is because of these facts that it would be equally wrong either to assert with Bentham that "pleasure" and "enjoyment" are synonyms or simply to deny Bentham's assertion. Hence also the misleading character of all such assertions is that pleasure is a species of enjoyment. For such assertions presuppose what is not the case, that the vocabulary of pleasure and enjoyment is a currency with fixed values. In my own elucidation I have annexed certain words for certain concepts in an arbitrary but, I hope, tolerably lucid way.

Some of the relations between the four concepts I have sketched are fairly clear: that a man has enjoyed much of his life is a good reason, although it may not be a sufficient one, for calling him happy; that an experience or activity was pleasurable may be cited as an explanation for having enjoyed it. But others of the relationships are more complex. The one on which I wish to lay stress is that between first-person reports of what I do or did take pleasure in or enjoy and statements about an experience or activity being enjoyable, pleasant, or pleasurable. When asked why I enjoyed an experience or why the experience was enjoyable

I may in both cases point to features of the experience which made it enjoyable. But if I fail to enjoy an experience and am asked to explain why I so failed, I may do one of two things. I may say that the experience just was not enjoyable, and I may cite features of the experience which made it unpleasant. Or I may account for my lack of enjoyment alternatively by explaining that although the experience had all the features of an enjoyable experience, none the less I failed to enjoy it because something was wrong with me: I had a cold, I was overtired, or even—the residual category—I just did not feel like it.

I lay stress on these alternative directions in which explanation may move (in calling them alternatives I do not mean to imply that it could not be the case both that the experience had unpleasant features and that I was in no fit state to enjoy it), both because this contrast between pointing to the state of the agent and pointing to the features of his experience or activity will recur later in the argument, and because attention to it enables us to diagnose certain errors. Ryle opens a discussion of pleasure by asking what sort of difference the difference is between a walk which one enjoys and a walk which one does not enjoy. The point of his question is partly to bring out that the difference is not that one walk is accompanied by a certain specific sensation and that the other is not. With this no one but a Benthamite could quarrel. But the question, as Ryle poses it, is almost as misleading as a Benthamite answer to it would be; for the form of the question suggests that one is looking for a single answer. And this is the kind of answer Ryle gives. A walk that one enjoys is one which has absorbed one's attention. So Ryle has written:

> To say that a person has been enjoying digging . . . is to say that he dug with his whole heart in his task; i.e., that he dug, wanting to dig, and not wanting to do anything else (or nothing) instead. His digging was a propensity fulfilment. His digging was his pleasure, and not a vehicle of his pleasure.[1]

This passage contains a mixture of true and false, When Ryle explains enjoying digging in terms of wanting to dig he gives us an important clue to a correct analysis. But he presents this clue as though there were only one answer to such questions as: "Why did you enjoy digging today?" or "What is the difference between that walk yesterday which you enjoyed and the one today which

[1] Gilbert Ryle, "Pleasure," *Proceedings of the Aristotelian Society, Supplement,* 1954 and *The Concept of Mind* (London: Hutchinson; New York: Barnes & Noble, 1949), p. 108.

you did not enjoy?" In fact the moment it is clear that we are talking about digging or walking on a specific occasion it also becomes clear that our enjoyment or lack of it has to be connected with features specific to the occasion. The difference between the walk today and the walk yesterday may be the difference between a walk when the sun was shining and a walk when it was cold and wet or the difference between a walk with Sarah who is charming and adores you and a walk with Selina who is boring and dislikes you. Suppose that it is objected that this is not the type of case Ryle had in mind. For a walk with Sarah is not the same activity as a walk with Selina, and a walk in the sun is not the same activity as a walk in the rain. What about the case where you enjoy and fail to enjoy the same activity on two successive occasions? The answer can only be that in that case the answer must be looked for in your state of body or mind and not in the activity. Again there will be no one general answer. You may on one occasion have had a cold or been overtired, or on the other have just had good news or felt unusually well.

So that we have to pass from the walking or the digging to the enjoyment by way of features of the walking or the digging. What makes these features relevant to cite is the fact that they are of a kind recognized as making a walk or a dig pleasurable. "I enjoyed the walk because the sun was shining" is intelligible as it stands; "I enjoyed the walk because of the cold drizzle" is not. Of course when someone says "I enjoyed . . ." his assertion does not mean the same as an assertion about what made the occasion enjoyable. What his assertion does mean, however, will not be understood if, as Ryle does, in the earlier of the discussions cited, we try to connect the enjoyment solely with the agent's mode of activity. Professor W. B. Gallie,[1] and Mr. C. C. W. Taylor[2] have both, for example, taken pleasure to be some form, mode, or species of attention. A general view of their case has been given by Professor H. L. A. Hart[3] who has written approvingly that,

> the outlines at least of a new and more realistic [than the Benthamite] analysis are clear. The elements previously treated as mere empirical evidence of a separately identifiable sensation of pleasure have now been introduced into the analysis of pleasure. The wish for prolongation of the activity or experience

[1] W. B. Gallie, "Pleasure," *Proceedings of the Aristotelian Society, Supplement*, 1954.
[2] C. C. W. Taylor, "Pleasure", *Analysis, Supplement*, 1962.
[3] H. L. A. Hart, "Bentham," *Proceedings of the British Academy*, 1962.

enjoyed; the resistance to interruption; the absorbed or rapt attention; the absence of some further end beyond the activity enjoyed—these are surely conceptually and not merely empirically linked with pleasure.

But these elements have by no means all the same status in relation to pleasure. Clearly it is right to link, for example, a wish for prolongation to enjoyment; but equally clearly that one is raptly attending to something is neither a necessary nor a sufficient condition for enjoyment. My attention may be absorbed by the thumbscrew's increasing pressure; my sleepy lack of attention may constitute part of what is enjoyable about lying on in bed, half-listening to the sounds of everyone else departing for work.

The mistake of those who have focused attention on attention is the opposite of one of Bentham's errors. Bentham wished to make the relation between pleasure and its external manifestations entirely contingent; these writers wish to make pleasure actually consist in its external manifestations. But while such manifestations as absorption and attention are perhaps highly characteristic of enjoyment, they are at best a criterion used by the observer to justify his third-person judgment on someone else's enjoyment. If someone says "I enjoy ..." or "I enjoyed ..." or "I am enjoying ..." he is not saying that he is attending or is absorbed. The criteria of enjoyment and the meaning of "enjoy" cannot be understood apart from one another, but they must none the less be distinguished.

At first sight a wish to prolong an experience or activity is no more intimately connected with enjoyment than attention is. For I may wish to prolong an experience which I am not enjoying (I do not enjoy the patient's struggle not to die, but I usually wish to prolong it and I may wish to prolong my stay at the bedside too); and I may wish to cut short an activity which I am enjoying very much. So that a wish to prolong is neither a necessary nor a sufficient condition of enjoyment. But if I have nothing else to do and if I do not wish to prolong an experience, I could not claim to be still enjoying it. The first condition has to be added, if we are to state a necessary condition for enjoyment accurately. But that this is a necessary condition of enjoyment is itself a consequence of a more central feature of enjoyment. If I enjoy an activity or experience, then I am satisfied with that activity or experience, as a way of spending time. To put the notion of satisfaction in its deservedly central place, we must again take up Ryle's point that a man who enjoyed digging "dug, wanting to dig, and not wanting to do anything else (or nothing) instead." Clearly, as it stands, the last point is incorrect. A man may want to do something other than what he is doing and yet enjoy what he is doing. There is indeed no paradox in a man's wanting to do something which he would not enjoy while doing something that he does enjoy. So a man may want to be called up in wartime because he considers it his duty to fight, although he knows he will hate the army, but still enjoy continuing his peacetime pursuits. Moreover, the sense in which a man who enjoys doing something must want to do it needs further clarification. A man may want to do something, do it, and not enjoy doing it. For him to enjoy doing it he must find in doing it that it is something he wants to do and would want to do even if it served no further end. Whether prior to doing it he wanted to do it or not is irrelevant. Furthermore, a man could not be said to enjoy doing something unless he wanted to do it again, provided only that there were not grave reasons in favor of not so doing, such as harm to himself or someone else. It is in this sense that enjoyment consists in the satisfaction of desire.

This analysis of enjoyment also applies when sensations, tastes, and smells are in question rather than activity. A sensation I enjoy, or from which I get pleasure, is one I want to feel in the same sense that when I feel it I want to feel and have felt it and would want to feel it even if it served no further end and even if it were not part, as it well may be, of a wider context of enjoyment. So sexual enjoyment is not just a matter of sensations, but the sensations are found pleasant even apart from the activity which gives them their context. Yet just at this point there is reason to pause in the argument. If I say that I took pleasure in an experience or enjoyed an activity, am I identifying my pleasure or enjoyment as distinct from the experience or activity? I have already suggested that it always makes sense to ask what made the experience or activity pleasurable and that the answer will be to point to features of the experience or activity. I may of course find an experience or activity pleasurable and be unable to pick out the relevant features. But if I can, they must, as I have also already suggested, be recognizable as pleasure-giving or enjoyable characteristics. In order to be so recognizable, a characteristic must give pleasure on standard occasions to most people. But what is the force of "most" here? If we recognize a characteristic as pleasure-giving, are we merely allowing that as a matter of purely contingent fact it is the sort of thing which most people happen to enjoy? Or are we asserting that some characteristics

may be enjoyable as such, as it were, or pleasant as such? That is,
are we asserting that if someone failed to find some particular
characteristic of a certain experience or activity pleasurable we
would have grounds for saying more than that he had minority
tastes?

The question can be put most sharply in terms of the sensations,
tastes, and smells which are so important to sensual pleasure. Is it
the case that most of us merely happen to like certain sensations,
tastes, and smells? Can we identify and characterize them independently of their being pleasurable? The belief that we can is
expressed most cogently by Mr. R. M. Hare[1] and expressed in
terms not of pleasure, but of pain.

<h1 style="text-align:center">III</h1>

"Objection might be taken to the claim that there could be a
'bare sensation' of pain which was not disliked. What, it might be
asked, would such an experience be like? Can we *imagine* such
an experience? I think that I can not only imagine it, but have had
it. . . ." So Hare, and much of his argument applies not only to
pain but to what he calls "unpleasant sensations"—itches,
tickles, electric shocks, and the like—and we can understand how
a partly parallel treatment of pleasure could be given.[2]

In the course of his argument Hare makes five important
points. He begins by criticizing Professor Kurt Baier[3] who had in
turn been criticizing Ryle's view that "pain is a sensation of a
special sort which we ordinarily dislike having."[4] Baier had criticized Ryle's view that the connection between pain and dislike is
a contingent one and had written that "whatever sorts of sensations we like and dislike, we only call pains those which we
dislike." Hare points to the fact that there are many different types
of sensation which we dislike (as there are also of course distinct

____

[1] R. M. Hare, "Pain and Evil," *Proceedings of the Aristotelian Society,
Supplement,* 1954.

[2] For Hare's own brief account see R. M. Hare, *Freedom and Reason*
(London and New York: Oxford University Press, 1963), pp. 125–29.
I would not want the case on pleasure, which I have constructed in
outline from Hare's views on pain, to be treated as though Hare could be
held responsible for it.

[3] K. Baier, *The Moral Point of View* (Ithaca, N.Y.: Cornell University
Press, 1958), pp. 268ff.

[4] Ryle, *op. cit.,* p. 109.

7

types of pleasurable sensations) and that we can segregate one group from these, the group of pains—that is, "burning pains, stinging pains, stabbing pains, aches, etc."—which is bound together therefore by something more and other than the fact of dislike. Hare then concedes that it may be that the use of the word "pain" in ordinary English does imply dislike; but if so this fact of usage can be countered by inventing a new term to name the sensation apart from our dislike of it.

Hare then draws two arguments from physiological evidence. The first is based on reports by experimental subjects in which the intensification of a sensation to the point to which it was painful is commented on in such a way by those who suffered it that Dr. C. A. Keele wrote that "the element of unpleasantness seems to be superimposed on a sensation which runs through the whole range."[1] That is, *the same sensation* is recognized as being when less intense painless but when more intense painful. So we can identify the sensation apart from its "painful", that is, dislikable qualities. The second piece of physiological evidence is drawn from experience of lobotomy. Patients who have had this operation appear still to feel pain, but their dislike of it appears to be reduced.

The two final points to which I wish to draw attention are not so much arguments for Hare's case as an answer to a possible objection and a statement of part of his purpose in propounding the earlier arguments. The possible objection is that we learn the meaning of the word "pain" when we are young only in contexts where dislike is being manifested. Hence we would have to grasp the meaning in such a way "that there is an analytic connection between having a pain and a manifestation of dislike." Hare's reply is that

> the teaching procedure would work perfectly well if the connection between pain and the manifestations of dislike were not analytic but contingent, provided that cases of pain without the manifestations, or *vice versa*, were rare. For me to succeed in teaching children the use of the word "pain", it is sufficient for me correctly to *guess*, on one or two occasions, that they are in pain because they are doing what normally manifests dislike of pain.

Finally Hare points out that an argument used against his own distinction between descriptive and evaluative judgments has been that "I am in intense pain" is both descriptive and—because

[1] *The Assessment of Pain in Man and Animals*, edited by Keele and Smith, as cited by Hare in "Pain and Evil", *op. cit.*

pain is necessarily disliked and to dislike something is clearly to evaluate it—evaluative, and that therefore Hare's distinction breaks down. But on the basis of his earlier arguments Hare replies that we must distinguish between reports of the sensation of pain and avowal of the dislike of pain. The first is description, the second evaluation,[1] and even if our ordinary use of "pain" combines them there is no necessary or logical connection between them.

This last point of Hare's is more relevant to my present argument than might appear. The critics to whom Hare refers surely went quite the wrong way about impugning Hare's distinction. For even if they could produce an example of a judgment which was both descriptive and evaluative, they would not thereby have shown that there were not two distinct classes of judgment. The discovery of borderline cases is evidence for, not against, the existence of borderlines. My own objection to Hare's view is that it presents the distinction between what is factual or descriptive and what is action-guiding or evaluative as a distinction between two classes of judgment or kinds of statements. Whereas, in fact, whether a statement is factual is a matter of what is said in it and of how it would be shown to be true or false; whereas whether a statement is action-guiding or evaluative depends on such matters as the intention with which and the context in which and the audience for whom it is uttered. Consider the difference between the statement "The White House is on fire" uttered as a news report by a broadcaster and uttered as a warning by a Presidential aide to the President. The same statement with precisely the same meaning can be put to very different uses, and to suppose that by putting a statement to a different use one had necessarily thereby changed its meaning would only be possible if one had illegitimately conflated the notions of meaning and use. It is worth making this point, even if the key question thereby raised of the meaning of such a word as "good" has to be put on one side, because it brings out the fact that a statement only provides someone with a reason for action if it is relevant to his wants or needs. Outside the context of human wants and needs no statement can function as such a reason. The question that I posed at the end of the last section was whether there are predicates of a factual kind which have meaning and application only in terms of desire and aversion; that is, whether there are kinds of property which can only be identified and characterized if we identify them

[1] I have compressed this argument and the reader is referred to Hare's own exposition.

as objects of desire or aversion. If there are such predicates and properties, their existence presupposes that certain desires and aversions are standard for human beings, standard not only in being statistically usual, but in providing norms for desire, to such an extent that our descriptive vocabulary embodies these norms. Hence certain types of statements would furnish us with reasons for action in a special sense. Hare's view on pain might be generalized into the contention that there are no such statements.

My first problem about Hare's thesis is equally a problem about the statements of Ryle and Baier from which Hare's exposition started. All speak of sensations which we dislike. Now certainly we dislike many sensations, and pains are among these; but the variations in my dislike of my pain are not to be confused with variations in the pain. That is, it is just not the case that the more painful my pain the more I dislike it. For my dislike may intensify or lessen depending on how well able I feel to bear the pain; and there are times when I may feel better able to bear a greater pain than I am able to bear with equanimity at other times. Equally, my dislike of the same pain of unchanging intensity may vary greatly. Thus, the connection between pain and characteristic pain behavior is unlikely to be elucidated at all by putting this concept of liking or disliking in the center of the picture.

Consider instead the notion of "the same sensation." What are the criteria for identity or similarity of sensation? Certainly identity of stimulus is not enough. It always makes sense to inquire whether the same stimulus is producing the same sensation as it did before, or whether it is producing the same sensation in you as it is in me. Equally, reactions to sensations vary. It makes sense to inquire whether the same sensation produces the same or different reactions in me as it does you, or in me at different times. But what criterion have we for characterizing sensations at all, if this is so? It is considerations such as this that lead either to skepticism or to behaviorism. The behaviorist attempt to outlaw the sensation itself breaks down, among many other reasons, because I may, when I cannot observe a stimulus, infer correctly what it is from a sensation (as when I infer that someone has stabbed me in the back). But the comparison of one sensation with another—which is presupposed, for example, in such correct inferences to true conclusions—is only possible because a relatively uniform intervening sensation between stimulus and behavioral response is presupposed. Take the notions of tickles and itches. We have to acquire these notions in terms both of their characteristic causes and of the characteristic responses to such causes.

If tickling in certain parts of the body did not characteristically produce laughter, we should lack the concept of a tickle. Again, if a feeling did not characteristically produce an impulse to scratch we should hesitate to call it an itch.

When I speak of a behavioral response, I mean a natural, primary response; I may always learn to inhibit such responses, and there is no logical limit to such learning. So the notion of an itch that I do not any longer want to scratch or a tickle that produces no laughter is perfectly intelligible. So is the notion of a pain that produces neither clutching nor screaming. But is it then true that having used the behavioral concomitants to acquire a sensation vocabulary, I can then use the vocabulary without any behavioral reference? Consider the notion of severe and less severe pain. What can this be but pain to which the natural response would be more and less extreme forms of avoidance or aversion behavior? Or, if one prefers, pain which requires more or less inhibition of such behavior. Equally, *the same pain* must be pain whose natural response would be avoidance behavior of the same degree, although it must also be pain of the same kind—stabbing, throbbing, or aching, for example. What otherwise could "the same pain" mean? Suppose the reply to this is: the criterion of identity is just that the two feel the same, they are phenomenologically identical. Can we make sense of the notion of two sensations feeling the same but being associated with different natural behavioral responses? If this were so, ascriptions of sameness of sensation in different people would not be possible. Predicates ascribing sensation would be egocentric predicates, which they are not in fact. Of course, we have the concept of the phenomenological feel of sensations; but the vocabulary in which we express it depends on a notion of sensations as comparable, which depends in turn on the association of sensation with behavioral responses.

This dependence is neither purely contingent, as Hare supposes, nor purely analytic. In fact, half our difficulties have arisen from too rigid an application of an analytic/synthetic dichotomy. Consider a parallel case, that of fear. We certainly have feelings of fear, which sometimes simply arise in us inexplicably and which we recognize by their phenomenological feel, although we may know perfectly well that at that moment there is nothing to be afraid of. Should we therefore conclude that the connection between feelings of fear and the belief that something harmful or dangerous is at hand, which occurs in the majority of cases of fear, is a purely contingent connection? This absurd conclusion is avoided by distinguishing between primary cases of fear and secondary cases. We are only able to use the concept in the secondary cases because we understand it in its primary application. So also with pain. There may be cases where we wish to assert an identity of sensation, sufficient to call the sensation "pain" between the central cases where the notion of pain is conceptually, though not analytically, tied to the notion of avoidance behavior and the marginal cases where learned inhibition or physiological interference has broken the link between the felt sensation and the behavior. If we say this, we are of course committed to disagreeing with Hare's view that we teach and learn the word "pain" by means of a guess based on the presence of a purely contingent criterion of pain, the external behavior. That Hare has to use the word "guess" to express his view is important; if he were right, there would always be room for doubt as to whether I had learned to understand the word correctly. But this doubt would apply to everybody, and where such a doubt applied there would be no sense to the notion of a correct understanding of the word. That is, the consequence to be drawn from Hare's view would in fact be that we had no clear concept of pain at all.

The view that I have outlined allows of course for the occurrence of cases of many kinds where pain is not accompanied by avoidance behavior; some of these cases present us with no difficulty at all, others such as the lobotomy cases are genuinely hard to understand. But it is crucial to note that the difficulty in understanding them does not arise from any philosophical theory about the meaning of "pain" and kindred words but from the language itself. The ordinary speaker is as puzzled as the philosopher by the avowals of such patients. The same is true of masochism.

The relevance of all this to pleasure has now to be brought out. It is, I hope, clear that there is no logical barrier to the existence of a vocabulary of pleasurable sensations, in which the identification of the sensation is tied to a certain type of behavioral response, so that where the response was lacking we should have at least a strong ground for inquiring whether the sensation could be the same. What is said of sensations would apply equally to tastes and smells. Let us apply the account I have given of pain to a parallel case of pleasure. If I put my hand in the fire and let it roast there, it can be explained either that I have trained myself to be heroically stoical in the face of pain and have some good reason for my action or that I am physiologically abnormal or anesthetized. What cannot be said is that I feel the pain just as anyone else would, am neither stoical nor abnormal or anesthetized, but just do not mind the pain. For my behaviour is a sufficient reason for concluding that if I am not being stoical, then, whatever I feel, it is not in any possible sense pain. Equally, if I when thirsty drink cold water from a mountain stream, and then spit it out in disgust, it may be explained that the water is polluted or that my mouth or throat is in an abnormal condition. But what cannot be said is that there is nothing wrong with the water and that my mouth and throat are in a normal condition, but that I just find the taste of cold water, which most people like, intolerable. For that someone finds such a taste intolerable is a sufficient reason for concluding that the taste cannot be the same taste that the rest of us experience. If someone finds sexual sensations not pleasurable but painful, he does not remark to himself that his likes and dislikes are those of a minority; he looks for a physiological cause of his abnormality.

That is to say, we do in fact treat certain tastes and sensations as pleasurable as such. If someone does not take pleasure in these, we look for an explanation of his failure in terms of the state of his body or his mind. The taste of cold water is not especially pleasurable perhaps; the tastes of Guinness or Chateau Yquem can be liked or disliked; we allow a wide range of variation to taste. But there is a limit to this range beyond which we explain lack of pleasure as we do lack of pain, in terms of the subject's discrepancy from norms of desire, norms which are embodied in parts of our vocabulary of pleasure and pain.

When I report what I enjoy, I am, unless there is reason to believe that I am insincere, the final authority on the truth of my report. When I report that an experience was or was not enjoyable or a sensation pleasurable, I can without insincerity be saying what is false. For the standard of the enjoyable and the pleasurable is not private, but public. *De gustibus est disputandum.* To call something pleasurable, therefore, is partly to say that it embodies the object of desire from the standpoint of the norms of desire. If I tell you that there is a fun-fair at the end of the pier I only give you a reason for going to the end of the pier if you happen to like fun-fairs and want to enjoy one now. If I tell you that fun-fairs are pleasurable, I may give you reason to believe that you would like them. Thus, statements about what is pleasurable do afford us in a special sense reasons for action. So the statement which I quoted from Dr. Kenny at the outset turns out to be true. It is also of course true that the prospect of pleasure will not move me to action unless I want pleasure at the given moment. But to ask why I want pleasure is indeed, as Dr. Kenny suggested, wrong-headed; because the notion of pleasure is the notion of a property of certain activities and experiences which are treated as standard objects of desire, which help to define not merely the desired, but the desirable. And to ask why I want what is desirable would only have point if I was thought to be in some way abnormal or perverse. That is, it may on occasion be asked why I should want pleasure. Moreover there are other desirable objects as well as pleasure; so that it makes sense to ask why I do *not* want pleasure at this moment. But it is after all not therefore true that, if a man wants pleasure, one can intelligently ask why. It is pleasant to discover that this obvious truth is an obvious truth after all.

18

The antecedents of action[1]

I

We are haunted by the ghosts of dead concepts. The trouble with
ghosts is that they do not replace the living satisfactorily and yet
do not leave us with an entirely vacant hearth either. One such
dead concept is the concept of the will; its ghost is the philosophical theory that the line which can be drawn between what is
a human action and what is a mere happening is such that actions
cannot have causes in the way that happenings can. When I speak
of the concept of the will I do not, of course, refer to pellucid
colloquialisms as in "Where there's a will there's a way" or "a
strong will"; I refer to the concept built up in post-medieval
philosophical psychology—in Hobbes, in Hume, and in Kant, for
example.

The exercise of the will in Hobbes distinguishes human action
from animal behavior because it presupposes a capacity for
deliberation. "In deliberation, the last Appetite, or Aversion,
immediately adhering to the action, or to the omission thereof, is
what we call the WILL; the Act (not the faculty) of *Willing*."[2]
The exercise of the will in Hume distinguishes human action
from muscular or nervous responses because it involves consciousness. "I desire it may be observed, that, by the *will*, I mean
nothing but the internal impression we feel, and are conscious of,
when we knowingly give rise to any new motion of our body, or
new perception of our mind."[3] The exercise of the will in Kant
marks out the human action from mere physical movement by
making action movement in accordance with and in obedience to

[1] Reprinted from *British Analytical Philosophy*, edited by Bernard
Williams and Alan Montefiore (London: Routledge & Kegan Paul;
New York: Humanities Press, 1966).

[2] *Leviathan*, I, 6.

[3] *Treatise*, II, iii, 1.

precepts or rules. "Everything in nature works according to laws. Rational beings alone have the faculty of acting . . . according to principles, i.e., have a *will*."[1]

The concept of acts of will which emerges from these quotations is one according to which the will is a special kind of efficient cause, the necessary cause of any human action. To make an act of will is to make a conscious and rational decision. It is to embody a precept for action in an instruction to oneself. Saying to oneself "So I will do such-and-such" sets one's limbs in motion. On occasion one may fail to set one's limbs in motion, just as any other cause may fail to operate if prior causes intervene. One's limbs are paralysed or shot away. The first requirement in explaining an action therefore is to assign a proximate cause to the action by pointing to a prior act of will. In Hobbes and Hume appetite or aversion inspire and inform such acts; in Kant the causal chains which terminate in inclination may always fail to operate because of the prior intervention of that uncaused cause, the autonomous rational will obeying its self-imposed categorical imperative.

This ancestry makes it less surprising that the concept of acts of will was later called upon to play opposite parts by different philosophers. In the mechanistic psychology which the utilitarians took over from Hartley all human actions are the determinate effects of prior causes, and in the causal chain the act of will is the immediate cause of the action. To some anti-determinist writers the will is the intervening cause which prevents human action being the mere outcome of events in the brain or the nervous system. So participants of both determinism and free will invoke "the will." For both parties, acts of will possess two characteristics which are used by later writers to attack their existence: they are events distinguishable from actions, always as a matter of contingent fact preceding them; and they are events necessarily connected with actions in that without them what followed would not be an action. It was in this way that H. A. Prichard, for example, wrote of acts of will. And it is in this way that his critics have written of them in order to cast doubt on their existence. But the point at which genuinely sharp criticism of the concept of the will began was not here; it was the dualism which the concept implied that first attracted hostile critical attention.

---

[1] *Fundamental Principles*, II.

II

The doctrine of acts of will from Hume to Prichard was formulated by philosophers who accepted a dualist view of body and
mind, and to this extent were true children of Descartes. This
dualism may have been refuted by Hegel, but in England, until
recently, Hegel and mystification were almost synonymous. The
refutation of Cartesian dualism was therefore in England the work
not of Hegel but of Professor Gilbert Ryle, a chapter of whose
The Concept of Mind is explicitly devoted to the will, but whose
argument throughout the book is extremely relevant.

The central argument of *The Concept of Mind* is that the criteria
for the application of those expressions which we use to describe
mental activity are all criteria of success or failure in performance
in the realm of overt behavior, and that therefore we neither
need nor have reason to postulate a realm of specifically mental
acts above and behind such behavior. Foremost among the
reasons which have misled philosophers into supposing that there
are such mental acts is a false view that those bodily movements
which are to count as human actions must have a special sort of
mental cause. The application of this doctrine to what I shall now
call the traditional view of acts of will is obvious.

Ryle in *The Concept of Mind* does not (at least nor usually) want
to deny the occurrence of any of the familiar "inner" events, such
as twinges or pains at one end of the scale or musings and interior
monologues at the other. What he does want to deny is that these
could have the characteristics which mental acts are alleged to have
in the traditional doctrine. In the case of acts of will, Ryle argues
that we cannot identify such acts (which he calls volitions) with
"such other familiar processes as that of resolving or making up
our minds to do something" or setting ourselves to do something.
For we know that there are many human actions which do not, in
fact, follow on such familiar processes, without thereby ceasing
to be human actions. But in the traditional doctrine any action
springs from an act of will. Hence these familiar processes and
events cannot be what the traditional doctrine wished to identify
as such acts.

Moreover, and here we return to Ryle's central argument, when
we describe actions by using such characteristic predicates as
"voluntary" or "responsible" or "done on purpose" or when we
insist that such-and-such a movement was not an action ("He was

pushed," "He slipped"), we seek to establish the truth of our description by reference to properties of the overt performance. We never deem it logically appropriate to inquire as to the presence or absence of acts of will. But if the traditional doctrine were correct, this would be the appropriate and the only appropriate question.

Ryle himself seems to place great weight on another line of argument with which it is less easy to be happy.

> No one ever says such things as that at 10 a.m. he was occupied in willing this or that, or that he performed five quick and easy volitions and two slow and difficult volitions between midday and lunch-time. ... Novelists describe the actions, remarks, gestures and grimaces, the daydreams, deliberations, qualms and embarrassments of their characters; but they never mention their volitions. They would not know what to say about them.

This appeal to what "no one ever says" or to what everybody does say is in itself ambiguous. It may simply be a way of underlining the point that actions can be adequately characterized in all possible ways without bringing in the notion of acts of will and that the occurrence of such acts is therefore an unnecessary hypothesis. But it suggests something else, in the form in which Ryle advances it; namely, treating ordinary nonphilosophical modes of speech as canonical for philosophical analysis.

If this is the thesis, it may once again be construed in two ways. A weak and unobjectionable version of the thesis is simply that any distinctions marked in ordinary language are likely to point to differences which philosophers ignore at their peril. But there is a stronger version of the thesis which must appear much more disputable. This is the thesis that "ordinary language is in order, just as it is" and that in the elucidation of what human action is, common speech is not merely a source of suggested distinctions, but provides us with hard criteria.

A quite different type of argument, which Ryle has used against what he takes to be mythological mental acts, has been advanced by A. I. Melden, specifically against the occurrence of volitions.[1] Melden argues that the concept of a volition involves an infinite and vicious regress. For, on the traditional view, to move my limbs I must first perform an act of will. But an act of will is itself an action which I peform. And every action has to be preceded by an act of will. So the performance of an act of will must itself be preceded by an act of will, and so proceed ad infinitum. So an

[1] *Free Action* (London: Routledge and Kegan Paul, 1961), Ch. 5.

infinite number of acts must precede any action and no action could ever be performed. This argument is clearly valid and effective, and, like Ryle, Melden supposes that whatever the traditional theorists were talking about when they spoke of acts of will, they were not speaking of our familiarly experienced making of resolutions, coming to decisions, and so on. About this one might be faintly dubious, if one remembered what Hobbes and Hume and Kant actually said. But for the moment let us put these doubts on one side.

III

The act of will was presented as the cause of the human action. But if there are no acts of will, as Ryle and Melden argue, do actions lack causes? Or have they quite other causes than acts of will? The discussion which has followed on from attempts to answer these questions can only be fruitful if we distinguish carefully between three senses of "cause," or at least between three ways in which causal questions can arise. There is first of all what is usually spoken of as Humean causality. This is the view of causality which springs from one of Hume's several and incompatible accounts and which was further developed by J. S. Mill. In this view one event is the cause of another, if and only if events of the former type have uniformly been observed to precede events of the latter type, and events of the latter type have uniformly been observed to follow events of the former type. The occurrence of the earlier event is both a necessary and a sufficient condition of the occurrence of the later event.

It is this concept of causality whose application has aroused controversy over determinism. If actions are the determined outcome of prior events, and presumably of prior physiological events, it has seemed difficult to draw a distinct line between an action and a mere reflex, and certainly difficult to draw the kind of distinction which would lead us to impute responsibility in one case and not in the other. It is, perhaps, because overtones of the determinist controversy lie in the background that discussions of the causality of actions have been directed so overwhelmingly toward Humean causality. But, in fact, no discussion could be carried to a successful conclusion unless it attended to at least two other senses or analyses.

One of these is the sense of "cause" which is equivalent to "necessary, but not necessarily sufficient, condition," a sense which is apparently rather than really simple. For very often when we speak of "the" cause of an event, for instance at a coroner's court in assigning responsibility for an accident, we point to a condition, by itself necessary but not sufficient for the occurrence of the accident. We do so when events were in train such that without the condition in question being satisfied the event would not have occurred. Taken by itself the condition was necessary but not sufficient. Taken in conjunction with all the other prior events, its satisfaction was sufficient to bring about the accident. So it is with the ice patch on the otherwise safe road. The point to note here is that what is by itself only a necessary condition for the occurrence of an event can be used to bring about the event, or can be referred to in giving a causal explanation of the event provided only that we know when its addition to other conditions is sufficient to produce the event. But by referring to such an occurrence as a cause we do not commit ourselves either to a generalization of the form "Whenever ice patches occur there is an accident" or to one of the form "There is never an accident unless there is an ice-patch," but only to one of the form "Whenever such-and-such other conditions occur, then, if there is an ice patch, there will be an accident." The importance of generalizations of this type needs much more attention, but for the moment we should only note that the task of detecting necessary conditions as it leads up to this type of generalization is inseparable from the task of detecting sufficient conditions and thus of formulating generalizations of the Humean type.

The third sense of "cause," or the third point about the sense of "cause," is one that is not incompatible with but required by the other two. This is the sense which was underlined by Professor H. L. A. Hart and Mr. A. M. Honoré in *Causation and the Law*. Here a cause is a lever, a means of producing some other event. There could be no well-established Humean generalizations unless we were able to interfere with the course of nature and so discover whether apparently uniform sequences were genuine ones or not. But the Hart-Honoré analysis brings out the importance for causality of the concept of what would have happened if the cause had not operated. All causal explanation presupposes a background of generalizations about what occurs in the absence of the cause. This is true of both cause understood in Hume's sense and of cause understood as necessary condition.

IV

This very inadequate sketch of causality is a necessary prelude to examining the two main attempts to show that actions cannot have causes, at least in the Humean sense. The first of these derives from an attempt to correct the assumption that the necessary and sufficient conditions of human action are to be found in prior physical events, an assumption which depends upon a companion assumption that human actions are in fact only extremely complex physical movements.

Against whom is this insistence directed? The answer is that a great deal of physiology and psychology has taken it for granted that this is correct. All attempts to explain human action by building cybernetic models assume that human actions are of the same kind as the movements of such models. The greatest of the behavior theorists of modern psychology, Tolman and Hull, set themselves the explicit goal of explaining human actions as very complex exemplifications of fundamentally simple patterns of physical movement. Those philosophers who have tried to show the falsity of this have clearly wanted a concept or set of concepts which will perform the function that the traditional concept of the will performed. But they have moved in a quite different direction.

In an article which tries to show that Hobbes and Hull were both essentially pursuing the same goal of mechanical explanations of human action, R. S. Peters and H. Tajfel have pointed out that bodily movements cannot be the genus of which human actions are a species, because the same bodily movements can be used in performing quite different actions and the same action can be performed by means of quite different bodily movements. So these bodily movements which are employed in writing a man's name may be used in signing a check, or giving an autograph, or authorizing a representative. Equally, the same action of paying a debt may be performed by those bodily movements involved in signing a check or by those involved in handing over coin. In other words, the criteria which we imply in judging that two bodily movements are the same or different are quite other than the criteria which we use in judging that two actions are the same or different.

Actions then cannot be identified with bodily movements. But while in the traditional view actions were bodily movements plus something else—namely, an act of will—for the more recent view this is equally incorrect and misleading. For to speak of human actions is to speak at a different logical level from that at which we speak of bodily movements. To call something an action is to invite the application of a quite different set of predicates from that which we invite if we call something a bodily movement. If I say "I moved my arm," I do not say either the same or more than I say if I say "My arm moved." I bring what occurred under a different form of description. We can bring out this difference in a number of ways. First, if we ask "Why did your arm move?" we invite a causal answer including perhaps a story about conditioned reflexes and a story about muscles and nerves. If we ask "Why did you move your arm?" we invite a story about intentions and purposes. Equally, if on being asked to explain a piece of behavior I start to give an account in terms of muscular and nervous mechanisms, I thereby treat the behavior as a piece of physical movement and not as an action. If, on the other hand, I talk about purposes, goals, desires, intentions, or the like, I thereby treat the behavior as an action. Secondly, if I say "I moved my arm," then the question "What reason did you have for doing that?" is always in place, even if the answer is, "I do not know why I did it." To say "I do not know" here is not to say "There is a reason, but I am ignorant of it" (except in psychoanalytic contexts, which demand special treatment). It is to say in effect "I had no reason, though I might have had." And nobody can know my reasons or lack of them, unless I tell or otherwise betray them. Here I have special and unique authority. But when it is a case where it is appropriate to say "My arm just moved," I have no such special authority in giving explanations. What is needed is not the authority of the agent as to his own intentions and purposes but the authority of the physiologist on matters concerning conditioned reflexes, nerves, and muscles.

Thirdly, in the standard cases at least where I say "I moved my arm," there is no room for the question "How do you know?" The reason for this can be brought out as follows. The point of asking "How do you know?" is to ask for the credentials of a claimant to knowledge in cases where the claimant to knowledge may be in either a better or worse position to back up his claim. "Pegasus won the 3.30." "How do you know?" "I was on the course," "I saw it on television," "My bookmaker told me," "I saw it in a dream" are all possible answers—of quite different value. But where self-knowledge of my own present actions is concerned, there is no question of being in a better or worse position to know.

And so there is no room for the question, "How do you know what you are doing?" But there is room for the question "How do you know?" where not actions but bodily movements are the subject of the inquiry. Usually, of course, the answer is very simple: "How do you know your arm moved?" "I felt it move," But from a partially anesthetized man, lying so that he could not see his arm, the answer "I saw it in the mirror" would make sense. And so would any other answer which appealed to observation or inference. Whereas this type of answer would make no sense as a reply to the question: "How do you know that you moved your arm?" (Indeed, this question, as I have already pointed out, lacks point except perhaps in some very special contexts. It does not follow that a man may not say "I moved my arm" outside those contexts and be mistaken. Where the question "How do you know?" lacks application there is still room for error.)

Fourthly, in cases where it is appropriate to say "I moved my arm" rather than "My arm moved" the future tense used before the event would express an intention, not a prediction, if used in the first person. Moreover, if it is appropriate to say of the event afterward "I moved my arm," then neither I nor anyone else could predict that I would move my arm except on the basis of a knowledge of my intentions. It does not however follow, as has sometimes been argued, that where an event is the object of my intention it cannot be the object of my prediction. What does follow is that the expression of my intention is never the expression of my prediction. But the expression of an intention and the expression of a prediction can be closely related; for if I express an intention, I license others to predict. Of course, whether they are wise to predict or not depends upon the evidence they possess as to how far I am usually faithful to my declared intentions. Now their beliefs (or their knowledge) on this point will be expressible upon occasion in the form of Humean generalizations. Moreover, I can acquire such knowledge about myself. A man may come to recognize his own reliability or unreliability. Consequently, even if it is psychologically out of the way, it is not conceptually odd for a man to say "I fully intend to do it tomorrow, but I know how unreliable I am, and so perhaps you are right and I will fail to do it again tomorrow." What is more, in the very framing of his intentions a man's self-knowledge and predictions about his own reliability inevitably come into play. Hence, in cases where it is appropriate to say "I shall move my arm," prediction is dependent upon knowledge of intention, but intention need not be entirely divorced from prediction; nevertheless, prediction depends not at all on knowledge of intention where it is in place to say "My arm will move."

Fifthly, the point of distinguishing between "My arm moved" and "I moved my arm" is brought out very clearly in just those borderline cases where we are uncertain which to say. We are all familiar—from novels if not from experience—with cases where, as we say,' the body seems to have taken control. In Sartre's novel *L'Age de Raison* the hero—no, the protagonist—Mathieu, intends to say to his mistress "I love you" and finds himself saying "I don't love you." Do we describe this as something he said or as words (or perhaps sounds) that come out of his mouth? Is it action or bodily movement? How we answer the question in this particular context does not matter for our present purposes. What does matter is that we cannot evade asking it, that we cannot escape the distinction between action and bodily movement.

Yet what follows about causality? Only that if we are to look for the causes of human actions, then we shall be in conceptual error if we look in the direction of the causes of the physical movements involved in the performance of the actions. It does not follow that there is no direction in which it would be fruitful to search for antecedent events which might function as causes. What has suggested this further conclusion is the way in which the investigation of concepts very close to the concept of action, such as that of intention, has been carried through. Wittgenstein wrote: " 'I am not ashamed of what I did then, but of the intention which I had.'[1] And didn't the intention reside *also* in what I did. ..."[1] Just because the intention resides *in* the action, it comes too close to it to play a causal role; nor could we say what the action was, apart from specifying the intention to at least some degree. An intention, unlike a cause, does not stand in an external, contingent relation to an action. When Miss G. E. M. Anscombe investigates the concept systematically in *Intention*, the whole discussion moves away from any kind of explanation in terms of causality, a topic to which Miss Anscombe alludes only in rare passages. One, but only one, reason why this is so can be brought out by considering how either in the kind of case which Miss Anscombe would classify as one of "mental causality" (I am startled by a noise and jump) or in the hard case where I make a decision and later act on it (with which Miss Anscombe does not deal) we should be missing the point if we looked for a Humean generalization to connect the noise and the jump or the decision and the action. I can know that I jumped because of the noise or

[1] *Philosophical Investigations*, Part I, para. 644.

that I acted because of the decision and know perfectly well that the generalizations "Whenever there is a noise of that sort, I jump in this way" and "Whenever I decide to do something, I do it" are false. Hence this kind of explanation of these actions at least must be in terms other than those of causality. Beginning from this point, the argument is sometimes generalized in the following way.

It is bodily movements which are to be causally explained and not human actions. Human actions are made intelligible by reference to intentions, purposes, decisions, and desires. These do not function as causes. They do not function as causes for at least two distinct reasons. The first is that to say "He did it because he intended so-and-so," or "He did it because he decided to" or "He did it because he wanted to" is in each case not necessarily to refer to two separately identifiable events, the doing on the one hand and the intending or desiring or deciding on the other. There may be cases where we first frame an intention, come to a decision, or experience a desire and then act; but the concepts of intention, decision, and desire are equally applicable where the action is itself the expression of intention, decision, or desire and to refer to our intention, decision, or desire in either explanation or justification of our action is not to refer to an antecedent event. But a cause must, so it is argued, always be a separate event from that which is its effect. So intentions, decisions, and desires cannot be causes. Secondly, intentions, decisions, and desires cannot be causes, for they are not causally but logically related to the relevant actions. How do I know that this intention relates to this action? Not by any observed correlation such as would be relevant in the case of causality. But because both intention and action are mine and the intention contained a description of the as yet unrealized action. The action is related to the intention as being what is described in the forming of the intention. "I'll have another cigarette in ten minutes' time." When I light up in ten minutes, I am faithful to my intention, but my intention has not made me light up.

Considerations such as these are invoked to support one of two theses. Either the weaker assertion is made which I have already described, that actions are to be explained in terms of intentions and kindred concepts and therefore, insofar as this is the case, they are not to be explained causally; or else the stronger assertion that causal explanations are out of court altogether so far as actions are concerned. Unfortunately, the most extended statement of this case is ambiguous to a certain extent. Melden says:

What I shall be concerned to deny . . . is that the term "cause" *when employed in these sciences* (physics and physiology) is applicable to those matters which, familiarly and on a common-sense level, we cite in order to explain action: the motives, desires, choices, decisions, etc., of human beings. I do not, of course, deny that there are appropriate senses of "cause" which can be intelligibly employed in these cases.[1]

And again he writes:

Indeed, it must appear problematic at best that the physiological psychologist who purports to be attempting to explain human action is addressing himself to his ostensible subject matter.[2]

While still later he says:

Here (in cases where I am predicting what someone whom I know will do) nothing is hidden; it is because I understand him, not because I am aware of events transpiring in some alleged mechanism of his mind or body, that I am able to say what he will do.[3]

These quotations can lend themselves to an interpretation in which all that Melden claims is that to explain actions citing purposes, intentions, desires, and the like is not to assign causes (in the Humean sense) or to another interpretation in which Melden is claiming that causal interpretations of human actions are ruled out of court altogether on conceptual grounds. The second quotation—apart from the fence-sitting use of "it must appear problematic at best"—seems to ensure that the latter is meant, but what I will presently try to do is to show that while the latter thesis is certainly untenable, even in the former interpretation, Melden's thesis needs amendment. Before that, however, an even more radical version of this view must be considered. It is more radical because it is more systematic. It arrives at the same conclusions as Melden's, but it derives them from independent foundations. The best-known exposition of this point of view is Dr. Friedrich Waismann's in *Language Strata*. Waismann wished to campaign against the view that language is unitary, all of a piece, that truth, rationality, and meaningfulness are one and the same for every sort of statement. Against this he urged the notion of language as composed of different strata, each with its own criteria

[1] *Free Action*, pp. 16–17.
[2] *Ibid.*, p. 72.
[3] *Ibid.*, p. 208.

of truth and meaning. An expression may be ambiguous in that it can figure in different contexts in different strata, and so take on different meanings. With this thesis so far my present argument does not require me to raise any questions. But Waismann then, although he allows that there are relationships between strata, characterizes the ambiguity of the word "action" in such a way as to exclude relationship between the stratum in which it is proper to speak of causes and that in which it is proper to speak of motives. It follows that anything which can be explained by reference to motives cannot be explained by reference to causes and vice versa.

In like manner we say that each stratum has a logic of its own and that this logic determines the meaning of certain basic terms. In some respects this is obvious. Whether a melody is a sequence of air-vibrations, of a succession of musical notes, or a message of the composer, depends entirely on the way you describe it. Similarly, you may look at a game of chess, or on the pattern of a carpet from very different aspects and you will then see in them very different things. Notice how all these words—"melody," "game of chess," etc.—take on a systematic ambiguity according to the language stratum in which you talk. The same applies to "doing a sum," "writing a letter," or to any action indeed. An action may be viewed as a series of movements caused by some physiological stimulus in the "Only rats, no men" sense; or as something that has a purpose or meaning irrespective of the way its single links are produced. An action in the first sense is determined by causes, an action in the second sense by *motives* or *reasons*. It is generally believed that an action is determined both by causes and by motives. But if the causes determine the action, no room is left for motives, and if the motives determine the action, no room is left for causes. Either the system of causes is complete, then it is not possible to squeeze in a motive; or the system of motives is complete, then it is not possible to squeeze in a cause. "Well now, do you believe that if you are writing a letter you are engaged in two different activities?" No; I mean that there are two different ways of looking at the thing; just as there are two different ways of looking at a sentence: as a series of noises produced by a human agent; or as a vehicle for thought. For a series of noises there may be causes but no reasons; for a series of words expressing thought there may be reasons, but no causes. What is understood is that the word "action" has a systematic ambiguity.[1] (pp. 30–31).

[1] *Language Strata*, pp. 30–31.

V

What is at stake in these arguments? Not only philosophical clarity, but also the question of the nature of the human sciences. For if philosophical argument can show that actions cannot have causes, then a good deal of science is fatally confused, since scientists do in fact attempt to offer causal explanations of action. Some physiologists have, indeed, done us a disservice by offering explanations of reflexes and calling these explanations of action, but in more than one field there appear to be genuine, if tentative, causal explanations of action. I refer to criminology and also to the study of the effects of drugs. (The study of hypnosis is interesting, but raises special issues.)

Some changes in the chemistry of the body which are brought about by taking drugs correlate with highly specific alterations in behavior. More than this, we can alter the way in which people behave by inducing such changes in body chemistry. These changes range from the medical use of insulin in highly artificial laboratory experiments to buying a man a drink. What is correlated with the chemical change is a type of action and not just a type of bodily movement. That is to say, the framing of intentions, deliberations, reflection on wishes and desires and the like all play their normal roles. It may be that in many cases the type of action which is produced by the chemical changes cannot be narrowly specified. That is, we can say that to give this type of man this type of drug will make him act more irritably or unscrupulously or excitably rather than specify in more detail what he will do. But in these cases we are none the less involved in explaining behavior.

Again, in criminology the work that has shown that there is a hereditary element in criminality is much to the point. The key studies on inherited characteristics in human beings are those which compare the degree to which such characteristics are shared by two siblings in the case of monozygotic and dizygotic twins respectively, for it would seem an unassailable conclusion that a clearly higher concordance in cases of monozygotic twins would indicate a hereditary factor. This is how the existence of a hereditary factor in tuberculosis was established for a study in New York in 1934, for example, which showed a 63 per cent concordance in monozygotic twins and only an 18 per cent concordance in dizygotic, while one in London in 1957 showed a 30 per cent concordance in monozygotic and only a 13 per cent concordance in dizygotic. Now, in exactly the same way, a hereditary factor in adult criminality can be established. For on the basis of five studies we have a concordance with monozygotic twins of 68 per cent and one with dizygotic of only 35 per cent. I need to insist that what were studied here were criminal actions, and that the fact that nobody supposes that heredity is more than a partial (and perhaps not enormously important) explanation of criminality does not make this any the less a causal explanation. Nor, if it makes sense to use such figures to provide an explanation, could it make nonsense if the figures turned out to be different, to be, for example, 100 per cent in the case of monozygotic twins and zero per cent in the case of dizygotic. This would make our explanation somewhat less partial.

What then are we to make of this situation in which some philosophers appear to assert that causal explanations of human action cannot be given, while some scientists assert that they have produced them? Can we safely treat the scientists as we would treat men who claimed to have invented a perpetual motion machine? Or are the philosophers like the old lady at the zoo who looked at the giraffe and said "It's impossible"?

VI

Let us begin with the most general form of the argument that actions cannot have causes, Waismann's. It is beyond the scope of this essay to question in general terms the widely influential, but profoundly misleading view of language contained in Waismann's paper. What one must note is that unless there were expressions and criteria which transcended the divisions between his language strata, he could not distinguish them in the way he does. He can, for instance, recognize, and has to recognize in order to specify the ambiguity of "action" in the way he does, that certain movements caused by physiological stimuli use the movements which are the "single links" of this particular action and of no other. So that we are able to say "These movements" (one stratum of language) "belong to this action" (a quite different stratum). It follows that statements are not necessarily confined to one particular logical order or type or stratum (however these are specified). And now we have to note that an expression that cannot be so confined is the word "cause" and its logical kith and kin. For Waismann speaks of the bodily movement by which an action is "produced." And "produce" is certainly a causal verb. Moreover, he speaks of a melody as though to speak of a sequence of air vibrations is to remain within one language stratum, but to speak of a succession of musical notes is to move to another. But clearly one cause, in a perfectly acceptable and unambiguous sense of "cause," of a set of notes succeeding one another in a piece of music to which we are listening is precisely the sequence of air vibrations which the orchestra have produced. Without having read Waismann, we might well want to say that the notion of color is of a different logical order from that of a wavelength of light. But we unhesitatingly explain alterations in color as caused by changes in the wavelength of light. So that, although the notion of bodily movements may be of a different logical order from that of an action, it certainly cannot follow that the word "cause" is restricted to the stratum to which "bodily movement" belongs and denied to the stratum to which "action" belongs.

If we then disallow Waismann's contentions, the arguments that actions cannot have causes are best dealt with not by denying the importance of the type of example to which such arguments appeal, but by considering counter-examples. The suggestion will be that all the ordinary senses of causality apply *in some cases* to human actions and that therefore the "ordinary language" use of "cause" in this connection is by no means as remote from Humean causality as some suggest. (For an "ordinary language" use, consider: "The Minister, receiving the Woman at her father's or friend's hands, shall cause the Man with his right hand to take the Woman by her right hand . . ." [Book of Common Prayer, Form of Solemnization of Matrimony.]

The first example is of *giving a reason* or *affording a motive* as causes. I may discover that when you are in a certain frame of mind I can get you to act by giving you information which affords a motive or a reason. Your action bears testimony to the fact that it was this motive or reason on which you were acting (as returning a ring with a reproachful letter is testimony that the girl's motive arises from her information about the man's behavior). Thus the connection between affording the motive and the action is not one of a Humean kind; we do not depend on a universal generalization of whose truth we need to be assured in order to make the connection. Even if another occasion affording the same kind of motive does not produce the same action, we should not have grounds for doubting what caused the girl to act in the way she did on the first occasion. And the word "caused" is in place precisely because of our third sense of causality. Affording a motive or a reason is performing a separately identifiable and desirable act, the performance of which is a lever that produces as its effects an action. And it is quite compatible with the thesis that motives, reasons, decisions, and intentions cannot be causes that affording motives, giving reasons, giving grounds for decisions, and for framing intentions can be. Nor is this merely something that others can do to me; I can in deliberation do this to myself. (This is not to be committed to the view that deliberation is always conversation with oneself, but only to the view that it can on occasion be.)

Secondly, "the" cause of an action may, like "the" cause of an accident, be a necessary condition, the satisfaction of which is with other circumstances sufficient to produce the action. An insult may not make me violent when I am sober; and when I am even mildly drunk I may be extremely pleasant except when and until I am insulted. So the insult plays in relation to the action the part that the icy patch on the road plays in relation to the accident.

Thirdly, we are already well on the way to formulating explanations of actions in terms of Humean causality. I am puzzled by why I become angry when playing cards. Both others and myself presently observe that it occurs five minutes after I have started to lose. This connection is uniformly observed to hold until I become aware of it. People who wish to make me angry have learned that I become angry and perform angry actions if they bring about my defeat at cards. This is a perfect case of Humean causality and nothing is affected if I change my behavior on discovering its cause. For the generalization which needed to be discovered by observation was that "Whenever I am losing at cards, and so long as I do not know what is going to happen to my behavior as a result, I shortly after become angry." Or it may be that I cannot alter my behavior. Obviously, it does not follow that I am inevitably going to be angry; but if I wish to avoid angry behavior then I must not lose at cards, and probably I must not play cards.

These examples only skim the topic of the causality of action. What they do show is the danger of any generalization of the form "Actions cannot have causes" or even "Actions cannot have Humean causes." Such generalizations are necessarily as erroneous as were the generalizations of the eighteenth-century mechanists who thought of every action as caused. What we need is a much fuller characterization of the concept of the human person in which the role of both causes on the one hand and of motives, reasons, and intentions on the other will become clear. But about two distorting features of the discussion hitherto we can now perhaps become clear.

The first is that the dichotomy "logical connection" or "causal connection" is much too easy, here as elsewhere. Consider the kind of case where an insult always leads to taking offense. "Every Celt when insulted uses whatever weapons lie to hand" can be the expression of a good Humean generalization (even if false). Now the description of the first action as "an insult" and of the second as "taking offense" brings them under descriptions which are conceptually and internally related. But the two events are separately identified and we can correlate them. We know what it would be for the causal generalization to be falsified by an insult not causing offense or offense being taken without insult. The root error here is to think of actions as standing in relationship to the agents' motives and reasons or to other agents' behavior independently of the alternative forms of description under which behavior can fall.

The second distorting factor is the fear of determinism. This perhaps springs from accepting a determinist view of the Hume-Mill concept of causality. But to show that an action is caused is not necessarily to show that it must have happened, that the agent could not alter what he did. For to assign a cause to a happening is to go some way to informing us both how to produce and how to inhibit the happening in question. It follows from this that to assign causal explanations to actions is not to show that the actions in question are inevitable and unalterable. Nor does it even follow that if the explanations in question are explanations of *my* actions, *I* cannot alter them. But it certainly does follow that the more I know about possible and actual causal explanations of my behavior the more likely I am to be able to intervene successfully and control what I do. Free, responsible, controlled behavior is, then, behavior where I have at least the possibility of successful intervention (though this is to state only a necessary, and not a sufficient, condition for being entitled to characterize a piece of behavior in this way).

This argument needs one addition. My freedom as an agent depends upon my ability to frame intentions which are capable of being implemented. This capability is dependent on the reliability of my beliefs about the world and about myself: it is not just that given motives, desires, and intentions of a certain sort, I act. A presupposition of successful action is a knowledge of what I will do unless I intervene in various ways. So the concept of intention cannot be understood in isolation from the role of belief and knowledge in our behavior. The way in which this is so is brought out most clearly by the argument of Stuart Hampshire in *Thought and Action*, especially Chapter 3. Hampshire uses the distinction between intention and prediction in a much more illuminating way than it is used by those who are trying to separate action and causation. For, as I argued earlier, there is a positive connection between intention and prediction. Unless I am able to predict what will happen if I do and again what will happen if I do not frame a given intention, I am in no position to frame intentions at all. Thus, what I can intend depends upon what I can predict, and the dependence of the concept of human action upon the concept of intention does not exclude the possibility of prediction based on causal explanation from the realm of human action, but actually depends upon that possibility. That others can predict my actions does not matter unless they are able to predict what these are, no matter what my intentions are. My freedom consists, as Hampshire has argued, not in my unpredictability but in my ability to form clear intentions *and* to implement them. And this freedom depends on my ability to intervene in causal sequences, including those which have resulted in parts of my own behavior to date.

The mistake that we might make in conclusion would be to suppose that because my main argument has been an attack on the generalizations of others, nothing definitive follows from it. I followed through the attack on the doctrine of acts of will and showed that the corollary to its destruction was the need to elaborate a much more complex view of the person. But some very simple conceptual truths still need emphasis, and one of them at least belonged to the view of the will which Ryle and Melden attempted to destroy.

The exponents of the traditional doctrine of acts of will were clearly wrong to hold that every act of a rational agent is preceded by an act of will which is its cause. They took what they thought to be the paradigm case of rational action, deliberation leading to conscious decision which issues in action, and supposed that the characteristics of the paradigm case must hold in every case. But were they wrong in their characterization of the paradigm? Where I act without deliberation or on impulse, where I provide one of the cases which appear to Ryle and Melden to destroy the traditional doctrine, what makes me responsible for what I do? Or where causal explanations of my anger are in place, what, if anything, makes me responsible? Presumably, that I could, had I reason so to frame an intention, decide not to do what I in fact do, not to let my impulses have their way or not to be angry; that I could deliberate (the "could" means here that it makes sense to speak of my deliberating; in many actual occasions I might have no time or opportunity to deliberate) and decide on some other course of action. In other words, that I could perform an act of will in the traditional sense. If we read Hobbes, Hume and Kant as characterizing not the necessary prerequisites for something to be classed as an action but as characterizing the type of action which one must be able to perform on occasion, the type of intervention, inhibiting one course of action or unleashing another, which one must be able to make on occasion if one is to be classed as a responsible and rational agent at all, then the arguments of Ryle and Melden become irrelevant. For acts of will are, as the traditional authors clearly state, the familiar and un-assailable processes of resolving, deciding, and intending and not the mysterious and occult "volitions" with which Ryle and Melden make so much play. There is nothing here with which novelists and ordinary agents are not familiar in their everyday transactions; and there is no requirement that every action shall be preceded by a volition, which may result in an infinite regress. There is only the requirement that we shall recognize that it is in virtue of what they can be and not of what they always are that men are called rational animals.

19

The idea of a social science[1]

My aim in this essay is to express dissent from the position taken in Mr. Peter Winch's book[2] whose title is also the title of this essay. Winch's book has been the subject of a good deal of misunderstanding, and he has been accused on the one hand of reviving familiar and long-refuted views[3] and on the other of holding views so eccentric in relation to social science as it actually is that they could not possibly have any practical effect on the conduct of that science.[4] In fact, however, Winch articulates a position which is at least partly implicit in a good deal of work already done, notably in anthropology, and he does so in an entirely original way. He writes in a genre recognizable to both sociologists and philosophers. Talcott Parsons and Alain Touraine have both found it necessary to preface their sociological work by discussions of norms and actions and have arrived at rather different conclusions from those of Winch; the importance of his work is therefore undeniable.

I

"Wittgenstein says somewhere that when one gets into philosophical difficulties over the use of some of the concepts of our language, we are like savages confronted with something from an alien culture. I am simply indicating a corollary of this: that sociologists who misinterpret an alien culture are like philosophers getting into difficulty over the use of their own concepts."

[1] © Aristotelian Society, 1967. Reprinted from the *Aristotelian Society Supplementary Volume* 1967, pp. 95–114.
[2] *The Idea of a Social Science* (London: Routledge and Kegan Paul, 1958).
[3] See, for example, Richard Rudner, *The Philosophy of Social Science* (Englewood, N.J.: Prentice-Hall, 1967), pp. 81–83.
[4] See A. R. Louch's review in *Inquiry*, 1963, 273.

This passage (p. 114) epitomizes a central part of Winch's thesis with its splendid successive characterizations of the figure baffled by an alien culture; a savage at one moment, he has become a sociologist at the next. And this is surely no slip of the pen. According to Winch, the successful sociologist has simply learned all that the ideal native informant could tell him; sociological knowledge is the kind of knowledge possessed in implicit and partial form by the members of a society rendered explicit and complete (p. 88). It is not at first entirely clear just how far Winch is at odds in this contention with, for example, Malinowski, who insisted that the native Trobriander's account of Trobriand society must be inadequate, that the sociologists' account of institutions is a construction not available to the untutored awareness of the native informant.[1] For Winch of course is willing to allow into the sociologist's account concepts "which are not taken from the forms of activity which he is investigating; but which are taken rather from the context of his own investigation," although he adds that "these technical concepts will imply a prior understanding of those other concepts which belong to the activities under investigation." Perhaps this might seem sufficient to remove the apparent disagreement of Winch and Malinowski, until we remember the conclusion of Malinowski's critique of the native informant's view. The sociologist who relies upon that view, he says, "obtains at best that lifeless body of laws, regulations, morals and conventionalities which *ought* to be obeyed, but in reality are often only evaded. For in actual life rules are never entirely conformed to, and it remains, as the most difficult but indispensable part of the ethnographer's work, to ascertain the extent and mechanism of the deviations."[2] This makes two points clear.

First, Malinowski makes a distinction between the rules acknowledged in a given society and the actual behavior of individuals in that society, whereas Winch proclaims the proper object of sociological study to be that behavior precisely as rule-governed. The second is that in the study of behavior Malinowski is willing to use notions such as that of mechanism which are clearly causal; whereas Winch warns us against comparing sociological understanding with understanding in terms of "statistics and causal laws" and says of the notion of

[1] Bronislaw Malinowski, *The Sexual Life of Savages in North-Western Melanesia* (New York: Harcourt, Brace & Jovanovich; London: Routledge & Kegan Paul, 1932), pp. 425–29.

[2] *Ibid.*, pp. 428–29.

function, so important to Malinowski, that it "is a quasi-causal notion, which it is perilous to apply to social institutions" (p. 116).

It does appear therefore that although Winch and Malinowski agree in seeing the ideal native informant's account of his own social life as incomplete by comparison with the ideal sociologist's account, they do disagree about the nature of that incompleteness and about how it is to be remedied. My purpose in this essay will be to defend Malinowski's point of view on these matters against Winch's, but this purpose can only be understood if one reservation is immediately added. It is that in defending Malinowski's views on these points I must not be taken to be endorsing Malinowski's general theoretical position. I have in fact quoted Malinowski on these matters, but I might have quoted many other social scientists. For on these matters Malinowski speaks with the consensus.

II

"A regularity or uniformity is the constant recurrence of the same kind of event on the same kind of occasion; hence statements of uniformities presuppose judgments of identity. But ... criteria of identity are necessarily relative to some rule: with the corollary that two events which count as qualitatively similar from the point of view of one rule would count as different from the point of view of another. So to investigate the type of regularity studied in a given inquiry is to examine the nature of the rule according to which judgments of identity are made in that inquiry. Such judgments are intelligible only relatively to a given mode of human behavior, governed by its own rules" (pp. 83–84).

This passage is the starting point for Winch's argument that J. S. Mill was mistaken in supposing that to understand a social institution is to formulate empirical generalizations about regularities in human behavior, generalizations which are causal and explanatory in precisely the same sense that generalizations in the natural sciences are. For the natural scientist makes the relevant judgments of identity according to *his* rules (that is, the rules incorporated in the practice of his science); whereas the social scientist must make his judgments of identity in accordance with the rules governing the behavior of those whom he studies. *Their* rules, not *his*, define the object of his study. "So it is quite mistaken in principle to compare the activity of a student of a form of social behavior with that of, say, an engineer studying the working of a machine. If we are going to compare the social student to an engineer, we shall do better to compare him to an apprentice engineer who is studying what engineering—that is, the activity of engineering—is all about" (p. 88).

What the type of understanding which Winch is commending consists in is made clearer in two other passages. He says that although prediction is possible in the social sciences, it "is quite different from predictions in the natural sciences, where a falsified prediction always implies some sort of mistake on the part of the predictor: false or inadequate data, faulty calculation, or defective theory" (pp. 91–92). This is because "since understanding something involves understanding its contradictory, someone who, with understanding, performs X must be capable of envisaging the possibility of doing not-X" (p. 91). Where someone is following a rule, we cannot predict how he will interpret what is involved in following that rule in radically new circumstances; where decisions have to be made, the outcome "cannot be *definitely* predicted," for otherwise "we should not call them decisions."

These points about prediction, if correct, reinforce Winch's arguments about the difference between the natural sciences and the social sciences. For they amount to a denial of that symmetry between explanation and prediction which holds in the natural sciences. (It has been argued often enough that this symmetry does not hold in the natural sciences; Professor Adolf Grünbaum's arguments in Chapter 9 of the *Philosophy of Space and Time* seem a more than adequate rebuttal of these positions.) But when we consider what Winch says here about decision, it is useful to take into account at the same time what he says about motives and reasons. Winch treats these as similar in this respect: that they are made intelligible by reference to the rules governing the form of social life in which the agent participates. So Winch points out that "one can act 'from considerations' only where there are accepted standards of what is appropriate to appeal to" (p. 82) and argues against Ryle that the "law-like proposition" in terms of which someone's reasons must be understood concerns not the agent's disposition "but the accepted standards of reasonable behavior current in his society" (p. 81).

From all this one can set out Winch's view of understanding and explanations in the social sciences in terms of a two-stage model. An action is *first* made intelligible as the outcome of motives, reasons, and decisions; and is then made *further* intelligible by those motives, reasons, and decisions being set in the context of the rules of a given form of social life. These rules logically determine the range of reasons and motives open to a given set of agents and hence also the range of decisions open to them. Thus Winch's contrast between explanation in terms of causal generalizations and explanations in terms of rules turns out to rest upon a version of the contrast between explanations in terms of causes and explanations in terms of reasons. This latter contrast must therefore be explored, and the most useful way of doing this will be to understand better what it is to act for a reason.

Many analyses of what it is to act for a reason have written into them an incompatibility between acting for a reason and behaving from a cause, just because they begin from the apparently simple and uncomplicated case where the action is actually performed, where the agent had one and only one reason for performing it, and where no doubt could arise for the agent as to why he had done what he had done. By concentrating attention upon this type of example, a basis is laid for making central to the analyses a contrast between the agent's knowledge of his own reasons for acting and his and others' knowledge of causes of his behavior. For clearly in such a case the agent's claim that he did X for reason Y does not seem to stand in need of any warrant from a generalization founded upon observation; while equally clearly any claim that one particular event or state of affairs was the cause of another does stand in need of such a warrant. But this may be misleading. Consider two somewhat more complex cases than that outlined above. The first is that of a man who has several quite different reasons for performing a given action. He performs the action; how can he as agent know whether it was the conjoining of all the different reasons that was sufficient for him to perform the action or whether just one of the reasons was by itself alone sufficient or whether the action was over-determined in the sense that there were two or more reasons, each of which would by itself alone have been sufficient? The problem arises partly because to know that one or other of these possibilities was indeed the case entails knowing the truth of certain unfulfilled conditionals.

A second case worth considering is that of two agents, each with the same reasons for performing a given action; one does not in fact perform it, the other does. Neither agent had what seemed to him a good reason or indeed had any reason for not performing the action in question. Here we can ask what made these reasons or some subset of them productive of action in the one case, but not in the other? In both these types of case we need to distinguish between the agent's having a reason for

8

performing an action (not just in the sense of there being a reason for him to perform the action, but in the stronger sense of his being aware that he has such a reason) and the agent's being actually moved to action by his having such a reason. The importance of this point can be brought out by reconsidering a very familiar example, that of post-hypnotic suggestion.

Under the influence of post-hypnotic suggestion a subject will not only perform the action required by the hypnotist, but will offer apparently good reasons for performing it, while quite unaware of the true cause of the performance. So someone enjoined to walk out of the room might, on being asked why he was doing this, reply with all sincerity that he had felt in need of fresh air or decided to catch a train. In this type of case we would certainly not accept the agent's testimony as to the connection between reason and action, unless we are convinced of the untruth of the counter-factual. "He would have walked out of the room, if no reason for doing so had occurred to him" and the truth of the counter-factual, "He would not have walked out of the room, if he had not possessed some such reason for so doing." The question of the truth or otherwise of the first of these is a matter of the experimentally established facts about post-hypnotic suggestion, and these facts are certainly expressed as causal generalizations. To establish the truth of the relevant generalization would entail establishing the untruth of the second counter-factual. But since to establish the truth of such causal generalizations entails consequences concerning the truth or untruth of generalizations about reasons, the question inevitably arises as to whether *the possession of a given reason* may not be the cause of an action in precisely the same sense in which hypnotic suggestion may be the cause of an action. The chief objection to this view has been that the relation of reason to action is internal and conceptual, not external and contingent, and cannot therefore be a causal relationship; but although nothing could count as a reason unless it stood in an internal relationship to an action, *the agent's possessing a reason* may be a state of affairs identifiable independently of the event which is *the agent's performance of the action*. Thus it does seem as if the possession of a reason by an agent is an item of a suitable type to figure as a cause, or an effect. But if this is so then to ask whether it was the agent's reason that roused him to act is to ask a causal question, the true answer to which depends upon what causal generalizations we have been able to establish. This puts in a different light the question of the agent's authority as to what roused him to act;

for it follows from what has been said that this authority is at best prima facie. Far more of course needs to be said on this and related topics; but perhaps the argument so far entitles us to treat with skepticism Winch's claim that understanding in terms of rule-following and causal explanations have mutually exclusive subject matters.

This has obvious implications for social science, and I wish to suggest some of these in order to provide direction for the rest of my argument. Clearly if the citing of reasons by an agent, with the concomitant appeal to rules, is not necessarily the citing of those reasons which are causally effective, a distinction may be made between those rules which agents in a given society sincerely profess to follow and to which their actions may in fact conform, but which do not in fact direct their actions, and those rules which, whether they profess to follow them or not, do in fact guide their acts by providing them with reasons and motives for acting in one way rather than another. The making of this distinction is essential to the notions of *ideology* and of *false consciousness*, notions which are extremely important to some non-Marxist as well as to Marxist social scientists.

But to allow that these notions could have application is to find oneself at odds with Winch's argument at yet another point. For it seems quite clear that the concept of ideology can find application in a society where the concept is not available to the members of the society, and furthermore that the application of this concept implies that criteria beyond those available in the society may be invoked to judge its rationality; and as such it would fall under Winch's ban as a concept unsuitable for social science. Hence there is a connection between Winch's view that social science is not appropriately concerned with causal generalizations and his view that only the concepts possessed by the members of a given society (or concepts logically tied to those concepts in some way) are to be used in the study of that society. Furthermore, it is important to note that Winch's views on those matters necessarily make his account of rules and their place in social behavior defective.

III

The examples which Winch gives of rule-following behavior are very multifarious: games, political thinking, musical composition, the monastic way of life, an anarchist's way of life, are all cited. His only example of non-rule-governed behavior is "the pointless behavior of a berserk lunatic" (p. 53), and he asserts roundly "that all behavior which is meaningful (therefore all specifically human behavior) is *ipso facto* rule-governed." Winch allows for different kinds of rules (p. 52); what he does not consider is whether the concept of a rule is perhaps being used so widely that quite different senses of *rule-governed* are being confused, let alone whether his account of meaningful behavior can be plausibly applied to some actions at all.

If I go for a walk, or smoke a cigarette, are my actions rule-governed in the sense in which my actions in playing chess are rule-governed? Winch says that "the test of whether a man's actions are the application of a rule is ... whether it makes sense to distinguish between a right and a wrong way of doing things in connection with what he does." What is the wrong way of going for a walk? And, if there is no wrong way, is my action in any sense rule-governed? To ask these questions is to begin to bring out the difference between those activities which form part of a coherent mode of behavior and those which do not. It is to begin to see that although many actions must be rule-governed in the sense that the concept of some particular kinds of action may involve reference to a rule, the concept of an action as such does not involve such a reference. But even if we restrict our attention to activities which form part of some coherent larger whole, it is clear that rules may govern activity in quite different ways. This is easily seen if we consider the variety of uses to which social scientists have put the concept of a role and role concepts.

Role concepts are at first sight peculiarly well-fitted to find a place in the type of analysis of which Winch would approve. S. F. Nadel wrote that "the role concept is not an invention of anthropologists or sociologists but is employed by the very people they study," and added that "it is the existence of names describing classes of people which make us think of roles." It would therefore be significant for Winch's thesis if it were the case that role concepts had to be understood in relation to causes, if they were to discharge their analytic and explanatory function.

Consider first a use of the notion of role where causal questions do not arise. In a society such as ours there are a variety of roles which an individual may assume or not as he wills. Some occupational roles provide examples. To live out such a role is to make one's behavior conform to certain norms. To speak of one's behavior being governed by the norms is to use a sense of "governed" close to that according to which the behavior of a chess player is governed by the rules of chess. We are not disposed to say that the rules of chess or the norms which define the role of a headwaiter constrain the individual who conforms to them. The observation of the rules constitutes the behavior and what it is; it is not a causal agency.

Contrast with this type of example the inquiry carried on by Erving Goffmann in his book *Asylums*. One of Goffmann's concerns was to pose a question about mental patients: how far are the characteristic patterns of behavior which they exhibit determined, not by the nature of the mental disorders from which they suffer, but by the nature of the institutions to which they have been consigned? Goffmann concludes that the behavior of patients is determined to a considerable degree by institutional arrangements which provide a severely limited set of possible roles both for patients and for the doctors and orderlies with whom they have to deal. Thus the behavior of individual patients of a given type might be explained as the effect of the role arrangements open to a person of his type. In case it is thought that the role structure of mental hospitals only has a causal effect upon the patients because they are *patients* (and the implication might be that they are not therefore rational agents but approach the condition of the exception Winch allows for, that of the berserk lunatic) it is worth noting that Goffmann's study of mental hospitals is part of a study of what he calls "total institutions." These include monasteries and armed services as well as mental hospitals. A successful terminus to his inquiry would therefore be the foundation of generalizations about the effects upon agents of different types of character of the role structure of such different types of institution.

If Winch were correct, and rule-governed behavior were not to be understood as causal behavior, then the contrast could not be drawn between those cases in which the relation of social structure to individuals may be correctly characterized in terms of control or constraint and those in which it may not. Winch's inability to make this contrast adequately in terms of his conceptual scheme is the counterpart to Durkheim's inability to make it adequately in terms of his; and the resemblance of Winch's failure to Durkheim's is illuminating in that Winch's position is, roughly speaking, that of Durkheim turned upside down. Durkheim in a passage cited by Winch insisted, first, "that social life should be explained, not by the notions of those who participate in it, but by more profound causes which are unperceived by consciousness" and, secondly, "that these causes are to be sought mainly in the manner according to which the associated individuals are grouped."[1] That is, Durkheim supposes, just as Winch does, that an investigation of social reality which uses the concepts available to the members of the society being studied, and an investigation of social reality which utilizes concepts not so available and invokes causal explanations of which the agents themselves are not aware, are mutually exclusive alternatives. But Durkheim supposes, as Winch does not, that the latter alternative is the one to be preferred. Yet his acceptance of the same dichotomy involves him in the same inability to understand the different ways in which social structure may be related to individual action.

Durkheim's concept of *anomie* is the concept of a state in which the constraints and controls exercised by social structure have been loosened and the bonds which delimit and contain individual desire have therefore been at least partially removed. The picture embodied in the Durkheimian concept is thus one according to which the essential function of norms in social life is to restrain and inhibit psychological drives. For Durkheim, rules are an external imposition upon a human nature which can be defined independently of them; for Winch, they are the guidelines of behavior which, did it not conform to them, could scarcely be human. What is equally odd in both is the way in which rules or norms are characterized as though they were all of a kind. Durkheim is unable to recognize social structure apart from the notions of constraint and control by the structure; Winch's concept of society has no room for these notions.

Just as Winch does not allow for the variety of relationships in which an agent may stand to a rule to which his behavior conforms, so he does not allow also for the variety of types of deviance from rules which behavior may exhibit. I quoted Malinowski earlier on the important gap between the rules professed in a society and the behavior actually exhibited. On this Winch might well comment that his concern is with human behavior as rule-following, not only with mere professions of rule-following, except insofar as professing to follow rules is itself a human and (for him) *ipso facto* a rule-following activity. Moreover he explicitly allows that "since understanding something involves understanding its contradictory, someone who, with understanding, performs X must be capable of envisaging the possibility of doing not-X." He makes this remark in the context of his discussion of predictability; and what he does not allow for in this discussion is that in fact the behavior of agents may exhibit

[1] Review of A. Labriola's *Essays on Historical Materialism*.

regularities of a Humean kind and be predictable just as natural events are predictable, even though it can also be characterized and in some cases must also be characterized in terms of following and deviating from certain rules. That this is so makes it possible to speak not only, as Malinowski does in the passage quoted earlier, of mechanisms of deviation, but also of mechanisms of conformity. Of course those who deviate from the accepted rules may have a variety of reasons for so doing, and insofar as they share the same reasons their behavior will exhibit rule-following regularities. But it may well be that agents have a variety of reasons for their deviance and yet deviate uniformly in certain circumstances, this uniformity being independent of their reasons. Whether in a particular case this is so or not seems to me to be an empirical question and one which it would be well not to attempt to settle a priori.

I can put my general point as follows. We can in a given society discover a variety of systematic regularities. There are the systems of rules which agents professedly follow; there are the systems of rules which they actually follow; there are causal regularities exhibited in the correlation of statuses and forms of behavior, and of one form of behavior and another, which are not rule-governed at all; there are regularities which are in themselves neither causal nor rule-governed, although dependent for their existence perhaps on regularities of both types, such as the cyclical patterns of development exhibited in some societies; and there are the interrelationships which exist between all these. Winch concentrates on some of these at the expense of the others. In doing so he is perhaps influenced by a peculiarly British tradition in social anthropology and by a focus of attention in recent philosophy.

The anthropological tradition is that centered on the work of Professor E. E. Evans-Pritchard, work which exemplifies the rewards to be gained from understanding a people first of all in their own terms. Winch rightly treats Evans-Pritchard's writing as a paradigm case of a social scientist knowing his own business,[1] but neglects the existence of alternative paradigms. Edmund Leach, for example, in his *Pul Eliya, a village in Ceylon* has remarked how ecological factors do not in fact genuinely figure in the explanatory framework of Evans-Pritchard's *The Nuer.* Now it is clear that such factors may affect the form of social life either in ways of which the agents are conscious (by posing problems to

[1] In "Understanding a Primitive Society," *American Philosophical Quarterly*, Vol. I, No. 4.

which they have to formulate solutions) or in ways of which they are unaware. This elementary distinction is perhaps not given its full weight in a recent discussion by Walter Goldschmidt[1] in which the very problems discussed by Winch are faced from the standpoint of an anthropologist especially concerned with ecological factors. Goldschmidt offers the example of the high correlation between agnatic segmentary kinship systems and nomadic pastoralism as a form of economy. He argues that nomadic pastoralism, to be a viable form of economy, has to satisfy requirements which are met most usually by segmentary lineages, but "age-sets can perform some of the same functions—especially those associated with the military—with equal effectiveness. . . . " Goldschmidt's claim is at least superficially ambiguous. He might be read (at least by a critic determined to be captious) as asserting that first there are economic forms, these pose problems of which the agents become aware and segmentary or age-set patterns are constructed as solutions by the agents. Or he might be read (more profitably, I imagine) as moving toward a theory in which social patterns (including kinship patterns) represent adaptations (of which the agents themselves are not aware) to the environment and to the level of technology prevailing. It would then in principle be possible to formulate causal laws governing such adaptations, and work like Leach's on Pul Eliya or Goldschmidt's on East Africa could be placed in a more general explanatory framework. This type of project is at the opposite extreme from Evans-Pritchard's concern with conceptual particularity.

Secondly, in Winch's account the social sciences characterize what they characterize by using action descriptions. In his stress upon these, Winch follows much recent philosophical writing. It is on what people *do* and not what they *are* or *suffer* that he dwells. But social scientists are concerned with the causes and effects of *being unemployed, having kin relations of a particular kind, rates of population change*, and a myriad of conditions of individuals and societies, the descriptions of which have a logical character other than that of action descriptions. None of this appears in Winch's account.

IV

The positive value of Winch's book is partly as a corrective to

[1] *Comparative Functionalism* (Berkeley: University of California Press, 1966), pp. 122–24.

the Durkheimian position which he rightly castigates. But it is more than a corrective because what Winch characterizes as the whole task of the social sciences is in fact their true starting-point. Unless we begin by a characterization of a society in its own terms, we shall be unable to identify the matter that requires explanation. Attention to intentions, motives, and reasons must precede attention to causes; description in terms of the agent's concepts and beliefs must precede description in terms of our concepts and beliefs. The force of this contention can be brought out by considering and expanding what Winch says about Durkheim's *Suicide* (p. 110). Winch invites us to notice the connection between Durkheim's conclusion that the true explanation of suicide is in terms of factors outside the consciousness of the agents themselves such that the reasons of the agents themselves are effectively irrelevant and his initial decision to give the term "suicide" a meaning quite other than that which it had for those agents. What is he inviting us to notice?

A number of points, I suspect, of which one is a central insight, the others in error. The insight is that Durkheim's particular procedure of giving to "suicide" a meaning of his own *entails* the irrelevance of the agent's reasons in the explanation of suicide. Durkheim does in fact bring forward independent arguments designed to show that reasons are either irrelevant or inaccessible, and very bad arguments they are. But even if he had not believed himself to have grounds drawn from these arguments, he would have been unable to take reasons into account, given his decision about meaning. For Durkheim arbitrarily equates the concept of *suicide* with that of *doing anything that the agent knows will bring about his own death* and thus classifies as suicide both the intended self-destruction of the Prussian or English officer who shoots himself to save the regiment the disgrace of a court martial and the death in battle of such an officer who has courageously headed a charge in such a way that he knows that he will not survive. (I choose these two examples because they both belong to the same category in Durkheim's classification.) Thus he ignores the distinction between *doing X intending that Y shall result* and *doing X knowing that Y will result*. Now clearly if these two are to be assimilated, the roles of deliberation and the relevance of the agent's reasons will disappear from view. For clearly in the former case the character of Y must be central to the reasons the agent has for doing X, but in the latter case the agent may well be doing X either in spite of the character of Y, or not caring one way or the other about the character of Y, or again finding the character of Y desirable, but not desirable enough for him for it to constitute a reason or a motive for doing X. Thus the nature of the reasons *must* differ in the two cases, and if the two cases are to have the same explanation the agent's reasons can scarcely figure in that explanation. That is, Durkheim is forced by his initial semantic decision to the conclusion that the agent's reasons are in cases of what agents in the society which he studies would have called suicide (which are included as a subclass of what he calls suicide) *never* causally effective.

But there are two further conclusions which might be thought to, but do not in fact, follow. It does not follow that all such decisions to bring actions under descriptions other than those used by the agents themselves are bound to lead to the same a priori obliteration of the explanatory role of reasons; for this obliteration was in Durkheim's case, as I have just shown, a consequence of certain special features of his treatment of the concept of suicide, and not a consequence of any general feature of the procedure of inventing new descriptive terms in social sciences. Secondly, from the fact that explanation in terms of reason ought not to be excluded by any initial decision of the social scientist, it does not follow that such explanation is incompatible with causal explanation. Here my argument in the second section of this essay bears on what Winch says about Weber. Winch says that Weber was confused because he did not realize that "a context of humanly followed rules . . . cannot be combined with a context of causal laws" without creating logical difficulties, and he is referring specifically to Weber's contention that the manipulation of machinery and the manipulation of his employees by a manufacturer may be understood in the same way, so far as the logic of the explanation is concerned. So Weber wrote, "that in the one case 'events of conciousness' do enter into the causal chain and in the other case do not, makes 'logically' not the slightest difference." I also have an objection to Weber's argument, but it is in effect that Weber's position is too close to Winch's. For Weber supposes that in order to introduce causal explanation he must abandon description of the social situation in terms of actions, roles, and the like. So he proposes speaking not of the workers being paid, but of their being handed pieces of metal. In so doing Weber concedes Winch's point that descriptions in terms of actions, reasons, and all that falls under his term "events of consciousness" cannot figure in causal explanations without a conceptual mistake being committed. But in this surely he is wrong.

Compare two situations: first, one in which managers minimize shop-floor trade-union activity in a factory by concentrating opportunities of extra overtime and of earning bonuses in those parts of the factory where such activity shows signs of flourishing; and then one in which managers similarly minimize trade-union activity by a process of continual transfers between one part of the factory and another or between different factories. In both cases it may be possible to explain the low level of trade-union activity causally by reference to the managers' policies; but in the former case the reasons which the workers have for pursuing overtime and bonuses can find a place in the explanation without it losing its causal character and in both cases a necessary condition of the managers' actions being causally effective may well be that the workers in question remain ignorant of the policy behind the actions. The causal character of the explanations can be brought out by considering how generalizations might be formulated in which certain behavior of the managers can supply either the necessary or the sufficient condition or both for the behavior of the workers. But in such a formulation one important fact will emerge; namely, that true causal explanations cannot be formulated—where actions are concerned—unless intentions, motives, and reasons are taken into account. That is, it is not only the case as I have argued in the second section of this essay that a true explanation in terms of reasons must entail some account of the causal background; it is also true that a causal account of action will require a corresponding account of the intentions, motives, and reasons involved. It is this latter point that Durkheim misses and Winch stresses. In the light of this it is worth returning to one aspect of the explanation of suicide.

In modern cities more than one study has shown a correlation between the suicide rate for different parts of the city and the proportion of the population living an isolated, single-room apartment existence. What are the conditions which must be satisfied if such a correlation is to begin to play a part in explaining why suicide is committed? First it must be shown that at least a certain proportion of the individuals who commit suicide live in such isolated conditions; otherwise (unless, for example, it was the landlord of such apartments who committed suicide) we should find the correlation of explanatory assistance only insofar as it pointed us toward a common explanation of the two rates. But suppose that we do find that it is the individuals who live in such isolated conditions who are more likely to commit suicide. We still have to ask whether it is the pressure on the emotions of the isolation itself, or whether it is the insolubility of certain other problems in conditions of isolation which leads to suicide. Unless such questions about motives and reasons are answered, the causal generalization "isolated living of a certain kind tends to lead to acts of suicide" is not so much an explanation in itself as an additional fact to be explained, even though it is a perfectly sound generalization and even though to learn its truth might be to learn how the suicide rate could be increased or decreased in large cities by changing our housing policies.

Now we cannot raise the questions about motives and reasons, the answers to which would explain why isolation has the effect which it has, unless we first of all understand the acts of suicide in terms of the intentions of the agents and therefore in terms of their own action descriptions. Thus Winch's starting-point proves to be the correct one, provided it is a starting-point. We could not even formulate our initial causal generalization about isolation and suicide, in such a way that the necessary question about motives and reasons could be raised later, unless the expression "suicide" and kindred expressions which figured in our causal generalizations possessed the same meaning as they did for the agents who committed the acts. We can understand very clearly why Winch's starting-point must be substantially correct if we remember how he compares sociological understanding with understanding a language (p. 115). The crude notion that one can first learn a language and then secondly and separately go on to understand the social life of those who speak it can only flourish where the languages studied are those of peoples whose social life is so largely the same as our own, so that we do not notice the understanding of social life embodied in our grasp of the language; but attempts to learn the alien language of an alien culture soon dispose of it. Yet the understanding that we thus acquire, although a necessary preliminary, is only a preliminary. It would be equally harmful if Winch's attempt to make of this preliminary the substance of social science were to convince, or if a proper understanding of the need to go further were not to allow for the truth in his arguments.

V

These dangers are likely to be especially inhibiting in the present state of certain parts of social science. Two important essays by anthropologists, Leach's *Rethinking Anthropology* and Goldschmidt's *Comparative Functionalism* (to which I have referred earlier), focus upon problems to which adherence to Winch's conclusions would preclude any solution. At the outset I contrasted Winch with Malinowski, but this was in respects in which most contemporary social scientists would take the standpoint quoted from Malinowski for granted. We owe also to Malinowski, however, the tradition of what Goldschmidt calls "the detailed internal analysis of individual cultures" with the further comparison of institutional arrangements in different societies resting on such analyses. This tradition has been criticized by both Leach and Goldschmidt; the latter believes that because institutions are defined by each culture in its own terms, it is not at the level of institutions that cross-cultural analyses will be fruitful. The former has recommended us to search for recurrent topological patterns in, for example, kinship arrangements, with the same aim of breaking free from institutional ethnocentrism. I think that both Leach and Goldschmidt are going to prove to be seminal writers on this point and it is clear that their arguments are incompatible with Winch's. It would therefore be an important lacuna in this essay if I did not open up directly the question of the bearing of Winch's arguments on this topic.

Winch argues, consistently with his rejection of any place for causal laws in social science, that comparison between different cases is not dependent on any grasp of theoretical generalizations (pp. 134–6), and he sets limits to any possible comparison by his insistence that each set of activities must be understood solely in its own terms. In so doing he must necessarily reject for example all those various theories which insist that religions of quite different kinds express unacknowledged needs of the same kind. (No such theory needs to be committed to the view that religions are and do no more than this.) Indeed in his discussion of Pareto (pp. 104–11) he appears to make such a rejection explicit by the generality of the grounds on which he rejects Pareto's comparison of Christian baptism with pagan rites. I hold no brief for the theory of residues and derivations. But when Winch insists that each religious rite must be understood in its own terms to the exclusion of any generalization about religion or that each social system must be so understood to the exclusion of any generalization about status and prestige, he must be pressed to make his grounds precise. In his later discussion of Evans-Pritchard, one aspect of Winch's views becomes clear; namely, the implication of his remark that "criteria of logic are not a direct gift of God, but arise out of, and are only intelligible in the context of, ways of living or modes of social life" (p. 100). Winch's one substantial point of difference with Evans-Pritchard in his treatment of witchcraft among the Azande is that he thinks it impossible to ask whether the Zande beliefs about witches are true.[1] We can ask from within the Zande system of beliefs if there are witches and will receive the answer "Yes." We can ask from within the system of beliefs of modern science if there are witches and will receive the answer "No." But we cannot ask which system of beliefs is the superior in respect of rationality and truth; for this would be to invoke criteria which can be understood independently of any particular way of life, and in Winch's view there are no such criteria.

This represents a far more extreme view of the difficulties of cultural comparison that Goldschmidt, for example, advances. Both its extreme character and its error can be understood by considering two arguments against it. The first is to the effect that in Winch's view certain actual historical transitions are made unintelligible; I refer to those transitions from one system of beliefs to another which are necessarily characterized by raising questions of the kind that Winch rejects. In seventeenth-century Scotland, for example, the question could not but be raised, "But are there witches?" If Winch asks, from within what way of social life, under what system of belief was this question asked, the only answer is that it was asked by men who confronted alternative systems and were able to draw out of what confronted them independent criteria of judgment. Many Africans today are in the same situation.

This type of argument is of course necessarily inconclusive; any historical counter-example to Winch's thesis will be open to questions of interpretation that will make it less than decisive. But there is another important argument. Consider the statement made by some Zande theorist or by King James VI and I, "There are witches" and the statement made by some modern skeptic, "There are no witches." Unless one of these statements denies what the other asserts, the negation of the sentence expressing the former could not be a correct translation of the sentence expressing the latter. Thus if we could not deny from our own standpoint and in our own language what the Azande or King James assert in theirs, we should be unable to translate their expression into our language. Cultural idiosyncrasy would have entailed linguistic idiosyncrasy and cross-cultural comparison would have been rendered logically impossible. But of course translation is not impossible.

[1] *American Philosophical Quarterly*, Vol. I, No. 4, p. 309.

Yet if we treat seriously, not what I take to be Winch's mistaken thesis that we cannot go beyond a society's own self-description, but what I take to be his true thesis that we must not do this except and until we have grasped the criteria embodied in that self-description, then we shall have to conclude that the contingently different conceptual schemes and institutional arrangements of different societies make translation difficult to the point at which attempts at cross-cultural generalization too often become little more than a construction of lists. Goldschmidt and Leach have both pointed out how the building up of typologies and classificatory schemes becomes empty and purposeless unless we have a theory which gives point and criteria to our classificatory activities. Both have also pointed out how, if we compare for example marital institutions in different cultures, our definition of "marriage" will either be drawn from one culture in terms of whose concepts other cultures will be described or rather misdescribed, or else will be so neutral, bare, and empty as to be valueless.[1] That is, the understanding of a people in terms of their own concepts and beliefs does in fact tend to preclude understanding them in any other terms. To this extent Winch is vindicated. But an opposite moral to his can be drawn. We may conclude not that we ought not to generalize, but that such generalization must move at another level. Goldschmidt argues for the recommendation: Don't ask what an institution means for the agents themselves, ask what necessary needs and purposes its serves. He argues for this not because he looks for functionalist explanations of a Malinowskian kind, but because he believes that different institutions, embodying different conceptual schemes, may be illuminatingly seen as serving the same social necessities. To carry the argument further would be to raise questions that are not and cannot be raised within the framework of Winch's book. It is because I believe writers such as Goldschmidt are correct in saying that one must transcend such a framework that I believe also that Winch's book deserves close critical attention.

---

[1] See Kathleen Gough, "The Nayars and the Definition of Marriage," in P. B. Hammond, ed., *Cultural and Social Anthropology* (New York: Macmillan); E. R. Leach, "Polyandry, Inheritance and the Definition of Marriage with Particular Reference to Sinhalese Customary Law," in *Rethinking Anthropology* (London: Athlone Press); and Goldschmidt, *op. cit.*, pp. 17–26.

20

Emotion, behavior and belief

In this essay I intend to attack behaviorism and I may therefore seem to have an initial obligation to specify precisely which of the many kinds of behaviorism I am attacking. But this I do not need to specify, since my arguments, if correct, hold against anything that it would be worth calling behaviorism. Consider for example the following four theses about the emotion of resentment, all of which might be called behaviorism.

1. "Smith resents what Jones did" means the same as some specifiable statement or set of statements about Smith's behavior.

2. "Smith resents what Jones did" is true, if, and only if, some specifiable statement or set of statements about Smith's behavior is true.

3. Although "Smith resents what Jones did" does not mean the same as some statement or set of statements about Smith's behavior, there is nothing more to Smith's feeling resentful than that Smith behaved, and was disposed to behave, in certain specifiable ways.

4. Although it is not the case that "Smith resents what Jones did" is true, if, and only if, some specifiable statement or set of statements about Smith's behavior is true, it is the case that if it is true that "Smith resents what Jones did" is true, then either some specifiable statement or set of statements about Smith's behavior is true, or else some special explanation is necessary as to why the behavior which, if it had occurred, would have made that statement or those statements true did not occur.

These theses are importantly different. The truth of (1) entails the truth of (2), but not vice versa; the truth of (3) entails the truth of (2), but the falsity of (1); and the truth of (4) entails the falsity of (1), (2), and (3). But, different as they are, they all have in common the following thesis: there is a connection between the emotion of resentment and certain specific and specifiable forms of behavior such that, even if there is more to resentment than the exhibition of the behavior in question and even if resentment may be felt without the behavior in question being exhibited, none the less behavior of that specific kind is the behavior-which-is-ex-hibited-when-resentment-is-expressed-in-behavior. I understand this thesis in such a way that it entails, first, that the connection between behavior and emotion is not merely contingent, as the connection between a twitching of my ear and my feeling resent-ment might be (it might just happen to be the case that whenever I feel resentment my ear twitches) and, second, that there is a limited and specifiable number of forms of behavior in which and through which resentment may be exhibited. It is precisely this last point that I wish to deny, and the argument of the first section of this essay will be directed to showing that resentment and some other emotions may be expressed by any form of be-havior whatsoever, and that there is, therefore, no necessary connection between some emotions at least and particular forms of behavior.

I

A man who yesterday chatted pleasantly with an academic colleague today crosses the street to avoid meeting him. Why? He has in the interval read a review of his latest book by this colleague and resents what he takes to be his unjust verdict. He expresses his resentment by crossing the road. Suppose that he knew that this colleague had a peculiar love of a rare fruit which he could only procure at one store; he might then buy up the entire stock of that fruit and so express his resentment. Or suppose that he knows that what his colleague prizes is an invitation to a particular party; he might then express his resentment by inter-cepting the invitation. Crossing a road, buying up fruit, stealing mail: these actions have nothing in common with each other and yet they can all express resentment. Precisely because there is no characteristic which they have to possess in order to function as expressions of resentment, precisely because, except as possible expressions of resentment, there is no reason for including these items in the list rather than any others, it seems plausible to suppose that any action whatsoever can function as an expression of resentment.

Consider now three possible criticisms of this argument. Surely, it might be argued, all such items of behavior do fall under some one single description other than "resentful"; they are all, for example, items of *hostile* behavior. This is of course true, but it does not affect my point. First of all, just as any action at all can be an expression of resentment, any action at all can be a hostile action. Crossing a road, buying up fruit, stealing mail can all be hostile in specific contexts, just as they can be resentful in specific contexts. To this it might be objected that there are some actions which *could* not be hostile, if by that is meant "directed to the harm of others"; how could suicide be in this sense hostile? The answer is, of course, that there is a well-recognized class of suicides, the so-called "revenge" suicides ("I'll kill myself and *that* will teach them a lesson!") where the point of the suicide is precisely that it is a hostile action. Moreover, the variety of types of action which can be characterized as expressions of resentment can also be characterized as hostile just because "hostile" is partially synonymous with "resentful," in turn because resentment is a species of hostility. So that the fact that we can find another description under which all these actions fall does not in any way show that we have found an additional common characteristic shared by all these actions.

A second objection to my thesis might be that I am able to understand all these actions as expressions of resentment only by establishing a context of a given kind. It is not crossing the road or buying fruit or stealing mail that is the expression of resentment, but crossing-the-road-to-avoid-speaking-to-someone-who-has-un-justly-criticized-me or buying-fruit-especially-desired-by-some-one-who-has-unjustly-criticized-me, and so on. This is in a way correct. We are only able to construe the actions in question as behavior expressive of resentment by connecting them with the reasons that the agent has for doing what he does. But these reasons cannot be identified with what the agent does nor are they ex-hibited in doing what he does. Certainly it is only because the action is done for a certain kind of reason that it is an expression of resentment. But to say this is to say that *qua* action, and *qua* the action that it is, the relation between the action and the resentment is purely contingent. To make the point in this way does perhaps help us to understand better why many philosophers may have thought otherwise. They may have envisaged the action under some description, such as the descriptions above, that links the action to the reason for performing it and passed from asserting truly that such a description is conceptually connected with the characterization of the emotion in question as resentment to asserting falsely that the action itself was not merely contingently connected to the resentment.

A third point might be raised not so much as an objection to my initial thesis as an objection to drawing possibly illegitimate conclusions from it. For it might be suggested that while what I have said is true of the emotion of resentment, it is not true of emotions in general. What is special about the emotion of resentment? A man cannot be said to resent something unless he has a particular type of belief. He must believe that he has been wronged in the light of what it is established that a man in his position has a right to expect. Unless he has such a belief, what he feels may be characterized perhaps as anger but not as resentment. What then of anger? Is there some belief which a man who is said to be angry must possess? It is clearly the case that usually and characteristically a man who is angry believes that something has been done that is harmful to or an affront to himself or his interests or those about whom he cares. But is it not sometimes the case that a man just feels angry? And, therefore, does not anger perhaps differ in a not irrelevant way from resentment?

The relevance of this point to the argument is as follows. In the case of resentment it is because the circumstances, tastes, and other relevant characteristics of the person against whom resentment is directed are indefinitely variable that the actions which may express that resentment are indefinitely variable. Hence, the indefinite variability of the actions which express resentment is connected with the belief which a man to whom resentment is correctly ascribed must possess. But if in the case of anger there is no such belief, then may not anger be connected with behavior expressive of anger in some way quite different to that in which resentment is connected with behavior expressive of resentment?

It is important to stress first that where anger is divorced from the belief that usually and characteristically accompanies it, (namely, the belief that some identifiable person has done some identifiable harm), we are confronted not with anger as it basically is (that is, with the emotion in a pure form, so to speak), but rather with an uncharacteristic and marginal case, which is less easily intelligible to us than anger in its usual form and which we understand by its resemblance to these forms. (Try to imagine a culture in which everyone is all the time in a rage with no one in particular about nothing in particular, but is never angry with specific individuals about specific harms. I am inclined to think that we would treat this as a different emotion.)

Secondly, anger in these special cases is not in fact unaccompanied by belief; it is just that the belief is expressed in sentences containing more variables. The belief that someone or anyone has done something harmful or affronting to me, although I know not who or what, is still a belief, and the belief that connects the feelings accompanying it to other feelings of anger. Hence anger, like resentment, is connected with a belief and although the belief is a less complex one, the persons or actions against whom anger is directed are as indefinitely variable as are the objects of resentment. Hence also the forms of behavior by means of which anger too may be expressed are indefinitely variable.

I take it therefore that the lack of any necessary connection between emotion and behavior holds in the case of anger as well as in that of resentment. But if anger and resentment resemble each other in this way, how do they differ? It seems plausible to suggest that the only difference is in the beliefs of the agents in question. The emotion of anger involves the belief that someone, whether I deserve it or not, has done harm or has affronted me or my interests or those about whom I care; the emotion of resentment involves the belief that someone has done undeserved harm or offered an undeserved affront to me or my interests. The difference is not in the phenomenological feel of the two emotions: introspective reports do not reveal different sensations in the case of anger from those present in the case of resentment. Nor is the difference in the behavior through which each is expressed, since each may be expressed in the same behavior. The beliefs alone provide a difference.

To this it may be retorted that the relationship of anger to resentment is a special case. For after all resentment is a species of anger. It may therefore be true that the felt quality of the emotion and the behavior do not differ in this case. But if, instead of asking for the difference between anger and resentment, we were to inquire what is the difference between anger and elation or between resentment and gratitude, the same would not hold. Consider resentment and gratitude. To feel grateful is to feel pleased that someone has done more for your good or for the good of those about whom you care than you had a right to expect. But like resentment any kind of behavior may express gratitude; the fact that one emotion is one of pleasure in something and the other of displeasure at something does not entail that the very same behavior may not express gratitude which expresses resentment. If I am grateful to you for what you have done and I know that you resent what someone else has done, I may express my gratitude to you by doing to him what if you did it to him would express your resentment. Hence the difference between gratitude and resentment is not a difference in behavior. I take it that it is also not a difference in the felt quality of inner states. The feelings of a man in the extremity of an emotion such as gratitude is customarily described by novelists in ways that are remarkably like the ways in which the feelings of a man in the extremity of an emotion such as fear are described. His throat goes dry, his temples throb, his pulse rate rises, his eyes prick with tears, and so on. The physiological symptoms of emotion seem remarkably constant and the physiologists seem to agree with the novelists about this.

If I conclude then that the difference between emotions lies in the belief and not in the behavior, I cannot possibly identify emotions with patterns of behavior. But a behaviorist might try at this point to recover his position by an argument of more general import. For he might contend that the notion of belief itself is to be analysed in terms of behavior, asserting that "X believes that p" is logically equivalent to or means the same as "X has a disposition to manifest certain patterns of behavior" and also that to manifest a belief is to manifest patterns of behavior, so that the appropriate evidence which would warrant the assertion that "X believes that p" is that X has on occasion exhibited the relevant behavior. In order for these assertions to be defensible, the behavior in question would have to include what X says as well as what X does, what some behaviorists have quaintly called "linguistic behavior." More specifically it is what X asserts and not just what X says which has to be included in the list of relevant items: unless on certain types of possible occasions a man was prepared to assert that p and to deny that p he could not be said to believe that p. It follows, therefore, that if the notion of belief is to be analysed in terms of behavior, the behavior in terms of which it is analysed must include acts of assertion and denial. But not what is it to assert that p? It is to give one's hearers or readers to understand that one believes that p and that p is worthy of belief. That is to say, the notion of assertion has to be explained by referring to the notion of belief. So it turns out that the notion of belief has not been analysed in terms of behavior, for the type of behavior to which reference has to be made in the course of the analysis can itself only be understood by referring to the concept of belief. The concept of belief is at least as fundamental a concept, and possibly a more fundamental concept than that of behavior.

To this it might be answered that to assert and to deny are just forms of behavior. There is clearly a sense in which this is true. If I say of someone that he behaved disgracefully in denying that he was to blame, I say something intelligible to every user of standard English. But in this idiomatic sense of "behavior" we cannot give a behaviorist account even of behavior. For to assert of someone that he asserts that p is to go beyond saying that he utters the sentence "p" even if he did in fact assert that p by uttering the sentence "p." It is to construe his utterance in terms of his intention in uttering the sentence. The intentions that inform that utterance, like all intentions, presuppose beliefs. So that we have once again, in the course of trying to analyse the concepts of belief, been brought back to it.

Finally it ought to be noticed that in discussing behaviorism I have not ascribed to the behaviorist that extreme view which equates behavior with physical movement. When I argued that there are at least certain emotions which can be expressed by any behavior whatsoever, my examples—those of crossing the road, buying fruit, and stealing mail—were all examples of actions and their descriptions were descriptions which specified an intention embodied in what was done. If the behaviorist wants to insist that he means more than this by behavior, that in his view behavior has not been characterized adequately until it is characterized by the emotions it expresses, if any, and that therefore resentful behavior for example is just a species of behavior and not behavior informed by something other than that behavior, namely an emotion, his thesis becomes trivial. If he wants, on the other hand, to insist that he means less than this by "behavior," perhaps equating behavior with physical movement, then my preceding arguments hold with as great or greater force than they do against behavior equated with human action.

The outcome of my arguments is then that behavior stands in indirect and complex relationship to emotions. Without accepting classical introspectionism, the introspectionist and indeed ordinary language usage according to which we speak of emotions as lying behind behavior and as being concealed as much as revealed by it does not seem exaggerated. But if this is so, what are we to say about our knowledge of the emotions of others? How far can we know what they feel?

II

Paul Ziff in his *About Behaviorism* considers the contention that "You can in principle if not in fact always find out whether or not I am behaving in certain ways. But you cannot even in principle always find out whether or not I am angry," and even waiving all difficulties about the locution "you can in principle find out" finds what he takes to be two fatal objections to it. One which I shall not consider, since I agree with it, is that it is false that you can in principle always find out how I am behaving. The other objection he puts as follows: "You can in principle always find out whether or not I am angry because I can tell you. Hence you need attend only to my verbal behavior. (I assume that it would be generally odd to speak of my being mistaken about whether or not I am angry.) To suppose that you cannot in principle find out whether or not I am angry would be to suppose that I cannot in principle tell you whether or not I am angry. I find such a supposition unintelligible." Agreeing with finding this last supposition unintelligible, I still want to disagree with the main point.

From the fact that, if I *am* angry, I can always tell you that I am angry, it does not follow that from what I say you can always tell if I *am* angry or not. The reason for this is that I can always deceive you by lying or otherwise misleading you and that I can always simply refuse to reveal what I feel. The use of "can in principle," which Ziff overgenerously adopts from the antibehaviorists whom he is criticizing, is one source of trouble. For it may lead us to concede not only that I may always when angry tell you that I am, but also that your knowledge of my anger is unproblematic. But it isn't.

When Ziff talks of verbal behavior, he may be suggesting that what I say about my emotions stands to my emotions in the same relationship that the behavior which expresses my emotions stands to my emotions. But this is surely false either in a behaviorist or in a nonbehaviorist view. In a behaviorist view it is false because, in that view, my having an emotion consists in my exhibiting a certain pattern of behavior: the behavior which expresses the emotion is the emotion. But when I tell you what I feel, I do not express the emotion, I report it. Or rather, I may be expressing the emotion in the act of reporting it or not, but I am certainly reporting it. This is partly a matter of to whom I am speaking. If I am angry with you and I say "I am angry with you," I am undoubtedly expressing my anger in the act of reporting it. But if I am angry with you and say to someone else "I am angry with Smith," then it would be odd to say that I was expressing my anger. It is in any case utterances and neither sentences nor statements that are expressive of emotion, and utterances may certainly stand to an emotion just as other behavior stands to it. But what I say when I so utter does not stand in the same relationship to the emotion, and as a counterpart of my thesis that in certain cases at least emotions do not stand to the behavior that expresses them in such a way

that there is any conceptual connection between the characterization of the emotion and that of the behavior. I now want to develop
a second key thesis to the effect that statements about their own
behavior made by agents are not expressions of that behavior
at all because statements about their own behavior made by
agents stand in no different relationship to that behavior than do
statements made by others about their emotions. I thus have to
attack directly the Wittgensteinian view that first-person reports
are—just because they are expressions of feeling—not symmetrical
with second- and third-person ascriptions.

Against this I want to contend that there is no asymmetry, so
far as emotions are concerned (and if I restrict the point to emotions
in this essay this must not be taken to imply that I hold different
views about sensations), between first-person sentences on the one
hand and second- and third-person sentences on the other or
between statements expressed by means of first-person sentences
and statements expressed by means of second- and third-person
sentences. I take it that to understand personal pronouns at least
two conditions must be satisfied: first no one understands personal
pronouns who does not understand that they are blanks for which
personal proper names may be substituted. I do not understand
personal pronouns unless I am able to make the inference from
hearing someone say "MacIntyre is drunk" to "He is saying that
I am drunk." To have understood this is to be able to see what is
wrong with attempts to suggest that for "I" what can be substituted is not a proper name, but a description such as "the
present speaker." Of course, first-person statements can often be
correctly paraphrased by statements using such expressions as
"the present speaker." But "the present speaker" is not necessarily self-referential in the way that "I" is. While I am speaking,
someone may say "The present speaker is drunk" and he would not
normally be taken to mean that he is drunk, but that I am; while
if I hear someone say "MacIntyre is drunk," I must if I understand him see that it follows that if what he says is true then I am
drunk, but I do not need to have even learned the use of the
expression "the present speaker" to understand "I" and to use it
correctly.

Secondly, it is a condition of my understanding personal pronouns that I understand that if I say truly of you that "You are
drunk," then you are able to say truly of yourself (provided that you
are not too drunk—perhaps this is what "can in principle" means)
"I am drunk"; and I can say truly of you to a third person, "He is
drunk"; *and* in addition that if you can say truly of me that "You

are drunk," then I can say truly of myself "I am drunk"; and so on. In other words, to have extricated oneself from the egocentric predicament—insofar as this is a matter of grammar rather than of beliefs—is a necessary condition for the exercise of the ability to use those parts of speech which are held by some philosophers to generate it.

It is these facts about personal pronouns which make it clear that if the sentence "MacIntyre is angry" can be used truly to make a statement about me, then "I am angry" can be used by me to make the same true statement. This statement is, let us say, on this particular occasion true, but it could have been false. The statement made by my saying "I am angry" truly is thus a statement which stands in the same relationship to my anger that the statement "MacIntyre is angry" said by someone else stands to it. But if this is so, then the *statement* cannot be an expression of my anger, let alone the sentence. Certainly I may so utter the sentence "I am angry" with clenched lips, gnashing teeth, and all the conventional accompaniments of anger, whatever they are, in such a way that my utterance is an expression of my anger. But my utterance of "$E=MC^2$" can be an expression of my anger in just the same way as my utterance of "I am angry."

It is not to the point that I cannot be mistaken about whether MacIntyre is angry if I am MacIntyre. I cannot be mistaken because I cannot fail to have all the necessary evidence for what I assert. But whenever I have all the necessary evidence for what I assert, I cannot be mistaken either. Placed with vision unimpaired in front of a tray containing a bottle and two glasses, I cannot be mistaken in asserting that here are a bottle and two glasses. Yet of course in both cases although I cannot be mistaken as to what is true and what is false I can of course knowingly assert what is false. Thus Ziff's acknowledgement that sometimes at least I can only know whether you are angry if you will tell me implies that I cannot know whether you are angry or not unless I know that you are a trustworthy reporter of your emotions. But can I ever know this?

It is not just that a great deal of behavior does not bear its meaning on its face and that we cannot tell what intentions inform it simply by observing it, because it is susceptible of more than one and perhaps of many interpretations. But behavior which is *qua* behavior unambiguous can be put to the service of a pretence, just as assertions can be lies. This is the point at which to note that when behaviorists have assimilated what I say to my behavior, using such expressions as "linguistic behavior" or "verbal behavior" they have been wrong not so much in that they assimilated them as in that they tried to reduce uses of language to forms of behavior instead of seeing that certain forms of behavior are best understood as at least resembling uses of language. One reason why one of the key positions of this essay has not been accepted by some philosophers—namely, that any behavior at all can be expressive of certain emotions at least—is that there is a behavioral iconography of emotion. That is, there are certain forms of behavior which are by convention understood to symbolize the presence of a particular emotion. To exhibit such behavior is equivalent to saying "I am angry" (or whatever emotion is in question). It is because of this symbolic character of such behavior—of shaking the fist and clenching the teeth in relation to anger, for example—that it can be put to different uses just as speech can. In Japan and Korea there is a tradition of visiting a recently bereaved person who will then laugh and joke with his guests without making reference to the bereavement. The host by doing this asserts to his guests that he does not wish to burden them with his grief; the guests assert in reply that they would not wish to burden the host with the belief that he has in fact burdened them with his grief. It is the conventional, symbolic character of the behavior that makes this possible. So far as this iconographic aspect of behavior is concerned, the conventions could, of course, be other than they are. We could express anger by touching our toes or gratitude by performing cartwheels. If it is objected that very often the behavior expressive of anger or gratitude is evoked from us by some action, is not a voluntary, deliberate, or controlled response, it must be pointed out that very often too what we say about our emotions is similarly evoked. An involuntary utterance of a statement about my behavior does not, because it is involuntary, lose its conventional character. So too with behavior symbolic of emotion.

There is, of course, a difference between speech and such symbolic behavior which ought to be noted. I cannot use such behavior to indicate to you that I am angry without being taken to have expressed and not merely indicated the fact of my anger. But this difference does not affect the preceding argument. What follows from that argument is that whether I say to you that I am angry or show you that I am angry I may be misleading you, and from this, two additional consequences follow. The first is that over large areas I can sometimes have no way of knowing what you feel. Any performance of behavior by you, no matter how extended, may be a pretence at the service of some further unrevealed intention and emotion. This gap between performed behavior on the one hand and intention and emotion on the other is what goes unnoticed in a sociological perspective such as Erving Goffmann's, in which there is nothing to human beings but their performance of the behavior appropriate to different roles and the behavior (equally and in precisely the same way rule-governed) necessary to produce the behavior appropriate to the roles. I introduce the doctrines of Goffmann in *The Presentation of Self in Everyday Life* at this point because in identifying what is omitted from an account of social stituations which is restricted to overt performances I have identified not merely what is omitted from this particular piece of sociological inquiry and description, but what it is at once essential and very difficult to include. The early behaviorists believed that their doctrine provided the only basis for a scientific knowledge of human beings and believed that such knowledge could have a firmer basis than our everyday knowledge of each other has. Goffmann resembles them in believing that the notion of "a true self" behind the role- and rule-governed performances is an antiscientific myth perpetrated by those who, as he puts it, wish to keep part of the human world "safe from sociology." But in liquidating the distinction between the self and its performances, Goffmann loses sight of the way in which we can only take what others do seriously if we trust what they say on certain key occasions.

It is not just that the possibility of deception and of being misled are so large; it is also that our beliefs about others have to be founded so largely on trust if the preceding arguments are correct. I may argue on an inductive basis about other people's emotions insofar as these are not exhibited in or deducible from their behavior; but however well contrived my inductive learning policies are, the evidence from which I argue will include at crucial points what others have said; and my willingness to treat what they have said as trustworthy or untrustworthy cannot itself be inductively based. Why not? Could I not learn that Smith is generally trustworthy about his inner life too? The problem here is that we could only derive well-founded inductive generalizations about the connection between a man's trustworthiness in his monetary transactions, say, and his trustworthiness in reporting his emotions if we already had independent access to his emotions—which we do not. Every piece of behavior is open to doubt. Does this entail skepticism about the emotions of others? Or to compare the not quite ridiculous with the not completely sublime, does my conclusion about the emotions of other people resemble Kant's conclusion about God: that the removal of knowledge has left room for faith?

To put matters like this would be unhelpful; for clearly faith in God is something that is dispensable. It is indeed of the essence of faith that one can fail to have it. But if our beliefs about the other people depend upon a presumption of their trustworthiness, so that there is indeed a moral element in our beliefs about others —and those who have wanted to mark a difference in this respect between our knowledge of nature and our knowledge of others have thus been right—it is not the case that we can rationally decide not to make this presumption. For emotions are not occurrences in the lives of individuals, insulated from similar occurrences in the lives of other individuals. As Hume points out in his discussion of sympathy in the *Treatise*, what I feel is in large part a response to what I take others to feel or not feel. You are resentful of my lack of gratitude at your generosity in the face of my anger at your lack of sympathy for my depression over your sentimentality. Such chains of emotion are characteristic of the emotional life; the plot of a novel often traces just such a chain. It follows that systematic skeptical doubt about the emotions of others, based on an acknowledgement of the opaque quality of their behavior and a refusal to trust their avowals, would produce an inability to respond to others, for we would not know to what to respond and the reliefs that inform our emotions would not specify adequate intentional objects for our emotions. We have to trust one another at this basic level or be paralysed in our humanity. This is not a choice.

There is one final point worth attending to. Small children exhibit certain emotions spontaneously before they have learned to pretend and about their emotions animals never learn to pretend. So in these cases the element of trust in avowals is obviously absent. Rage is an example of this. Small children also sometimes learn in the case of certain other emotions to exhibit behavior symbolically expressive of the emotion before they have learned to feel the emotion. This is often true in the case of gratitude. But what they have to learn in order to exhibit adult emotions involves them in learning how to pretend, how to be ironic, how to lie, and how to produce these stock responses which sustain fatigued human relationships. In so doing they become, like the adult world, opaque. Behaviorists were in the right when they stressed that sometimes we want to claim that we can recognize what others are feeling better than they can; but in repudiating what introspectionists seemed to imply—that we are all continually opaque to each other all the time—they may have underrated the extent to which we are very often opaque to each other a great deal of the time. Misunderstanding and not understanding are at the core of human life, a fact perhaps standing in the way of the project of scientific inquiry about human beings, even if we view it as an obstacle to be circumvented rather than as a final barrier. This conclusion I find disconcerting. But perhaps the nature of reality is such that we ought to have learned by now never to be disconcerted at being disconcerted.

21

Rationality and the explanation of action

I

It is distinctly unfashionable to attempt to characterize and to understand the history of human societies in terms of an opposition between reason and irrationality. There was a time—in the closing decades of the last century—when to do so was in fashion. Anthropologists such as Frazer and Tylor, historians of thought such as Lecky and Dickson White all took the possibility of so doing for granted; and it is of course in part against their parochialism and against that misdescription of other cultures and other ages which resulted from too great a confidence in the categories of their own age that we have been reacting. Or overreacting, as I shall argue in this essay. It is not that I want to return to the concepts of rationality and irrationality of the late Victorian Age; it is rather that I do not want to see the perception of those concepts as culture-bound to lead to a blindness to the importance of ascriptions of rationality and irrationality in the human sciences.

The contemporary attitude is strikingly exemplified in the strictures passed by H. R. Trevor-Roper[1] on the nineteenth-century liberal historians of witchcraft, strictures with which it would be difficult to quarrel. None the less, even if with Trevor-Roper we reject such notions as that intellectual history is "a direct contest between reason and faith, reason and superstition," we may find reasons for holding that, when we have conceded that, as Trevor-Roper holds, "such a distinction between 'reason' and 'superstition' is difficult to maintain, the making of some such distinction is unavoidable. Indeed, we may find those reasons in Trevor-Roper's own essay. Trevor-Roper explains the European witch-craze of the sixteenth and seventeenth centuries as the outcome of certain social

[1] "The European Witch-Craze" in *Religion, the Reformation and Social Change* (London; Macmillan, 1967).

strains and conflicts. He speaks of "a scapegoat for social frustration," of "the mythology of the witch-craze" as "the articulation of social pressure" and of "social tension." I do not want to, I am of course not competent to question the truth of his explanation; but I do want to try to understand its logical structure, and the attempt to do this will lead me to use terms which are not used by Trevor-Roper himself. I hope therefore that I do not misrepresent. When it is said that social pressures generate a belief, as Trevor-Roper asserts that social tensions between the people of the mountains and the people of the plains partly generated the sixteenth-century belief in witches, I take it that something like the following is meant. A certain social situation generates certain emotions, in this case a certain kind of fear. Emotions are intentional; that is, they presuppose beliefs and we cannot characterize the emotion except in terms of the relevant object of belief. So an expression of fear is the expression of a belief that something harmful or dangerous is at hand. The belief may, of course, be false; and of course the frightened person may both express his fear and yet assert sincerely that he does know that there is really nothing to be afraid of. But where an emotion is generated which has no adequate intentional object, such an object will under certain circumstances be supplied. Jews, witches, and Communists have all at certain periods been available as such objects for fear; not the Jew, the witch, or the Communist of course as he or she is, but as the social stereotype has him or her. The form of explanation is thus as follows: we explain the belief as brought into being by a need to supply a rationale for the emotion; and we explain the emotion as generated by the social structure.

It is noteworthy that, although Trevor-Roper scorns the use of "superstition" by Lea and Lecky, he himself is quite prepared to call the belief in witches "a mythology" and a "fantastic" mythology at that, and perhaps this is not as marginal a matter as he himself seems to think. For we have to ask whether the type of explanation which he advances would be equally appropriate for the explanation of *any* set of well-established beliefs, or whether we must not distinguish a class of beliefs for which it would be appropriate and a class for which it would be inappropriate. Consider, for example, the beliefs of a deviant minority in the early seventeenth century, beliefs whose incompatability with the socially established doctrines of the dominant institutions led to some sporadic persecution. I refer to the astronomers. If we ask why by 1630 most astronomers believed that Jupiter had satellites, the explanation must begin not only from Galileo's observations, but from what had become accepted canons of observation and of argument. If we ask why those canons were accepted, the only possible answer will be a historical one. This history may reveal to us certain conditions which appear to have been necessary prerequisites for the exercise of the rationality embodied in those canons; but just because they will only be necessary conditions, they will in no way provide an explanation of, for example, why those canons rather than any others were adopted. Moreover, what such a history would not and could not reveal to us would be antecedent sufficient conditions, sufficient, that is, to bring about the social practice of arguing in terms of those canons. My reasons for asserting this can be put as follows. Once we have asserted that the explanation of why men came to believe and believed something or other is that their behavior and procedures were governed by the appropriate rational criteria, we have already in so doing asserted that they had made themselves independent of these psychological or social factors which on occasion lead men to act or to believe regardless of where reason points. If some antecedent condition, such as a form of social structure or the prevalence of certain emotions, is sufficient to produce a belief, irrespective of the reasoning appropriately to be invoked, then explanation in terms of the procedures of rationality is clearly out of place. So when Trevor-Roper cites the beliefs of modern anti-Semitism, of medieval anti-Semitism, and of McCarthyism as parallels to the sixteenth- and seventeenth-century witch-craze, he points to, although he does not formulate precisely, a generalization of the form "Whenever the social structure is of a certain kind, beliefs of a certain kind will be generated independent of any rational support they may or may not have." In cases where such a generalization holds, the belief in question will clearly be generated if the antecedent sufficient conditions are satisfied, whatever the state of the processes of argument and deliberation appropriate to the rational formation of such a belief. Where, however, a belief is intelligible only in terms of an antecedent process of reasoning and could only be generated as the outcome of such a process, it would follow that its being held cannot be ascribed to antecedent sufficient conditions of the kind invoked by Trevor-Roper to explain the witch-craze.

It thus appears that there is at least a preliminary case for holding that not all beliefs are to be explained in the same way. The form of explanation appropriate to rational beliefs seems to be not the same as the form of explanation appropriate to irrational beliefs. We can well understand at a semi-intuitive level why this should be so. To characterize a belief as irrational is to characterize the intellectual procedures and attitudes of those who hold it. It is to say in effect—at least in the extreme case—that the believer is invulnerable to rational argument. But to say this is precisely to say that the belief is held as the outcome of antecedent events or states of affairs which are quite independent of any relevant process of appropriate deliberation. Thus, *pace* Trevor-Roper, a crucial distinction between rationality and irrationality or superstition must continue to be made and we cannot simply remark, as he does, that we have now learned that the mental structures of one age are not the same as the mental structures of another. For the explanation of rational belief terminates with an acccount of the appropriate intellectual norms and procedures; the explanation of irrational belief must be in terms of causal generalizations which connect antecedent conditions specified in terms of social structures or psychological states—or both—with the genesis of beliefs.

Suppose to this it were to be retorted that the explanation of rational beliefs cannot terminate with an account of the relevant norms and rule-governed procedures. For any social practice which is informed by such a body of norms and procedures must itself be explained by references to prior antecedent conditions. This retort might be grounded in the conviction that every event or state of affairs must have a cause. Now certainly one may be able to identify many conditions necessary for the establishment and maintenance of such social practices and more especially conditions which favor or inhibit their institutionalization. But sufficient conditions? What could these be? The notion of a causal explanation for the genesis of an intellectual tradition is like the notion of such an explanation for the genesis of a style of painting. All attempts to give such explanations have foundered. The most that any specification of antecedent conditions can give us (as Antal unintentionally demonstrated in his work on Florentine painting) is a set of necessary and predisposing conditions which might be shown to make a given audience receptive to works of art characterized as falling under some very general description. But the style which in fact procures the reception always does so by virtue of characteristics which escape such descriptions. The specific characteristics of Florentine painting which make it great painting can in no way be deduced from the market situation of the Florentine painter. As with art, so with astronomy or arithmetic.

Two points ought to be noted about the argument so far. The

9

first is that, even if we accept it, Trevor-Roper's strictures upon the liberal historians of thought remain justified to a very large degree. This is because what is in question in his discussion is not merely the propriety of ascribing rationality or irrationality to the beliefs which the social historian and the sociologist study; there is also the question of whether the liberal historian's conception of rationality was coherent and adequate. In fact it was not, for they tended to confuse the question of rationality with that of truth. This confusion has often been repeated;[1] the importance of not repeating it will emerge later in my argument. For the moment I will simply point out that "true" and "false" are predicated of *what is believed*, namely of statements, and the truth or falsity of a statement is a matter quite independent of whether that statement is believed by anyone at all. Rationality is predicated of the attitudes, dispositions, and procedures of those who believe; a man who uses the best canons available to him may behave rationally in believing what is false, and a man who pays no heed to the rules of evidence may behave irrationally in believing what is true. The parochialism of the liberal historians of the late Victorian Age lay in their treating as one of the criteria of rationality assent to the truth of certain propositions which they themselves affirmed; false belief they took to be a symptom of irrationality. In taking this to be the case, they certainly believed what is false and they were perhaps irrational in so doing. For what entitles us to call the belief in witchcraft irrational is not its falsity, but the fact of its incoherence with other beliefs and criteria possessed by those who held it.

Secondly, I would like to emphasize that this preliminary thesis —that the type of explanation appropriate to a rational belief is different from that appropriate to an irrational belief—is to be distinguished from the thesis that human actions cannot be causally explained. I have advanced reasons for denying this thesis elsewhere.[2] But it is of course the case that the present thesis is not without implications for the explanation of actions. What some of these are will be considered in the third section of this essay. Before I consider them, however, another issue must be raised.

---

[1] Most recently in the *European Journal of Sociology*, 1967, by S. Lukes, p. 62., and J. Torrance, p. 276.

[2] "The Antecedents of Action," pp. 191–210 and "The Idea of a Social Science," pp. 211–29.

II

From the conclusion of my argument in the previous section—that the explanation of the genesis and maintenance of irrational beliefs must be of a different order from the explanation of the genesis and maintenance of rational belief—it follows that the sociologist cannot, in setting himself the task of such explanation, abstain from judgment concerning the rationality or irrationality of the beliefs which he studies. It follows that the "neutrality" thesis expressed by Bryan Wilson for the sociology of religion can only be held in a tempered version. Bryan Wilson has argued that the sociologist of religion, so long as he studies religious belief and the religious believer *qua* sociologist, may and ought to remain neutral as to the truth and reasonableness of the beliefs which are part of the object of his study. *Qua* man he will doubtless be theist or atheist, Catholic, humanist, or Parsee. But this need not affect his work as a sociologist. About this thesis I should want to make two comments. The first is that, for reasons I have already given, the question of the truth or falsity of the belief studied is to some degree independent of the question of its rationality; but, although this distinction must not be ignored, truth and rationality are both conceptually and empirically related. For to advance reasons is always to advance reasons for holding that a belief is true or false; and rational procedures are in fact those which yield us the only truths of which we can be assured. Thus, to recognize a belief as rationally held is to lay oneself open to at least the possibility of its truth. Hence, if the sociologist *qua* sociologist must, in order to determine what form of explanation is appropriate to the genesis and maintenance of the beliefs which he is studying, pass a verdict upon the reasonableness or unreasonableness of the procedures of those who hold the belief, he may find that he is at least partially committed in respect of truth or falsity.

Secondly, we must not as a result of the present argument elaborate a picture of the sociologist as approaching his material with *his* canons of rationality which he uses to sit in judgment upon the irrationalities of those whom he studies. We must distinguish at least two elements in rationality. The first element is a matter of language. To understand what is said in a given culture, we must learn to classify the forms of utterance, to distinguish assertions from requests, wishes from commands, and so on. We shall not be able to do this except on the assumption that the laws of logic are embodied in the linguistic practice of the community which we are studying. If we cannot identify negation and such laws as $\sim\sim p \equiv p$ as embodied in this practice, I do not understand how we can be confident in our identification of the speech acts of assertion and denial. It follows that any notion of pre-logical thought, if it is taken to be thought which displays *no* regard for the laws of noncontradiction, for example, is extremely difficult to understand. Perhaps Lévy-Bruhl never did seriously mean anything as extreme as this—although in his earlier writings he does seem to. So far as this element in rationality is concerned then, there is no question of *us* judging the rationality of alien cultures in terms of *our* criteria. For the criteria are neither *ours* nor *theirs*, but simply *the* criteria, and logic is the inquiry which formulates them.

This has sometimes been recognized, however, in such a way as to draw a sharp and quite misplaced contrast between this element and another. For it is suggested that on matters of substance, rather than matters of logic, what is believed to be a good reason for holding a certain belief in one culture will appear as in no way a good reason for holding that belief in the context of another culture. Hence, it appears that what is counted as rationality in one culture must be something quite different from what is counted as rationality in another. Peter Winch has written that "We start from the position that standards of rationality in different societies do not always coincide."[1] In his view we thus *can* speak of *our* criteria and of *theirs*, where criteria rationality are concerned. But this view fails—quite apart from the point about logic made above—for two reasons. First, no belief is rational or irrational except relative to some other belief or beliefs. Thus, to predicate rationality or irrationality of the complete set of beliefs held in a given culture is always a mistake. To say that a belief is rational is to talk about how it stands in relation to other beliefs, given a background of yet further beliefs as to what counts as a good reason for holding beliefs on a particular type of subject matter in a given culture. Because this is so, we can only ascribe rationality to others on the basis of their criteria of rationality. Or rather, the distinction between *ours* and *theirs* again breaks down. If we indict others for contradiction or incoherence, the contradiction or incoherence is a feature of their beliefs, but the standards of contradiction and incoherence must be the same for

[1] "Understanding a Primitive Society," *American Philosophical Quarterly*, 1964, p. 317.

them and for us. Secondly, as we have been urged by anthropologists such as Leach and Beattie, we have to be careful how to construe the genre to which any particular utterance or set of utterances belongs. We cannot begin to evaluate the rationality of procedures until we know what is being said on the relevant occasions, and we cannot know what is being said until we know into what genres the utterances of a given culture may be classified. But now consider an apparent counter-example to my thesis.

In *Purity and Danger* Mary Douglas has argued that the pollution and taboo rules of primitive societies are not to be construed as, for example, unsophisticated exercises in practical hygiene. When we place these rules in the context of the world-view of the way of life of the people who uphold them, we begin to understand the connection for those people between the notion of harm or danger and the notion of an anomaly. An anomalous person or animal or thing, one that cannot be fitted into the classificatory scheme whereby the world is grasped, threatens the order of the cosmos. The response to the recognition of its presence is not to revise the classificatory scheme or to modify the beliefs underlying or springing from it; it is to expel the offending instance. Now the procedures in which this response is embodied are notably different from what we have learnt from Pierce and Popper to regard as characteristic of science. What is anomalous relative to our present classificatory schemes, what constitutes a counter-example to our present beliefs, is to be sought for in order that we may revise and modify our present beliefs and expectations. So far as science is concerned, the discovery of an anomaly is always a victory. Surely it may then be argued the procedures of science and the procedures described by Mary Douglas cannot both be called rational. If the scientific mode of dealing with counter-examples is rational, then the primitive mode must be irrational. But to judge thus would surely be to judge *their* procedures in terms of *our* criteria, in just the way that I have suggested need not occur.

We must at once grant that if a contemporary scientist adopted the attitude to the classification of animal species which, in Mary Douglas's interpretation, was exhibited by the writer of Leviticus we should at once have to suppose him at least prima facie guilty of irrational behavior. But notice that in ascribing irrationality to him we should be pointing to the incoherence and incompatibility between the beliefs and criteria which he already possessed and his new behavior. It is not just that his behavior would be at odds with what we believe to be appropriate; it would be at odds with what we know him to believe to be appropriate. But in the practices codified by the writer of Leviticus, there is no such incoherence; those who engaged in such practices were not trying to be Linnaeus and failing. The point of their enterprise was quite different. Can we say what it was?

Here my previous point about the need to identify genres correctly becomes crucial. To a Frazer, who classified primitive rites as inept technology, we are apt to reply that such rites are not science but, for example, a kind of poetry or drama. Thus John Beattie asserts that magic is not technology but "the acting out of the expression of a desire in symbolic terms" (*Other Cultures*, p. 72). I am not competent to question Beattie's ethnographic findings, insofar as these are empirical. It is, however, right to wonder whether, sophisticated as we are, we may not sometimes at least continue to make Frazer's mistake, but in a more subtle way. For when we approach the utterances and activities of an alien culture with a well-established classification of genres in our mind and ask of a given rite or other practice "Is it a piece of applied science? Or a piece of symbolic and dramatic activity? Or a piece of theology?" we may in fact be asking a set of questions to which any answer may be misleading—although doubtless Beattie's answers are far less misleading than Frazer's. For the utterances and practice in question may belong, as it were, to all and to none of the genres that we have in mind. For those who engage in the given practice the question of how their utterances are to be interpreted—in the sense of "interpretation" in which to allocate a practice or an utterance to a genre is to interpret it, as a prediction, say, rather than as a symbolic expression of desire, or vice versa—may never have arisen. If we question them as to how their utterances are to be interpreted, we may therefore receive an answer which is sincere and yet we may still be deceived. For we may, by the very act of asking these questions, have brought them to the point where they cannot avoid beginning to construe their own utterances in one way rather than another. But perhaps this was not so until we asked the question. Perhaps before that time their utterances were poised in ambiguity. It would follow that questions of rationality and irrationality cannot be appropriately posed until in a given culture the relevant utterances are given a decisive interpretation in terms of genres. Myths would then be seen as perhaps potentially science *and* literature *and* theology; but to understand them as myths would be to understand them as actually yet none of these. Hence the absurdity involved in speaking of myths as misrepresenting reality; the myth is at most a possible misrepresentation of reality, for it does not aspire, while still only a myth, to be a representation.

In the cases where we are right to allocate utterances and practices to genres, it is with reference to the speakers' own implicit or explicit allocations that we ascribe rationality or irrationality. In the areas where we would be mistaken in so allocating utterances, we are not entitled to ascribe either. In both cases it is clear that, even though we are now concerned with criteria other than those with which formal logic is concerned, there is once again no question of being able to distinguish between *our* criteria of rationality (the anthropologists' or sociologists') and *their* criteria (those of the agents whose culture is the object of study). Rationality is nobody's property. It is necessary to re-emphasize this point in order even more clearly to discriminate the position defended in this essay from that of the Victorian defenders of reason, and in order to show that a rationalist standpoint is not merely (as Winch takes it to be) the ideological standpoint of a Western culture which aspires to be the judge of others without being judged itself. The argument of this essay implies the possibility of ascribing irrationality to modern Western culture on precisely the same grounds as we should make this ascription elsewhere. One final footnote to this section of the argument: the community of shared rationality to which I have argued that all recognizably human societies must belong must of course also be a community of shared beliefs to *some* extent. For there are some commonsense beliefs (about day and night, the weather and the material environment generally) which are inescapable for any rational agent.

III

If we discriminate the rational and the irrational in the way that I have suggested in the second section of this essay, and if the form of explanation appropriate to irrational beliefs differs from that appropriate to rational beliefs, as I have suggested in the first section, what follows so far as the explanation of action is concerned?

Beliefs and actions are, after all, intimately related, since it is a central feature of actions that they are expressive of beliefs; and this is not just a contingent fact about actions. An action is identifiable as the action that it is only in terms of the agent's intention.

An intention can only be specified in terms of a first-person statement. The expressions used in formulating such a statement (even if the agent does not himself formulate it explicitly) will presuppose certain beliefs on the agent's part. An everyday intention to spray my roses to kill the green-fly or an exceptional intention to assassinate an archduke and liberate Bosnia alike presuppose an extended web of beliefs, botanical in the one case, political in the other. It is for this reason that it is possible to predicate of actions characteristics which it is the province of logic to consider. An action may be consistent or inconsistent with an agent's other beliefs, and one action may be consistent or inconsistent with another in terms of the beliefs presupposed. As Aristotle pointed out, an action may conclude a syllogistic argument in a way analogous to that in which the utterance of a statement may. It follows that the sociologist or anthropologist will not even have succeeded in identifying correctly the actions which are the object of his study unless and until he has identified the web of beliefs expressed in those actions.

It is important to underline this because there is a tendency, perhaps at its strongest in contemporary political science, to suppose that the object of study in the human sciences is behavior, and "behavior" is an expression understood in these quarters in a behaviorist sense. Haunted by the ghosts of philosophical controversies about dualism, such theorists wish to analyse all mental predicates in behavioral terms and "belief" is an important candidate for such an analysis. But no such analysis can succeed in the case of "belief" at least. For all such analyses must, as their proponents allow, include reference to what they quaintly call "linguistic behavior." More particularly, if we try to analyse the notion of belief in behavioral terms, then to say that someone believes that such-and-such is the case will have to be analysed not only in terms of dispositions to do and to expect certain things, but also in terms of dispositions to say certain things. What sort of disposition to say will be involved? The answer must be a disposition to make certain assertions. But what is an assertion? It is the utterance of a statement in such a way as to give a hearer or reader to understand that the statement is believed by the speaker or writer and is worthy of belief. Thus, the notion of belief has not been analysed away into behavioral terms, for the notion of assertion—which any analysis that sought to be convincing would have to employ—can itself be understood only in terms of the notion of belief. So the notion of belief turns out to be ineliminable, and the contemporary project of a science of behavior is seen to invert the proper relationship between belief and action. Actions must be understood in terms of their character as expressions of belief; beliefs are not simply patterns of behavior plus dispositions to produce such patterns.

I have already noted that to say that rational belief cannot be explained in causal terms is not to say or to imply that actions, even the actions of a man who acts upon a rational belief in a rational way, cannot be explained in causal terms. Indeed, as I have argued elsewhere,[1] to treat an agent's actions as the outcome of the reasons which he possessed for acting in the way that he did is precisely to point to one kind of cause as operative and to exclude other possible causal explanations. The notion that an agent's having a reason to do something may be the cause of his doing it is necessary if we are to distinguish reasons which are genuinely effective from mere rationalizations which are not. But although actions can have causes (in the sense of sufficient and not merely of necessary conditions), the close link between actions and beliefs would suggest that the asymmetry between the explanation of rational belief for which I have argued ought to entail some asymmetry between the explanation of rational action and the explanation of irrational action. That it does so is made clear if we consider two distinct types of cases which lie at opposite ends of a dimension on which the relation of belief and action can be charted.

At one end of this spectrum there is the case where an agent acts rationally on the basis of his beliefs; at the other end there is the case where the agent's beliefs only affect his actions in the most minimal way. There are cultures where the occurrence of the latter type of case is a characteristic feature of social life; in parts of Latin America, for example, belief in sacramental monogamous marriage is part of the Catholicism of the inhabitants, but the actual forms of their sexual unions rarely, if ever, conform to the Catholic pattern. There are other cultures (Campbell's account of a Greek highland village is one example) where the professed beliefs of the agents actually inform the detail of their day to day social life. The difference between these types of cases is in the first instance a difference in what requires explanation. For actions which accord with the beliefs of an agent stand in need of no further explanation than do the beliefs themselves; actions which do not so accord clearly do stand in need of an independent explanation, and the gap between belief and action itself requires to be explained. It follows that once again there is an asymmetry,

[1] See pp. 215–17.

although a rather different one. Where actions do accord with beliefs, the form of explanation will be one in which the whole complex of belief and action is to be explained together; and when the beliefs are rational, explanation will terminate with the account of the norms involved. Where, on the other hand, the beliefs are irrational or the actions do not accord with beliefs, explanation will have to go beyond the delineation of the relevant norms; for we shall need to know at least why discrepancies and incoherencies, contradictions and other irrationalities are tolerated by the agents concerned. Sociological discovery will be an uncovering of those mechanisms which blind agents to or enable them to ignore the irrationalities of their own social order. Hence, the asymmetry in what demands explanation will be matched by an asymmetry in the forms of explanation given. Irrational action—whether irrational because expressive of irrational beliefs or because of inconsistency between beliefs and actions—will be explicable in terms other than those in which rational action is to be explained, just as irrational beliefs are to be explained in terms other than those in which rational beliefs are to be explained.

The nature of the gap between belief and action has traditionally provided matter for the philosophical problem of ἀκρασία. But treatments of that problem fastened upon the gap that sometimes exists between the moral beliefs of an individual agent and his actions. The gap with which I am concerned here is one that is institutionalized so that there is a systematic discrepancy between the norms dominant in the culture and the characteristic behavior of agents in that culture. For the problem of rationality is a problem of the relationship of the beliefs and norms which define the roles which structure action in a given social order and the beliefs and norms of the agents whose behavior is characteristically governed or defined by these roles. Consider, for example, the contrast between a society such as Britain where articulate beliefs about the hierarchy of status and class cohere well with the role-governed behavior of agents in status and class situations and a society such as the United States where behavior expresses an implicit recognition of hierarchies of status and class, the existence of which at the level of articulate belief a surprisingly large proportion of the population deny. What needs to be explained is why this contradiction is tolerable and the hypotheses about comparative rates of mobility or about social identity which are sometimes advanced on this subject will only have explanatory power if they can explain this. To adopt this perspective may be procedurally important for the empirical investigator in directing his attention to one set of facts rather than another. If we wish to explain the civil rights movement among American Negroes, for example, we shall do well to pause and ask what needs to be explained. Is it why since 1953 Negro students have acted on the beliefs which they are taught in school that all American citizens, indeed all men, have certain rights? or is it, rather, why they failed for so long or were unable to act on their beliefs? If the latter, we shall expect no general, as it were positive explanation of the Negro civil rights movement, but only a series of explanations of why the different particular obstacles to such a movement were removed in the early 1950s. These examples are large, obvious, and unsophisticated, but perhaps the obviousness will compensate for the lack of sophistication.

IV

Consider now an example of a very different kind. The weight of my initial argument was directed against the contention that we did not need to discriminate between rational and irrational beliefs in order to explain the origin and the maintenance of those beliefs. But I now wish to press further another contention, namely that in discriminating between what is rational and what is irrational we must not mistake the standards of normal belief and behavior in our own age for the standards of rational belief and behavior as such. This mistake seems to me embodied in Norman Cohn's *The Pursuit of the Millennium*. It is to the point that Cohn's exploratory apparatus is psychological and that he appears to believe that the key psychological terms which he deploys can be deployed without reference to the criteria of the culture which is the object of his inquiry. So we find in his pages[1] the following argument: J. A. Boullan, the nineteenth-century sectarian, was declared by psychiatrists on the evidence of his actions and his handwriting to suffer from paranoia; J. A. Boullan's beliefs and behavior resemble those of the late medieval Brethren of the Free Spirit; therefore the medieval Brethren of the Free Spirit may be presumed to have suffered from paranoia. Now to suffer from paranoia is precisely to have delusions as to one's importance and as to one's relations to others. But which beliefs count as delusions and which as rational is a matter of the standards of a given time and place.

When we examine the case of Thomas Münzer, for example—

[1] 1962 edition, pp. 185–86.

of whom Cohn treats—we find that Münzer accepts, just as his Protestant and Catholic enemies did, the standard of scripture. But he is more, rather than less, rational than they in interpreting scripture, if anything. For he takes at their face value certain New Testament injunctions, for which his opponents have to provide special explanations. Münzer, after much careful study, took on the office of a *propheta*, an office of whose place in the early church he read in the New Testament, but which he found absent in sixteenth-century churches. It is very difficult to see that Münzer's apocalyptic reading of the New Testament is less rational than the faith of the bishops who condemned Münzer or of Luther, both of whom have to flout New Testament texts in which they professedly believe.

Cohn's error resides in making the *content* of beliefs and not their irrationality the criterion of their being delusional. It is not perhaps surprising that apocalyptic prophesying should be condemned in a book whose ethos is as much a reflection of the climate in which the end-of-ideology thesis was born as Cohn's is. But the true conclusion to be drawn reflects not on the rationality of those sixteenth-century revolutionaries, such as Münzer, whom Cohn so dislikes, as on the defensibility of contemporary views of the nature of rationality.

V

Two final morals: the first is that, if I am correct in supposing rationality to be an inescapable sociological category, then once again the positivist account of sociology in terms of a logical dichotomy between facts and values must break down. For to characterize actions and institutionalized practices as rational or irrational is to evaluate them. Nor is it the case that this evaluation is an element superadded to an original merely descriptive element. To call an argument fallacious is always at once to describe and to evaluate it. It is highly paradoxical that the impossibility of deducing evaluative conclusions from factual premises should have been advanced as a truth of logic, when logic is itself the science in which the coincidence of description and evaluation is most obvious. The social scientist is, if I am right, committed to the values of rationality in virtue of his explanatory projects in a stronger sense than the natural scientist is. For it is not only the case that his own procedures must be rational; but he cannot escape the use of the concept of rationality in his inquiries.

A second moral is that, if my arguments are correct, then the social scientist cannot evade the task of deciding what types of arguments and evidence are logically appropriate in different areas; he must be able to decide what constitutes the rationality of a scientific belief, or a moral belief, or a religious belief. But to do this is to do philosophy. It follows that the relationship of social science to philosophy must be other than the relationship of natural science to philosophy. The philosopher cannot be merely an external commentator on the social sciences; for philosophical arguments will actually enter into and forge critical links within the sociologist's explanations. The expulsion of philosophy from the social sciences—or at least the restriction of philosophy to *post eventum* comment on the social scientist's concepts and procedures—turns out to be another lost positivistic cause. Happily or unhappily, the philosophers cannot be restricted merely to interpreting the social sciences; the point of their activity is to change them.

22

Is a science of comparative politics possible?

There was once a man who aspired to be the author of the general theory of holes. When asked "What kind of hole—holes dug by children in the sand for amusement, holes dug by gardeners to plant lettuce seedlings, tank traps, holes made by roadmakers?" he would reply indignantly that he wished for a *general* theory that would explain all of these. He rejected *ab initio* the—as he saw it—pathetically common-sense view that of the digging of different kinds of holes there are quite different kinds of explanations to be given; why then he would ask do we have the concept of a hole? Lacking the explanations to which he originally aspired, he then fell to discovering statistically significant correlations; he found for example that there is a correlation between the aggregate hole-digging achievement of a society as measured, or at least one day to be measured, by econometric techniques, and its degree of technological development. The United States surpasses both Paraguay and Upper Volta in hole-digging. He also discovered that war accelerates hole-digging; there are more holes in Vietnam than there were. These observations, he would always insist, were neutral and value-free. This man's achievement has passed totally unnoticed except by me. Had he however turned his talents to political science, had he concerned himself not with holes, but with modernization, urbanization or violence, I find it difficult to believe that he might not have achieved high office in the APSA.

I

The ultimate aim of this paper is constructive; the skepticism which infects so much of my argument is a means and not an end. I do not want to show that there *cannot* be a general science of political action, but only to indicate certain obstacles that stand in the way of the founding of such a science and to suggest that the present practice of so-called political science is unlikely to overcome these obstacles. In writing more specifically of *comparative* political science I do not wish to suggest that there could be any other sort of political science; this the APSA recognized when it merged what was its section devoted to comparative politics into the general body. It is with the claim to be using legitimate *comparative* methods which could enable us to advance and to test genuine law-like *cross-cultural* generalizations that I shall initially be concerned. I shall not be concerned to question the possibility of genuine and relevant comparison and even of cross-cultural comparison for other purposes: to exhibit the march of the *Weltgeist* through history, for instance, or to draw moral lessons about the respective benefits of barbarism and civilization. These may or may not be reputable activities; I shall not argue for or against them here. I shall be solely interested in the project of a political *science*, of the formulation of cross-cultural, law-like causal generalizations which may in turn be explained by theories, as the generalizations of Boyle's Law and Dalton's Law are explained by the kinetic theory of gases; all that I say about the problem of comparability must be understood in this particular context. Moreover, my skepticism about any alleged parallel between theorizing about politics and theorizing about gases will not initially be founded on the consideration of the character of human action in general. I shall not argue, for example, that human actions cannot have causes, not just or even mainly because I believe that this proposition is false, but because I believe that, even if its falsity is agreed, we still have substantial grounds for skepticism about comparative political science. My method of proceeding in the first part of my argument will be as follows: I shall examine in turn the claim to have formulated law-like generalizations about political attitudes, about political institutions and practices, and about the discharge of political functions. I shall then in the second part of my argument suggest an alternative strategy to that now customarily employed, although the change in strategy will turn out to also involve a change in aim.

II

The study of political culture, of political attitudes, as it has been developed, seems to rest upon the assumption that it is possible to identify political attitudes independently of political institutions and practices. There are at least two reasons for thinking this assumption false. The first derives from Wittgenstein, who pointed out that we identify and define attitudes in terms of the objects toward which they are directed, and not vice versa. Our understanding of the concept of fear depends upon our understanding of the concepts of harm and danger and not vice versa. Our understanding of the concept of an aesthetic attitude depends upon our understanding of the concept of a work of art. It follows that an ability to identify a set of attitudes in one culture as political, and a set of attitudes in some second culture as political, with a view to comparing them must depend upon our having already identified as political in both cultures a set of institutions and practices toward which these attitudes are directed. In other words, the ability to construct comparative generalizations about attitudes depends on our already having solved the problem of how to construct comparative generalizations about institutions and practices. The notion of political culture is secondary to and parasitic upon the notion of political practice.

It follows that a necessary condition of a comparative investigation of political cultures is that the argument about the comparability of political institutions should have a certain outcome; but this is only a necessary end not a sufficient condition. It is also necessary if political attitudes are to be the subject of comparative inquiry that other attitudes shall be susceptible of comparison of a certain kind. I can explain what I mean by this by citing an example from *The Civic Culture* (Chapter IV, pp. 102–5) where Almond and Verba argue that Italians are less committed to and identified with the actions of their government than are Germans or Englishmen, offering as evidence the fact that the Italian respondents, as compared with the English and German respondents to their survey, placed such actions very low on a list of items to which they had been asked to give a rank order in terms of the amount of pride they took in them. At no point do Almond and Verba pause to ask whether the concept of pride is the same in the three different national cultures, that is, to ask whether the different respondents had after all been asked the same question. But in fact the concept of pride (" . . . si sente piu' orgoglioso . . .") in Italy is not the same as that pride in England. The notion of taking pride in Italian culture is still inexorably linked, especially in the South but also in the North, to the notion of honor. What one takes pride in is what touches on one's honor. If asked to list the subjects which touched their honor, many Italians would spontaneously place the chastity of their immediate female relatives high on the list—a connection that it would occur to very few Englishmen to make. These notions of pride and honor partially specify and are partially specified by a notion of the family itself importantly, if imperfectly, embodied in the actualities of Italian family life. Hence we cannot hope to compare an Italian's attitude to his government's acts with an Englishman's in respect of the pride each takes; any comparison would have to begin from the different range of virtues and emotions incorporated in the different social institutions. Once again the project of comparing attitudes independently of institutions and practices encounters difficulties. These particular difficulties suggest that a key question is: what are the units in each culture which are compared to be? To this question I shall of course return; but let me note that the difficulty which I have exemplified in the preceding argument is contingent on Almond and Verba's particular procedures. It does not arise from the project of comparison as such. For the difficulty which arises over any comparison between English and German culture on the one hand, and Italian on the other, from relying on the in fact false assumption that these cultures agree in their concept of pride would not arise in the same way if Italian attitudes were to be compared with Greek, for example. Not that there would not be other and perhaps more subtle pitfalls, but these would not arise merely because concepts of pride and honor are not shared.

We can now pose our problem in the following way: we wish to find identifiable units in different societies and cultures about which we may construct true causal generalizations. Political attitudes, for the two reasons I have given, are implausible candidates; what about political institutions and practices? The first point to be made here is that in turning to the discussion of political institutions and practices we have not left behind the topic of political attitudes. For attitudes to and beliefs about institutions and practices may sometimes be purely external phenomena; that is, the institution or the practice is what it is and does what it does independently of what certain people think and feel about it. But it is an obvious truism that no institution or practice is what it is, or does what it does, independently of what anyone whatsoever thinks or feels about it. For institutions and practices are always partially, even if to differing degrees, constituted by what certain people think and feel about them.

Consider the example of a currency system: a given type of piece of paper or of metal has the value that it has not only because it has been issued by a duly constituted authority, but because it is

accepted as having that value by the members of a particular
currency-using population. When this condition is not generally
satisfied, as in Germany and Austria in 1923, the currency ceases
to have value, and thus ceases to be currency. So also with an
army: an officer has the authority that he has not only because his
commission has been issued by a duly constituted authority, but
because he is accepted as having that status by the men serving
under him. When this condition is not generally satisfied, as in
Russia in 1917, an officer ceases to have authority, and thus ceases
to be an officer. Since such beliefs about social institutions are
partially constitutive of social institutions, it is impossible to
identify the institution except in terms of the beliefs of those who
engage in its practices. This fact is ignored in general by those who
wish to define political science as the study of political *behavior*,
with a view to thereby providing a public, neutral subject matter
for scientific enquiry. But if we identify behavior except in terms
of the intentions and therefore of the beliefs of the agents we shall
risk describing what they are doing as what we would be doing if
we went through that series of movements or something like it
rather than what they are actually doing. Nor do we avoid this
difficulty merely by finding *some* description of the behavior in
question which both the agents themselves and the political
scientist would accept. For clearly both agents and political scientist
might apply the description "voting behavior" to what they do,
but yet have a quite different understanding of what it is to vote.
But now what bearing does all this have upon the project of
comparing political institutions and practices?

III

I take it that if the generalizations which political scientists construct are to be part of a science, then among the conditions which
must be satisfied is this: that we shall be able to distinguish
between genuine law-like generalizations and mere *de facto* generalizations which hold only of the instances so far observed. I understand by this distinction, as many others have understood by it,
the difference between a generalization the assertion of which
commits one to the assertion of a set of corresponding counter-
factual conditionals and a generalization which does not so commit one. In the natural sciences the ground for treating a generalization as a law is generally not merely that as a matter of fact no
plausible counter-examples have yet been produced. It is also nor-

mally required that it be supported by a body of theory. But what then of these generalizations which we wish to assert as genuine law-like generalizations before we have any well-established theory? What about the generalizations of Kepler or of Galileo before Newton formulated his laws? What about Boyle's Law or Dalton's Law before the establishment of the kinetic theory? At this point the problems of confirmation theory become real.

The particular finding of confirmation theory that is relevant is that the degree to which a positive instance does genuinely confirm a generalization is in part a matter of the kind of environment in which it is found. For the greater the extent of the radically different environments in which confirmatory instances of a genera-lization are found, the less likely it is that the generalization is only confirmed in certain contingent environmental circumstances. Now it is a matter of contingent fact that nature is so structured that this condition is normally realizable. For nature could have been otherwise. If black ravens on being taken into laboratories for pigmentation tests, or if black ravens on being observed in the Arctic—in the course of our seeking confirmation or otherwise of the generalization that all ravens are black—promptly turned into philosphers of science or clouds of dust, generalizations about ravenly nigritude could not be as well founded as they are. But in fact the character of social life is such that in some respects it resembles this imaginary nature rather than nature as it—for-tunately for natural scientists—is.

Consider for example the alleged generalization that in two-party electoral systems the two parties will tend to move together in their policies and the alleged explanation for this generalization, that this is because neither party can hope to win those voters attracted by the furthest opposed wing of the other party, but only those nearest to it. Hence where, for example, the parties and their wings can be placed on a Left-Right dimension, each party tends to move its policies toward the center, having no hope of winning votes from the extreme Right or Left. Now consider two different kinds of attempts to provide counter-examples to this generaliza-tion. An example of the first would be Greece before the coup d'état of the colonels. This seems to be a straightforward refuta-tion of the generalization, even if we remember that a single counter-example in the natural sciences is never adequate to refute a well-established theory or a generalization with a huge weight of evidence supporting it, such as the generalization that all solids except bismuth, cast-iron, ice, and type metal expand when heated. For here we have nothing like a well-supported theory or generalization; it is rather as if the seventh raven we were to come across was colored magenta. Now consider a quite different kind of attempt to provide a counter-example.

Suppose that someone were to point to the rival parties in Sierra Leone immediately before the army seized power there, and to offer them as a counter-example. We ought at once to remember what Ruth Schachter wrote of African mass parties: "They and their cultural affiliates were interested in everything from the cradle to the grave—in birth, initiation, religion, marriage, divorce, dancing, song, plays, feuds, debts, land, migration, death, public order—and not only electoral success." At once the question cannot but be framed: "Why do we think of these as parties, rather than as, say, churches?" The answer, that they have some of the marks of American political parties, and that they call themselves parties, does nothing to show that in fact the meaning of "party" is not radically changed when the cultural context is radically changed, or that even if it is not changed the description has not become inapplicable. The intentions, the beliefs, the concepts which inform the practices of African mass parties provide so different a context that there can be no question of transporting the phenomena of party to this context in order to provide a suitably different environment for testing our generalization. Where the environment and where the culture is radically different the phenomenon is viewed so differently by those who participate in it that it is an entirely different phenomenon. In just this respect does society differ from nature. That is to say, the provision of an environment sufficiently different to make the search for counter-examples interesting will normally be the provision of an environment where we cannot hope or expect to find examples of the original phenomenon and therefore cannot hope to find counter-examples.

Note that my thesis is not that to transplant a phenomenon such as party is to subject it to causal influences which transform it. That is doubtless true. But the difficulty of studying political parties in alien social environments to test a generalization constructed about political parties in familiar social environments is not like the difficulty of studying viruses: that their own causal properties and/or those of the environment cause them to mutate too rapidly and too often. If this were the type of difficulty that we encountered in formulating cross-cultural generalizations about politics, then we might well ask if we could not insulate the object of study in its new environment from the disturbing causal influences at work. To ask this would be to mistake my point which is not about causal interference with the phenomenon of party, but with the absence of the same concept of party, or perhaps of any concept of party, as we understand it, in the alien culture.

Let me now consider a possible objection to this thesis which would base itself upon my choice of examples. A quite different choice of examples might provide us with more plausible candidates for cross-cultural generalization. Consider the alleged (and quite possibly false) generalization that in the government of cities, if a single non-transferable vote for single members is the method of election, then there will be over a certain time span a tendency for a two-party system to flourish. This seems to hold in the United States. But it might hold in other alien environments, even environments of an exotic kind, where we could identify the system as two-party, even if unclear in what sense the parties were parties. But this is surely therefore an example of at least a possible cross-cultural comparison which provides us with a law-like generalization and is therefore lethal to my entire thesis. Let me at once concede that I take this generalization to be law-like in that it does indeed entail counter-factual conditionals, and let me further concede that the counter-factuals in question might be true. But I do not concede that it injures my thesis. Why not?

The reason for not conceding that this example, if true, would injure my thesis is intimately connected with the fact that I should not be extremely surprised if the generalization in question did turn out to be true of cities outside North America as well as in North America. For what could make the generalization true, if true, is that voters prefer in general not to waste their votes in voting on matters that concern the administration of their daily lives; and it requires only a minimal and a very untheoretical understanding of the electoral system produced by such a voting procedure to understand that in the majority of cases votes for a third party will be wasted. The considerations from which we can deduce *this* particular generalization are thus concerned with human rationality in general; they do not have any specific connection with politics and they do not belong to political science, but to our general understanding of rationality. This will be true of all generalizations which concern the formal structures of human argument, even if they appear in political clothing, furnishing us with explanations of particular political choices and actions. So it must be, for example, with all applications of the theory of games to politics.

My thesis about the legitimacy or otherwise of the project of accumulating a stock of cross-cultural generalizations about political behavior to furnish the empirical foundation for a political science, as I have developed it so far, can now be stated disjunctively: *either* such generalizations about institutions will necessarily lack the kind of confirmation they require *or* they will be consequences of true generalizations about human rationality and not part of a specifically political science.

To complete this part of my argument I must now make three further observations. The first is that my statement of the difficulties in constructing true and warranted cross-cultural generalizations about political institutions is obviously akin to the arguments which some anthropologists—notably Edmund Leach and Walter Goldschmidt—have developed about cross-cultural generalizations in their discipline. But Goldschmidt has then argued that it is not institutions, but functions, or rather institutions only as serving certain functions, which we ought to aspire to compare; and this contention has already been advanced by some political scientists. We are, that is to say, to begin by identifying the same function in different societies and then to inquire how quite different institutions have this same effect; for I take it that to say that X performs, serves, or discharges a given function always entails that X is the cause of a particular effect, even if this does not exhaust the meaning of the statement in which function was ascribed. It is certainly not a final objection to this project that most political scientists who have tried to specify the functions in question have produced nothing but statements about institutions and their effects in which the word "function" may appear, but could be replaced not only without loss, but with gain. "Wherever the political party has emerged, it appears to perform some common functions in a wide variety of political systems . . . the organization called the party is expected to organize public opinion and to communicate demands to the center of governmental power and decision . . . the party must articulate to its followers the concept and meaning of the broader community . . . the party is likely to be involved in political recruitment . . . These similarities of function . . . suggest that the political party when the activities of a political system reach a certain degree of complexity, or whenever the notion of political power comes to include the idea that the mass public must participate or be controlled."[1] In a passage like this, the notion of function can be replaced entirely by either the notion of effect or the notion of purpose. When we so replace it, we notice also that the transition from previous

[1] J. LaPalombara and M. Weiner, eds., *Political Parties and Political Development* (Princeton, N.J.: Princeton University Press).

to tentative conclusion requires no reliance on any factual generalizations anyway; it is merely a matter of drawing out the consequences of definition. But even if in the writing of political
scientists as sophisticated as LaPalombara and Weiner the
function of the use of "function" is unclear, it does not follow
that this has to be so. But the condition of its not being so is that
we should have some criteria for identifying the functions served
by political institutions which is other than, and independent of,
the aims and purposes of political agents and the effects of political
institutions. The provision of such a criteria would require the
identification of a system, using the word "system" precisely, so
that concepts of feedback and equilibrium are applicable on the
basis of quantitative data which will provide values for variables
in differential equations. I scarcely need stress the remoteness
of this goal from the present state of all political science; if we
match the requirements that have to be satisfied to identify
such a system—which would involve, for example, being able
to distinguish between change that is part of the movement of
items through the system, change that is itself part of the struc-
turing of the system, and change that is the system decaying by
providing ways of measuring rates of change for all three—then
a work like David Easton's *A Systems Analysis of Political Life*
looks like a mad, millenarian dream. I therefore take it that any
attempt to answer my argument by suggesting that cross-cultural
generalizations about institutions may be provided by means of a
prior account in terms of functions is bound to fail.

My second observation is that my argument does not imply any
undervaluation of the importance of the work done by political
scientists in establishing both the facts about particular institutions
and the very limited generalizations they do establish. That the
conditions under which these generalizations hold necessarily
remain unclear to us for the kind of reason that I have given
does not mean that we do not need the best that we can get in this
case, which is what they give us; only this kind of accumulation
of data in no way leads toward the construction of a science. I
shall later suggest an alternative context in which these empirical
labors could perhaps be viewed more constructively. For the
moment I note that it is Machiavelli who ought to be regarded as
the patron saint of political studies and not Hobbes, and for this
reason: Hobbes believed—as presumably Almond and La-
Palombara and Easton (although Easton, in ways that I do not
entirely understand, tries to distinguish his enterprise from that of
Hobbes) believe—that the fortuitous, the surprising, the unpre-

dicted, arise in politics only because our knowledge of political motions is less adequate than our knowledge of planetary motions. Given time, labor, and foundation grants—the contemporary version of royal patronage—an unpredicted revolution—but for the sheer complexity of human affairs—ought to be as disgraceful to political scientists as an unpredicted eclipse to astronomers. But Machiavelli realized that in political life *fortuna*, the bitch goddess of unpredictability, has never been dethroned. To any stock of maxims derived from empirically founded generalizations the student of politics must always add one more: "And do not be surprised if in the event things turn out otherwise." The need to include this maxim follows from my argument, just as it follows from Machiavelli's.

My third observation is that in the history of political theory we have more than once been here before, and notably in the dispute between James Mill and Macaulay. James Mill argued, although in the interests of a quite different conclusion, even more that we cannot find reliable empirical generalizations about political behavior: "Absolute monarchy under Neros and Caligulas . . . is the scourge of human nature. On the other side, the public of Denmark . . . under their absolute monarch are as well governed as any people in Europe . . . the surface of history affords, therefore, no certain principles of decision." Mill then proceeded to argue from this that we ought to turn instead to the type of psychology favored by the utilitarians for our explanations, that there is no specifically political science. Against him Macaulay argued that the empirical facts about government *do* yield genuine lawlike generalizations, not least generalizations of a kind which enable us to predict future actions with great confidence. And it is clear that this practical use of law-like generalizations provides Macaulay with a crucial motive. The claim to technical expertise on the part of the political scientist is closely bound up with the defense of the possibility of formulating law-like generalizations. If the latter fails, the former is gravely impaired. When in our time on the basis of *his* generalizations Lipset predicts totalitarian horrors as the outcome of widespread political participation, he turns out to be the true heir of Macaulay who, on the basis of *his* generalizations, predicted cultural ruin if "the great number" were allowed to participate in government; "they will commit waste of every sort in the estate of mankind, and transmit it to posterity impoverished and desolate," so that "in two or three hundred years, a few lean and half naked fishermen may divide with owls and foxes the ruins of the greatest of European cities . . ." In both Macaulay and Lipset the claims of political science are closely linked to a claim about the political status of the political scientist, to a claim about the possession of political expertise, which entitles the political scientist to advise government. This claim too demands inquiry; but a prerequisite for such inquiry is a further development of my central argument.

IV

My doubts about identifying institutions in different cultures as "the same" and therefore as interestingly different are of course compatible with a recognition of the massive fact that the same actions are regularly performed in quite different cultures. One class of such actions are those that derive from implicit imitation. It is of course not necessarily or always the case that if one person imitates another he does what the other does. Indeed it is sometimes the condition of successful imitation that he who imitates shall not do what the other does precisely in order to seem to do what the other does. But when the intention to perform the same action as another *is* present, we always have an intelligible question as to why, if the corresponding action or its consequences or both are not the same as those produced by the agent imitated, they are not so. Of course it may be that even a particular intention to perform certain actions cannot be intelligibly embodied in some cultures; *Don Quixote* is the classical example. But we do have clear cases where the same intention is embodied in two different cultures, such intentions as to apply Roman Law or the Code Napoléon, or to bring about some particular course of economic development. What we shall achieve if we study the projects springing from such intentions are two or more histories of these projects, and it is only after writing these histories that we shall be able to compare the different outcomes of the same intention. We shall not, that is to say, begin by collecting data in the hope of formulating causal generalizations; we shall begin by looking at cases where a will to achieve the same end was realized with greater or lesser success in different cultural contexts.

There is of course a notable formula which seems to prescribe this approach: "Men make their own history, but they do not make it just as they please. They do not make it under circumstances chosen by themselves, but under circumstances directly encountered, given and transmitted from the past." But when Marx wrote these words he did not discriminate what

was implied by this approach from a search for causal generalizations, and he does not do so at least in part because he treats
what he calls the circumstances of action only as a causally
effective and limiting environment and not in addition, or rather
primarily, as a context of meaning-conferring symbols and rules.
So Marx speaks of "the burden of history" in the very next
sentence and Engels speaks of history as a "series of parallelograms of forces," and it is this model of Engels which creates for
Plekhanov the problem of the role of the individual in history
(since an individual can be no more than a point at which some
force operates). But the question with which Marx began in
the *Eighteenth Brumaire* does not require an answer in terms of
causal generalizations and parallelograms of forces. For what
Marx asks then is why, when someone aspires to perform the
same actions as a predecessor in some earlier cultural period—as
the English Puritans aspired to be Old Testament Israelites or the
French Revolutionary Roman republicans or Louis Napoléon
to do the deeds of Napoleon I—the actions should be so different.
A full answer to Marx's question would provide a genuine
starting point for historical comparison, but such an answer
could only be provided by first writing a history of each of these
episodes.

I therefore take it that if we wish to have a science of comparative politics, one first step is the writing of a series of comparative
histories; that comparative history is a more fundamental discipline
than comparative politics. But then the crucial question arises:
what can we legitimately expect the study of comparative history
to yield? And one of the best ways of answering this question is to
ask what the study of comparative history has in fact yielded.
Consider for example Isaac Deutscher's thesis about revolutions.
Deutscher asserted that in the English, French, and Russian
revolutions the same "broad scheme of revolutionary development"
could be discerned. This scheme involves three stages: a first
stage in which "popular energy, impatience, anger and hope"
burst out, and "the party that gives the fullest expression to the
popular mood outdoes its rivals, gains the confidence of the masses
and rises to power"; a second stage in which during the war on
behalf of the revolution the leaders of the revolutionary party and
the people are so well in accord that the leaders "are willing and
even eager to submit their policies to open debate and to accept
the popular verdict"; and a third stage in which weariness and
ruthlessness divide party and people, so that the revolutionary
party cannot listen to, but must indeed suppress the voice of the

people, thus in consequence splitting itself between the holders of revolutionary power and the caretakers of the purity of revolutionary doctrine. This pattern holds of "any party of the revolution, whether it be called Independent, Jacobin or Bolshevik."

That there are such patterns revealed by the rare studies of comparative history that we already possess and that there will be more is clear. But how are we to understand them? When we assert the recurrence of such a pattern, what are we asserting? Deutscher himself, following Engels and Plekhanov, understood this pattern of revolutionary behavior deterministically. Hence followed his very different assessment of Trotsky's relation to Stalin from Trotsky's own non-deterministic assessment of that relationship. Deutscher treats each stage, as he specified it, as satisfying both a necessary and a sufficient condition for the occurrence of the next stage, as he specified it; hence he takes it that Trotsky, the caretaker of revolutionary purity, could not but have failed to hold power, since maintaining the revolutionary doctrine and holding power are causally incompatible.

The evaluation of Deutscher's specific contentions about revolution is not relevant to my present argument; but the contention Deutscher almost takes for granted, namely that the discernment of recurring patterns in history has as its end-product the formulation of law-like generalizations, is precisely what I want to question. For when I suggested that the study of comparative politics would certainly benefit from, and perhaps require, a prior writing of comparative history, I did not intend to imply that what comparative history will provide us with is merely a stock of more adequate materials for the construction of these cross-cultural, law-like generalizations which the present methods of orthodox political science aspire to but in fact fail to provide; that the comparative history is not so much an alternative, as merely a necessary prelude to proceeding as before. What I want to suggest is that it is characteristic of the causal knowledge which history does provide us with that the antecedent conditions in terms of which we explain historical outcomes are sometimes necessary conditions for the occurrence of some specific outcome, but are never sufficient. If this is so, then the patterns which we discern in comparative history will always be *de facto* guides yielding Machiavellian maxims, rather than Hobbesian laws. But is it so? Is comparative political science, even when based on comparative history, precluded from formulating law-like generalizations?

To cast light on this, compare the situation of the political scientist with that of the political agent. The political agent confronts a situation in which he wishes to produce certain outcomes. He wishes, for example, to maintain two-party democracy in a new state, or he wishes to overthrow that state by revolutionary action. The situation he confronts consists of other political agents: party politicians, soldiers, trade union leaders, trade union rank and file, and so on. Some of each of these groups are keen readers of such works as *Political Man, Voting, Permanent Revolution*, and so on. Each of these derives certain inductively grounded maxims from these works; in an earlier age the maxims had different sources—Livy, Plutarch, what Napoleon did, or political folk wisdom—but the situation was essentially the same. The difficulty in applying the maxims is that the factors in the situation confronting the agent include the beliefs of every other agent about what each agent other than himself will do in applying the maxims, including the beliefs of every agent about what every other agent believes about his beliefs. "I know you know I know you know I know" is a crucial piece of poetic wisdom for political as well as for sexual behavior. The perception of any pattern or regularity in the behavior of the other actors, or in the behavior characteristic of this particular type of situation, is what particularly invites deviation from the pattern. "They all knew what Napoleon would have done," said Grant of the Union generals. "The trouble was that the rebel generals didn't know about Napoleon."

The key part that beliefs play in defining political situations, and the fact that beliefs are always liable to be altered by reflection upon the situation, including reflection about the beliefs of other agents, has a crucial consequence: that we cannot ever identify a determinate set of factors which constitute the initial conditions for the production of some outcome in conformity with a law-like regularity. To claim that we could identify such regularities and such sets of factors would be to claim that we can understand what occurs in politics independently of a knowledge of the beliefs of the agents, for it would be to claim that the beliefs do not play a causal role in political outcomes.

It makes no difference at this point if the alleged law-like regularity is framed in probabilistic terms: when the alleged probability of an outcome is ·7, the prediction is as vulnerable to reflection by agents as when the alleged probability of an outcome is 1. The conclusion that political agents are bound to be prone to error in their predictions of what other agents will do, and hence of political outcomes, has one important merit other than that of following validly from my premises: it would appear to be true. Nor is its truth incompatible with the fact that some political agents produce more correct predictions than others. It would perhaps be cynical to explain this latter fact by pointing out that given an entirely random relationship between prediction and outcome in a sufficiently large population of predictors, predictions, and outcomes, certain predictors would consistently predict correctly, just as certain predictors would consistently predict incorrectly. But without resorting to either cynicism or the theorems of statistics one can point out that success at prediction in practical affairs, including political affairs, can never be embodied into a method which can be taught, precisely because the maxims relied upon are open-textured and open-ended, and the sense of when which maxim is relevant cannot itself be unpacked into a set of maxims.

It may be asked: when I conclude that political agents cannot find law-like generalizations to aid them in their actions (other of course than those crucial and rock-like law-like generalizations of the physical senses which are available to us all, such that a bullet accelerates in the way that all moving bodies do, and that when a man's skull is crushed by an ice pick he dies), what is the force of "cannot"? Do I mean only that we have at the moment no technique for identifying determinate sets of antecedent conditions of the relevent kind, but that such a technique might well be discovered? Or do I mean that there is some confusion in the nature of such a technique? Am I saying what the limits of inquiry are *as of now*, or what the limits *as such* are?

I am strongly inclined to say that at the moment we have no grounds for answering this question as it stands in either way. We lack even the most minimal theoretical background against which to raise such questions. To say this is not to ignore the empirical work done by both psychologists and sociologists on such topics as prejudice, cognitive dissonance, and the relation of roles to beliefs; it is to say that the results of empirical studies in this field (which are not always obviously consistent with each other) are exceptionally difficult to interpret and to assess, in part just for the type of reason that I have given.

What I have been arguing in this latter part of my essay is that the political agent cannot rely on law-governed regularities in his activities. But just those premises, which entail that conclusion, entail that the political scientist is in no better position in this respect than the political agent. The political scientist may claim to know more (quantitatively, as it were) than many political agents;

but his knowledge is not of a different kind, and there seems no reason to believe that the chances that he will be able to apply the inductively grounded maxims which he derives from his studies in the course of political action successfully are any higher than they are for any other political agent.

If this is so, then the case for Machiavelli against Hobbes rests not merely on the impossibility of testing these law-like generalizations to which a true science of comparative politics would have to aspire; it derives also from the nature of the subject matter of political science. For the most that any study of comparative politics based upon comparative history can hope to supply us with in the foreseeable future is *de facto* generalizations about what has been an obstacle to or has facilitated certain types of course of action. There is available for the formulation of this type of generalization no vocabulary for political scientists which is essentially more sophisticated than the vocabulary of political agents themselves. And the advice given by political scientists turns out to be simply the advice given by a certain genre of political agent, agents as partial, as socially conditioned, as creative and as wayward as any others.

To this the defender of orthodox political science might well feel bound to reply as follows. *Qua* scientist, he may claim, he has a vocabulary that is not available to political agents; and he has this neutrality precisely because he restricts himself to the facts and to theorizing about them in an uncommitted way. Your redefinition of the tasks of political studies would, he might complain, destroy this neutrality. For the model of explanation implicit in your view of the relation of comparative history to comparative politics is as follows: Men in two different cultures seek to implement the same intention in action. Either their actions or the consequences of their actions may differ. If they do, by examining what was present in the one case and absent in the other, you make inferences as to what the obstacles or diversions were in either or both cases. You then explain in terms of the presence or absence of these obstacles or diversions the success or failure of the respective projects. But this is in fact a model of explanation familiar in our everyday understanding of action; and when we apply it in everyday life we cite as explanations for the success or failure of men's projects, not merely the external obstacles which they faced or the lack of such obstacles, but such factors as their reasonableness or un-reasonableness, their courage or their weakness, their willingness or reluctance to commit injustice and so on. That is to say, your model of explanation is that used by ordinary men in their political and other actions to assess themselves and each other and it is of the essence of this mode of explanation that we may cite in explanation evaluations both of intelligence and of moral character. The strength of orthodox comparative political science, this objector will go on, is that it has broken decisively with the evaluative commitments of the world of action. Just because it aspires to study these scientifically, it cannot share them. It must instead be objective in a sense that requires that it be neutral and value-free.

I accept from this objection the characterization of my own standpoint. It would certainly be an open empirical question whether it ever was in fact true that this or that project failed because of the unreasonableness or the injustice of the agents; but a priori nothing could rule out the possibility of these being true and relevant explanations. Political science would become in a true sense a moral science. But I do not take this to be in any way an objection. For what is the alternative, as it is exemplified in comparative political science as it is now usually practiced?

The type of comparative political science of which I have been highly critical is indeed generally and deeply committed to the view that its inquiries and explanations are indeed value-free. This results in an attempt to allow evaluative expressions into political life only in intentional contexts, in oratio obliqua, or in quotation marks. Hence, as John Schaar has pointed out,[1] such notions as those of legitimacy are in fact defined in terms of belief. Lipset says that "Legitimacy involves the capacity of the system to engender and maintain the belief that the existing political institutions are the most appropriate ones for the society" (*Political Man*, p. 77) and Robert Bierstedt writes that "In the tradition of Weber, legitimacy has been defined as the degree to which institutions are valued for themselves and considered right and proper."[2] These definitions are clearly mistaken in any case; not only would there be no contradiction in holding that a government was entirely legitimate, but that its institutions were morally ill-suited to a particular society, but in a society where this latter was widely believed, it would not follow either that the government was, or that it was considered, illegitimate. But it is not mere definitional ineptitude that I am concerned with here. Suppose that we define, as Lipset and the Weberian tradition according to Bierstedt do, evaluation in terms so that where "X"

[1] "Legitimacy in the Modern State," in Green and Levison, eds., *Power and Community*.
[2] "Legitimacy," in *Dictionary of Social Sciences*, p. 386.

is an evaluative expression it is always defined so that "A is X" is equivalent in meaning to an expression of the form "A is believed by some class of persons to be Y" where "Y" is another evaluative expression. Suppose further that, as both Lipset and some Weberians do, we try to explain legitimacy in terms of stability or vice versa. What is clear is that the original definitional move has preempted on a crucial causal and explanatory question: is it only beliefs about what is legitimate, what is appropriate, what is right which can be causally effective, or can the legitimacy of an institution, the appropriateness of an institution or an action, or the rightness or the justice of an action, themselves be causally effective? The definitional move of Lipset and Bierstedt removes a priori the possibility of a certain class of characteristics of intention and urgency being relevant in giving causal explanations.

Lipset and Bierstedt are thereby taking sides in an ancient philosophical argument: is it important for the ruler to be just, or is it only important for him to be thought to be just? What Lipset and Bierstedt do in defining legitimacy is not unlike what Thrasymachus did in defining justice and what Glaucon and Adeimantus did in developing Thrasymachus' case. We may now recall that Thrasymachus too claimed to be merely reporting how the world went, to be a neutral and value-free observer. My thesis on this last point can indeed be summarized as follows: to insist that political science be value-free is to insist that we never use in our explanations such clauses as "because it was un-just" or "because it was illegitimate" when we explain the collapse of a policy or a regime; and to insist on this is to agree with Thrasy-machus—even if for different reasons—that justice plays no part and can play no part in political life. The insistence on being value-free thus involves the most extreme of value commitments. Hence I take it to be no objection to the methodology which I propose that it is clearly not able to purge its explanations of evaluative elements.

Note that I have offered no arguments at this point for believing that Thrasymachus is, as a matter of fact, mistaken; what I have done is to suggest that those who maintain the stance of orthodox comparative political science are committed by their starting point and not by the empirical findings to the view that he was right. And this raises one more kind of doubt about their view. For the response to my parable about the man who aspired to be the author of the general theory of holes might well have been that such a man is intellectually misguided, but practically harmless. When, however, one has to recognize that this kind of intellectual mistake is allied to a Thrasymachean attitude to morality, it becomes clear that if this type of enterprise is to be ranked as a joke, it must be classed with the more dangerous kinds of practical jokes.

23

Political and philosophical epilogue: a view of The Poverty of Liberalism *by Robert Paul Wolff*[1]

Since I intend to criticize some of Mr. Wolff's positions[2] very sharply, I ought at the outset to express both my agreement with and my sense of indebtedness to him. In the task of criticizing liberalism from the Left in a way more creative than that of many Left polemics I am his ally; and Mr. Wolff has opened up the debate with a battery of arguments at once forceful and suggestive, from which we may all learn. It is thus not just because I aspire to be captious that I concentrate upon our disagreements. My strategy will be to begin with a set of genuine, but relatively superficial objections; to then suggest why these lead on to a profounder set of objections to Wolff's view of liberalism; and finally to object to Wolff's own radicalism.

Wolff's argument involves three central contentions (among others). The first is that the liberal case stands or falls with the utilitarian case. Wolff identifies liberal doctrine with the utilitarian doctrine of John Stuart Mill without apparent qualification. The second is that liberalism is an appeal only to individual and in-dividualist values. Wolff asserts that liberalism values social relationships only as means to the ends of individuals and that liberalism lacks any concept of community as an end or of communal life as a source of ends. The third contention of Wolff's, which I wish to take up initially, is one that concerns not Wolff's depiction of liberalism, but his own alternative stance. Wolff distinguishes himself from some other radicals by arguing that in modern American society "the people" are not in fact deprived of power, and deprived in such a way that they have no

[1] This paper will appear in the *Proceedings of the Conference for Political Theory*, New York, 1970.
[2] *The Poverty of Liberalism* (Boston: Beacon Press, 1969).

remedy, by a power elite. They are in fact ruled by default and evil policies such as those which issued in the Vietnam War were carried on with the active connivance of a public that was "too stupid or too vicious" (p. 114) to do otherwise.

All three points invite sharp comment. The first in particular invites the rejoinder that liberalism has in its time associated itself with and derived its warrant from many very different and indeed mutually incompatible theories, and hence that there is no reason to associate it peculiarly with utilitarianism. Locke, the French materialists, and T. H. Green are very different types of thinkers from J. S. Mill and from each other; but each provided philosophical support for attitudes that could certainly claim to be liberal. Moreover, on the second point it is clear that T. H. Green, who has as good a claim as any thinker to be called liberal, had a keen sense of the defects of individualism and of the importance of community as a source of ends as has Wolff. Liberalism was often, but certainly not always or necessarily, individualist in its values. On the third point I only want to note that Mr. Wolff has himself taken up an essentially liberal standpoint; that if "the people" do have constitutional access to the means of wielding power and they fail to use this access to institute enlightened policies, then they are either stupid or vicious. Liberalism, that is, views the people as either powerless or else morally responsible for political outcomes. That "the people" might have constitutional access to the means of wielding power, but suffer from an ideologically distorted vision which itself has deep social roots, and that this might be true in America today is a possibility which never seems to enter the liberal purview.

I shall return to this last point; but for the moment I shall note only that Wolff's portrait of liberalism is highly selective and appears arbitrarily selective. Yet I take this objection to his views to be relatively superficial, since, if what Wolff has given us is a partial and distorted cartoonists' version of liberalism rather than an adequate portrait, this is what liberalism itself in any one of its many versions also offers us in the course of presenting each particular version of liberalism as *the* essential doctrine. Why does liberalism present itself in this way? A much more serious defect in Wolff's presentation is that he offers us no means of answering this question. This may be because he does not notice two crucial aspects of liberalism, both of which must play an essential part in any explanation of why liberalism has been both able and willing to ally itself at various times and places with such a wide variety of philosophical theories and of factual analyses.

The first aspect of liberalism is that revealed by putting to liberalism a question that needs to be put to any political position which allies itself with a philosophical theory. In what relationship does the politics stand to the philosophy? When a particular political agent or group of political agents assert both a set of political principles and a philosophical theory in association with these principles (and the same would hold incidentally for a sociological or other such theory), the practical principles and the philosophical theory may stand in either of two quite different relationships. On the one hand the philosophical theory may consist, partially or wholly, in elucidations of the key expressions used in the statement both of the political principles and of their application to particular cases. In such a case, if we do not understand the philosophical theory, we shall fail to understand the political principles. But the theory and the principles may stand in a quite different relationship. For the theory may provide not an elucidation of the principles, but a mask behind which their true meaning and importance is concealed. The theory may be an ideological instrument, which enables those who profess the principles to deceive not only others but also themselves as to the character of their political action. I have already noticed that Wolff does not allow for the possibility of ideological distortion in his own explanations; I now want to stress the importance of his failure to see liberalism in a variety of guises as ideology.

It is important that Wolff in his abstinence from the concept of ideology is at one with the latest of liberalism's ideological masks, the end-of-ideology thesis. But before I go on to ask about the ideological content of all nineteenth- and twentieth-century versions of liberalism, including this one, I want to notice another central feature of liberalism unnoticed by Wolff. Liberalism always appears accompanied by and allied to, not only philosophical theories, but also political and economic stances of a non-liberal kind; belief in a free market economy and belief in welfare statism are both stances of this sort. The reason that this is always so and must always be so is that liberalism by itself is essentially negative and incomplete. It is a political doctrine about what cannot be justified and what ought not to be permitted: interference of a variety of kinds with individual liberty. This essentially negative character of liberalism derives from its eighteenth-century antecedents. Liberalism was the doctrine used to undermine the authoritarianism and the authority of the *ancien régime*. What is liberal in the writings of Jefferson and of Robespierre and their like are their demonstrations of the unjustifiable character of censor-

ship, of alien rule, of denial of the suffrage, of arbitrariness in the
courts, and of the enforcement of religious practice. It is from them
that liberalism inherits its character as a series of denials.

From this negative character derives both the virtue and the
vice of liberalism. The virtue resides in the affirmation of the
values of toleration and of freedom of expression; on this matter
I stand squarely with the liberal values and against Wolff. But I
have argued that case elsewhere and will not repeat it here.[1] The
vice of liberalism derives from the continuous refusal of liberals
to recognize the negative and incomplete character of their
liberalism. The precepts of liberalism enjoin upon us certain
constraints on our political activities; but they set before us no
ends to pursue, no ideal or vision to confer significance upon our
political action. They never tell us what to do. Hence no institution,
no social practice can be inspired solely or even mainly by
liberalism; and every institution or social practice that claims to be
so inspired—such as the "liberal" university or the "liberal"
state—is always a fraud.

Why do liberals fail to recognize this? Part of the answer is
that there is another constant element in liberalism, a way of
envisaging the social world and men's place in it, which is often
assumed at so deep a level that it is not identified as a contingently
alterable way of seeing the world, but is instead naively envisaged
as the way the world is. What are the key features of this ideologically distorted and distorting vision?

There is first of all an abstract moralism, an appeal to very
general principles on very concrete issues. Liberalism lacks what
the scholastics called "middle axioms," methods of interpreting
and mediating the application of first principles. Hence morality
is always being adduced, and liberals tend to be moral exhibitionists
with all the unsavoriness that attaches to the habitual use of a high
moral tone. Closely allied to this is a view of the individual as the
fount of all value and the locus of all value. The individual
confronts a realm of determinate facts with the value judgments
which he has chosen. Fact is one thing, value another, and even if
the individual commits himself to the values of community, as
Wolff wishes him to do and T. H. Green wished him to do, it is the
autonomy of the individual in judging which is of the essence of
morality. We can indeed understand the power of this liberal
picture of the relationship of individual choice, fact and value when
we notice how T. H. Green, whose philosophy was in some

[1] Cf. Alasdair MacIntyre, Herbert Marcuse: An Exposition and A
Polemic (New York: Viking; London: Collins, 1970).

fundamental respects at odds with it, did in fact have to compromise with it.

Thirdly, there is a consequent view of politics as the offering of alternatives to rational individuals who then make choices for which they are morally responsible. Right politics is offering the right values to individuals and if they reject them, then we are entitled to condemn them unless they were disabled by invincible ignorance. So the liberal view of politics is indeed precisely ideological in that it conceals from view all those social facts which have to do with ideology. It turns out to be no accident that liberals should turn to something like the end-of-ideology thesis.

On these three points I wish to make two comments. The first is that all these characteristically liberal positions turn up in Wolff's book as Wolff's own positions which, so he appears to believe, belong to a position to be sharply distinguished from Wolff's own liberalism. Why is this? Wolff himself argues, and rightly, that American conservatism and American liberalism are conceptually entangled in such a way that they have more in common than the adherents of either would like to believe. I take Wolff's own adherence to liberal positions in his book to be evidence that the same is also true of American liberalism and American radicalism. Engels once complained that England had a bourgeois proletariat and a bourgeois aristocracy as well as a bourgeois bourgeoisie; we may well complain that America has liberal conservatives and liberal radicals as well as liberal liberals.

In the case of conservatism, the moralistic stance is apparent. Liberalism—as contrasted with conservatism and socialism—in European contexts has been unique in its purely negative attitude to tradition, a negativism grounded in its general negativism. But American conservatism has no tradition, no past to repossess, except a liberal past; and the sermonizing tone of the abstract moralist is the dominant tone of modern American conservatism. Radicalism in America too is essentially yet another liberalism, a liberalism that has lost its temper with social reality for being so irremedially resistant to liberalism and that therefore turns, as Wolff turns, to blaming "the people." To free ourselves from liberalism therefore radicalism is the wrong remedy. Marx already saw this when he castigated the Young Hegelian radicals; and, if Marxism today will not do for us the work of providing us with a fundamental critique of liberal society and liberal thought that we need in order to transform society radically, we can at least learn from it where *not* to begin.